JOURNEY TO PERFECTION

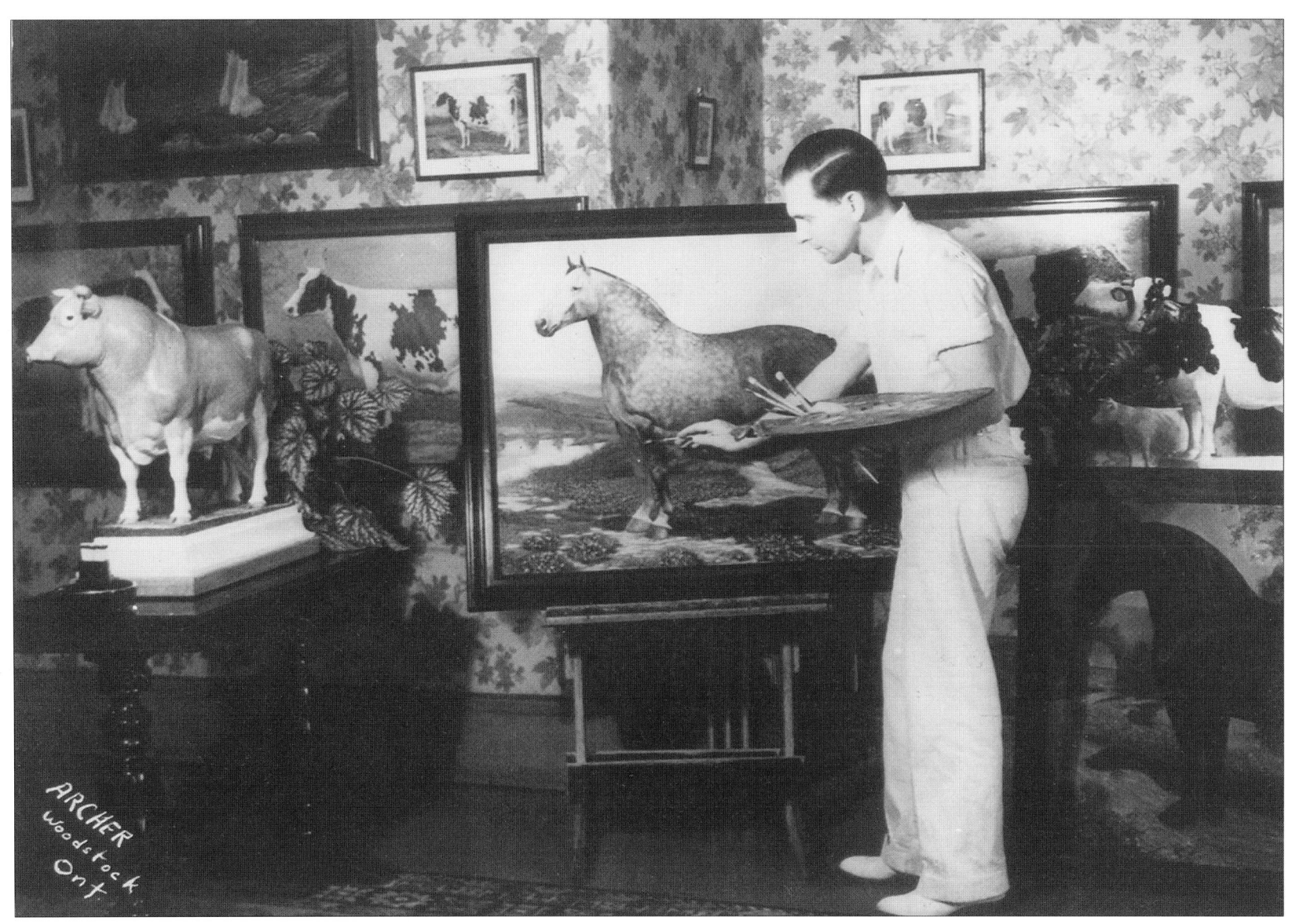

When we build, let us think we will build forever, not just for the present. — Ross Butler

Journey to Perfection
The Agricultural Art of Ross Butler

Irene Crawford-Siano

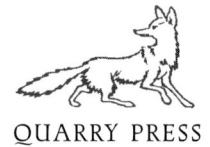

QUARRY PRESS

Acknowledgements

Text copyright © Irene Crawford-Siano, 1997.
Art, images, and foreword copyright © Ross Butler Studio, 1997.

All rights reserved.

The publisher gratefully acknowledges The Canada Council and the Department of Canadian Heritage for supporting the arts of writing and publishing in Canada.

ISBN 1-55082-212-8

Design by Susan Hannah.
Typeset by Larry Harris.
Printed and bound in Canada by AGMV/Marquis, Quebec.

Published by Quarry Press Inc.,
P.O. Box 1061, Kingston, Ontario K7L 4Y5
www.quarrypress.com

I WOULD LIKE TO ACKNOWLEDGE with thanks the assistance of David and Mary Butler, Ross Butler's son and daughter-in-law, who gave so generously of their time, as well as access to the Ross Butler Archives for his memoirs, scrapbooks, documents, letters, and files.

Many others have assisted with supplying information, namely the Canadian National Exhibition Archives (Amber Timmons): the Farm Museum; Norwich and District Archives (Mary Gladwin); Norwich & District Museum (Ian Bell); London Public Library, Regional Department; Meadowbrook Archives, Oakland University, Rochester, Michigan (Barbara Thorpe); University of Guelph Archives (Marilyn Cook); Woodstock Museum (Sheila Johnson); Woodstock Public Library (Stephen Nelson); Holstein Association of Canada (Elizabeth Mongeon); Jersey Canada (Russell Gammon).

Personal thanks for their input to Isabelle Baird, Keith and Mary Danbrook, Grant Butcher, Tom Dent Jr., Beth Deslippe, Jean Edwards, Grace Hall, Vera Innes, Margaret Kitchen, Wally and Peggy Knapp, Evelyn Lazenby & East Oxford Women's Institute, Wayne Lenhardt, Margaret Losee, Alfred Searles, Robt. C. Watkins, and Senator Eugene Whalen.

Special thanks to my editorial assistant, Andrea Roulston.

— *Irene Crawford-Siano*

Contents

Preface by Senator Eugene Whelan 7

Foreword by David Butler 9

One | Of Cold Feet, a Pasture Field, and a Cow Named Daisy 17

Two | Freedom To Create 30

Three | "The Greatest Animal Painter in the World" 37

Four | True Types 51

Five | Percheron Paintings and Sculptures 58

Six | An American Celebrity 67

Seven | Cows and Bulls Lined Up in Long Rows 89

Eight | Animal Photography 97

Nine | The Perfect Jersey and the Theory of Animal Proportion 103

Ten | Artificial Insemination 110

Eleven | Butter Sculptures 117

Twelve | The Jersey Islands and the Queen of England 123

Thirteen | Buying and Selling 130

Fourteen | Renewing the Dream 137

Fifteen | Southwood 145

Sixteen | Agri-Cultural Connections 150

Further Reading 158

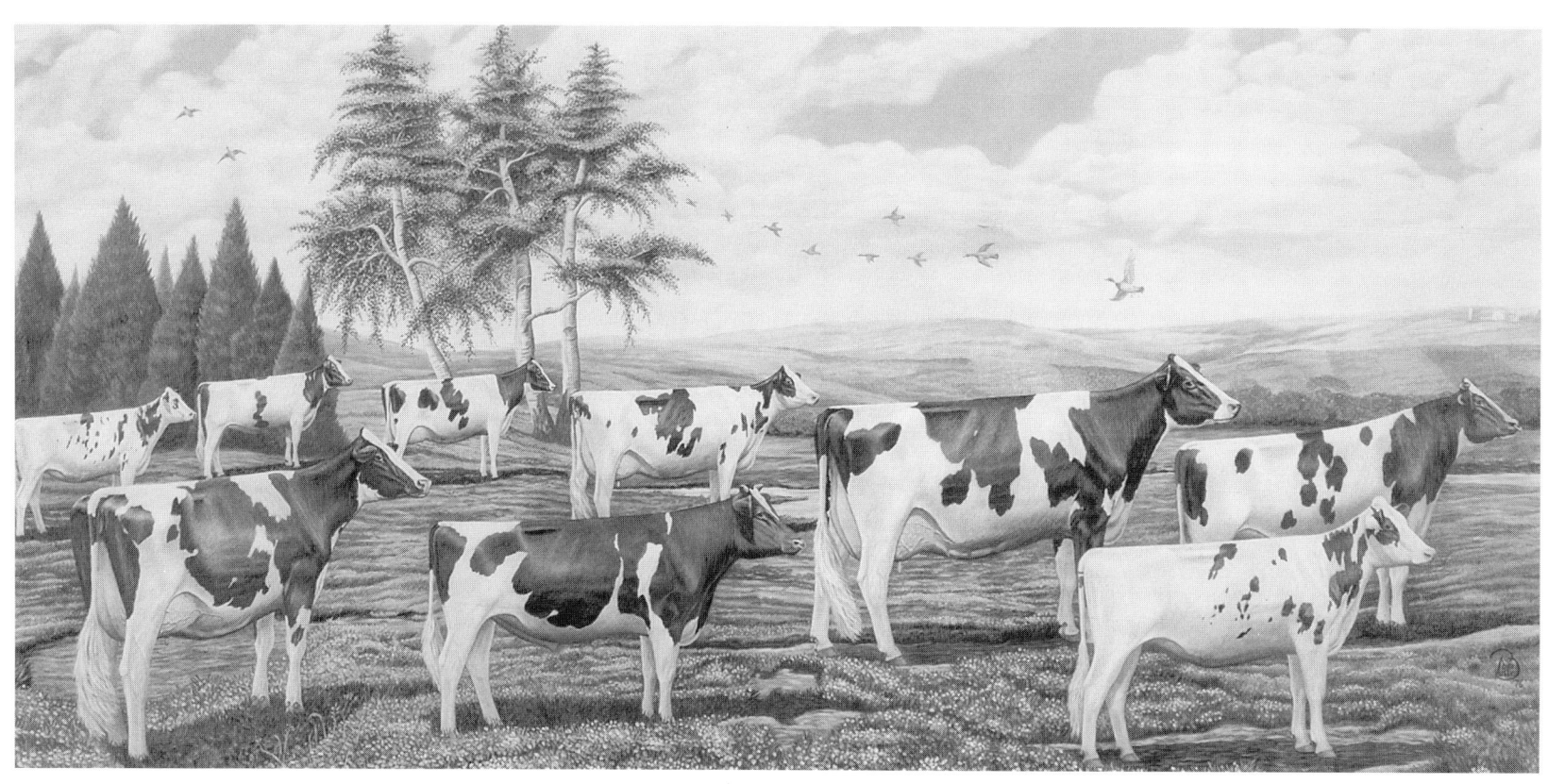

All Canadian Holsteins — The Cattle upon the Thousand Hills (48 x 96", oil on masonite, 1976), showing the best of the breed in each class for 1975, painted to serve as a breeding guide.

Preface

IT HAS BEEN SAID that one's early childhood experiences are a basic force in molding what a person will be in later years. Ross Butler's humble beginnings on a farm near Norwich, Ontario, were to lead him to worldwide recognition and to establish new frontiers in the knowledge of animal conformation. Who could have told then that the rather lonely, dreamer-son of an Ayrshire breeder's herdsman, a young boy who would rather draw than do his farm chores, would rise to such acclaim?

It was not until I was Canada's Minister of Agriculture that I was to meet Ross Butler, although, by then, his work was well known to me as it was to many others associated with agriculture, work that was outstanding not only for its artistic and emotive qualities but for the accuracy with which he, the artist, interpreted his subjects. The time that Ross spent studying the animals he painted and sculpted, and the accuracy with which he recorded his findings, established him not only as an authority on the conformation of animals, but also introduced new knowledge of animal proportion into the fields of both art and science.

Ross Butler had his ups and downs like many of us who place trust in their fellow man. Many took advantage of his trusting disposition, with the result that although his work was to reap rewards for others, he was never properly compensated for it. He was a true Canadian, working in a typically understated fashion, demanding little for his work except the satisfaction of knowing that he was doing what he loved to do, and doing it to the best of his ability. Yet he created sculptures and paintings that will withstand the tests of time and fashions to come.

As Minister of Agriculture I was well aware of Ross's brilliance, but much more than that, I considered him a great artist and also one of the leading contributors in making Canada's unique livestock industry known all over the world. Ross Butler was a man I am proud to have known, and even more proud to have been able to call my friend. A truly outstanding Canadian, joining those others who have plied their talents to making our Canada the great country it is today.

Thanks Ross. I see his Holstein cow and bull sculptures in my office everyday that I am there and they always bring his great contribution to Canadian agriculture to mind. Ross Butler, artist, outstanding Canadian, and my friend.

— *Eugene Whelan*

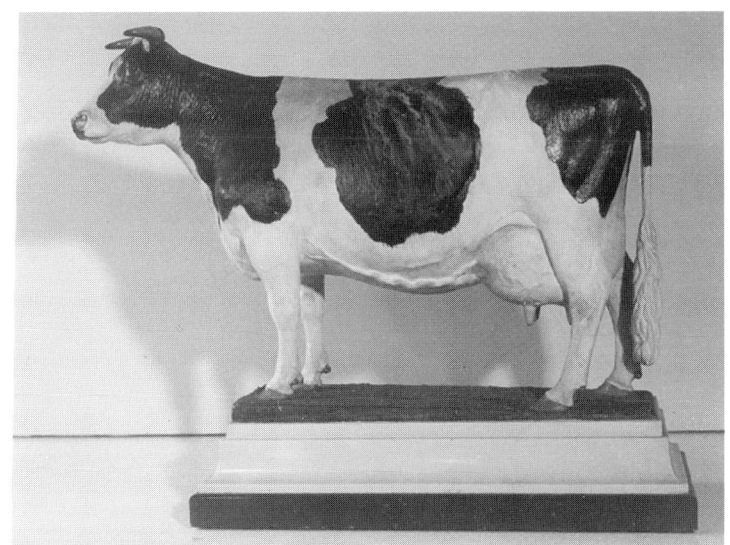 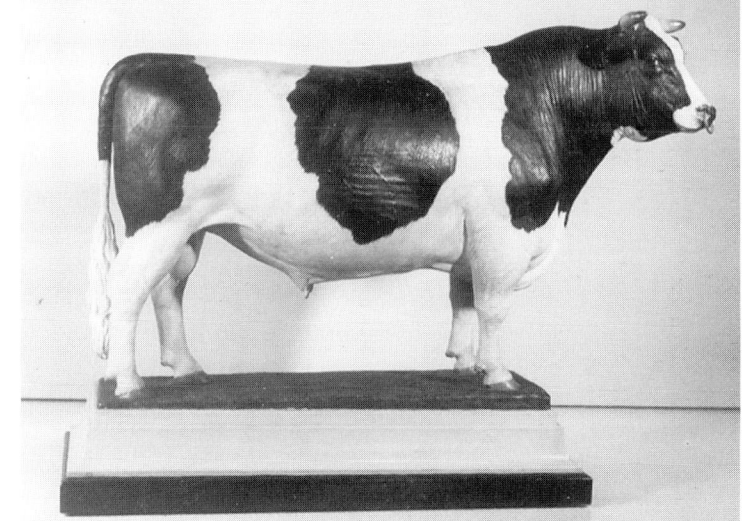

True type Holstein sculptures, 1938.

Foreword

ROY ROGER'S HORSE TRIGGER was a bone of contention among my childhood friends. They were skeptical about the fact that my father, Ross Butler, had met the famous horse and his rider in California (and subsequently fashioned Trigger's image in a butter sculpture at the Canadian National Exhibition). To avoid arguments or confrontation, we didn't dwell on the subject even though the Roy Rogers television show was a regular part of our young lives. This early memory would be associated with the attitude I would develop towards my father as we grew older. I was proud that he was a "famous" artist (although in those years I wasn't sure why or how he was famous), but part of me also wished he was more like other fathers who had jobs and did regular things.

Even though we lived "in the city," our sense of community was shaped by my father's visits to the fall fairs, drives in the country to see farmers and cattle, and our annual excursions to the Canadian National Exhibition and Royal Winter Fair. Here, he was in his element, rubbing elbows with the cattlemen, horsemen, and judges around the show ring.

The bulls were all gone from the Central Unit, the artificial insemination "barn" on Pavey Street in Woodstock, by the time I came along. But still hanging on the walls were dozens of my father's paintings, and shelves around the mangers were adorned by his models of cows and horses. The barn was also called "the studio," though my father still kept a few Jersey cows there. The barn and the studio, his art and his agriculture, always seemed to be inextricably linked. In the life of Ross Butler, there wouldn't have been any sense of one without the other.

I grew up with a fascination for art, if not for agriculture, and more than a bit of trepidation regarding each. It seemed that the artist's son was expected to have knowledge, talent, skill, and graces by association. I scorned any such attention. It wouldn't be until years later that I would have enough self confidence to honour my father by taking an active interest in his work. By then the years had mostly slipped away from him and the only pride we could share was in his three grandsons. My research into his place in agricultural art history came after the fact.

PERHAPS ANY DISCUSSION ON THE BROAD TOPIC of "Art or Agriculture" should begin with a qualified definition of terms. Art can be thought of as human effort that attempts to re-order nature in a way that affects a sense of beauty. Agriculture is the science or occupation of cultivating the soil, producing crops, and raising livestock, known simply as farming. We may say that the scientist observes the world in order to discover universal truths. The artist rearranges the world to express personal or cultural understanding. The farmer may be both artist and scientist. To this definition, I think my father would agree.

If we consider culture as not just intellectual and artistic activity, but all other products of human endeavour, then it would seem that art and agriculture should go hand in hand. The artistic representation of rural life became a customary practice. Artists may be driven by their creative energy, but they are also a product of their times, their environment and society. As society has changed from agrarian to urban, there have been fewer artists creating in a rural environment. The trends of art are influenced by not just the artist's creative wellspring, but by the galleries, patrons, and consumers who buy art. The styles, movements, and schools of art are also a result of the demand of these art galleries and collectors.

The art of Ross Butler is generally not well known in the art community in Canada. However, in agricultural circles, his name has been synonymous with farm animal portraiture and sculpture since the 1930s. He started sketching and painting in the early part of the great depression. It was a time of upheaval and change after World War I, a time of radical art. The modernist movement saw Dada, Surrealist, Expressionist, and Abstract art dominate the trends. These artists were trying to break with tradition and institutional values. These trends in art reinforced my father's sense of independence and perhaps isolation because his mind's eye saw art as an expression of the wonder and beauty of the world around him. The North American realist movement, influenced largely by the growing art of photography, also garnered a following in that era. It is this style with which Ross' work should be compared.

The history of animal portraiture is, of course, as old as the history of art. "The first subjects of painting were animals," Michael S. Quinn in an article on "Nature, Art and the Ideal Type" notes, "the first medium was probably animal blood." Paintings of domestic animals such as cattle and horses became the visual history of the natural evolution of these species until the 18th century when agriculturalists persuaded artists to create "breed studies" — and in turn farmers began to breed animals to match these images. Quinn tells the story of this interplay between cattle breeders and artists:

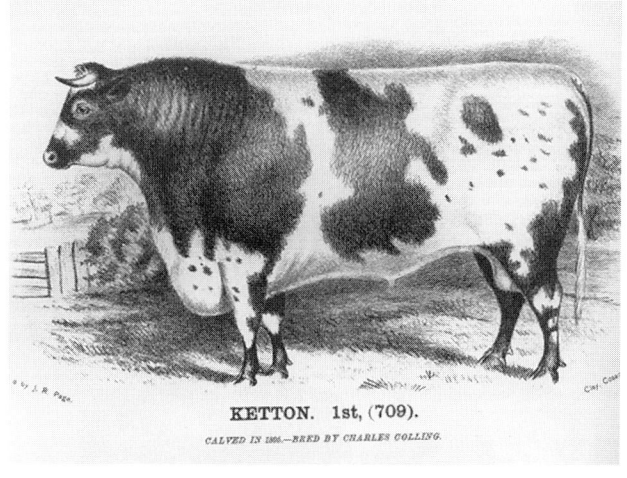

The Ketton Cow (a.k.a. "The Durham Ox"), bred by Charles Colling.

Cattle breeders in the middle of the 18th century set about to increase their profits through "improvement" of their beef-producing livestock. Improvement meant animals that gained weight faster, matured sooner and grew larger. . . . The pioneers of such improvement were Benjamin Tomkins, Richard Bakewell, and Charles Colling who began "systematic improvement" through selection in 1742, 1750 and 1784, respectively. It is important to remember that before this time there were no real breeds of cattle formally recognized. . . . A breed came into being through intensive breeding program driven by the selection of traits deemed desirable by the breeder. Much of the early breed establishment was wrought with rampant inbreeding.

During the late 18th and early 19th century various breeds — Longhorn, Hereford, Highlander, Aberdeen Angus — began to emerge, none so famous as the so-called "Durham Ox," an obese Shorthorn type that became a sort of side-show attraction, appearing on display throughout England and Scotland. In 1802, Quinn reports, "more than 2,000 people purchased a print of the squarish, roan ox." And so began the public fascination with art and agriculture:

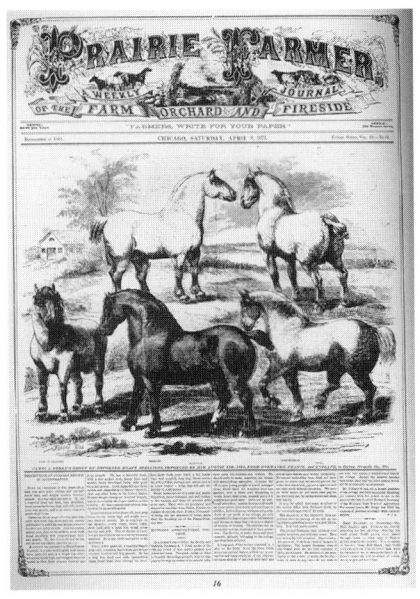

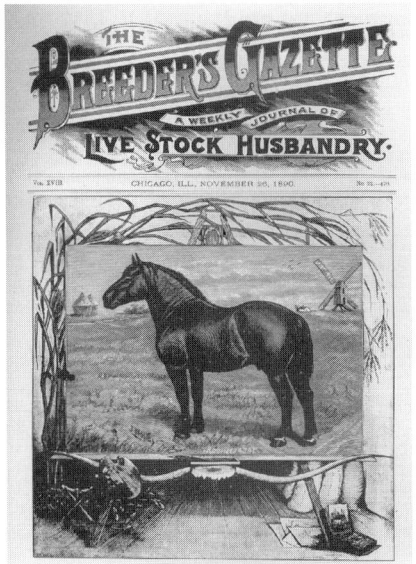

The demand for livestock portraiture blossomed in the first half of the 19th century. . . . Rich owners commissioned some of the better artists of the day to portray their favourite beasts. Engravers then made less expensive prints available to the rest of society. Several artists, such as George Gerrard, James Ward and Thomas Sidney "Cow" Cooper made a substantial living doing only cow portraits. Of this commercial art George Gerrard commented: "It has always been the practice of polished nations to unite the elegant with the useful, the polite with the necessary arts, which thus serve mutually to illustrate and assist each other, and render employment at the same time and upon the same subject for the man of genius and the man of labour."

Ross Butler embodied both components of this art and agriculture amalgam. A painter and a farmer, he not only created ideal types of cattle, horses, and poultry in his art based on his scientific theory of animal proportions, he worked on improving the various breeds of cattle by founding the first artificial insemination unit in Canada to offer semen from every major breed, breeding himself several prize-winning Jerseys. As Michael S. Quinn observes, "he quickly became established as the Canadian authority on what was called the True Type, Ideal Type or Standard of Perfection. He was granted one of the widest reaching commissions in Canadian art history when in 1937 he began work on 22 paintings depicting the perfect male and female of every major dairy breed, beef breed and draught horse." A full set of these paintings was sent to every school in Canada. "Few Canadians over the age of thirty," Michael Webster noted in a *Harrowsmith* profile of his career, "have not been exposed to the art of Ross Butler" — even if Ross Butler is neither a household name nor a name duly recognized in the history of agricultural art.

IN WESTERN ART IN THE 18TH and 19th centuries agriculture was a recurring theme as artists portrayed the landscapes of rural England and America. George Stubbs (1724–1806), a self-taught English painter and author of a treatise on the "Anatomy of a Horse," became known as the greatest horse painter of the age. John Constable

(1776-1837) painted *The White Horse* in 1819. His animal portraits and landscape art would influence one of Canada's great early landscape painters, Homer Watson (1855 - 1936), who featured domestic animals in his work. French painter Rosa Bonheur (1822-1899) portrayed horses dramatically with straining, bulging muscles and established a reputation as one of the foremost animal painters of her day. Horatio Walker (1858-1938) was born near Listowel, Ontario but lived in New York and Ile d'Orleans near Quebec City. His painting *Oxen Drinking* sold to the National Gallery in Ottawa for $10,000 in 1911. And, of course, Cornelius Krieghoff (1815-1872) portrayed the early life of rural Quebec, including farm scenes and animals.

These artists are all academically recognized and their work is sought after by museums and collectors. But there are other groups of artists from the 19th century whose work depicts farm life and the social realism of the day. Although valued by collectors, this genre of art is not as esteemed by the academies and institutions of the art world. Some of these early painters would work as magazine illustrators or engravers. Many early prints were made by artist/engravers who often relied on sketches or paintings for there subject matter. (Livestock photography didn't develop as an art form until the mid-1890s when photo-engraving was perfected to the point where it was available to the farm magazines.) The prints or engravings would often have two names associated with them: one of the artist who drew the picture denoted by "DEL" from Latin *delineavit* — he/she drew it; the other of the engraver who faithfully inscribed the picture onto the plate for printing followed by "SC" from Latin *sculpsit* — he/she carved or engraved it. A Golden Age of Livestock Art flourished in these agricultural publications.

A large number of agricultural books and journals in my father's studio are filled with these wonderful old engravings, mostly by American livestock artists from the 1800s. The names of some farm papers and agricultural periodicals include *The National Livestock Journal*, *Breeders Gazette*, *Prairie Farmer*, *Orange Judd Farmer*, *The American Agriculturalist*, *Country Gentlemen*, *Wallace's Farmer*, *The Poultry Tribune*, and *The American Poultry Journal*. It was the poultry journals, with the many varieties of perfectly coloured chickens, that my father referred to when he was inspired to paint the

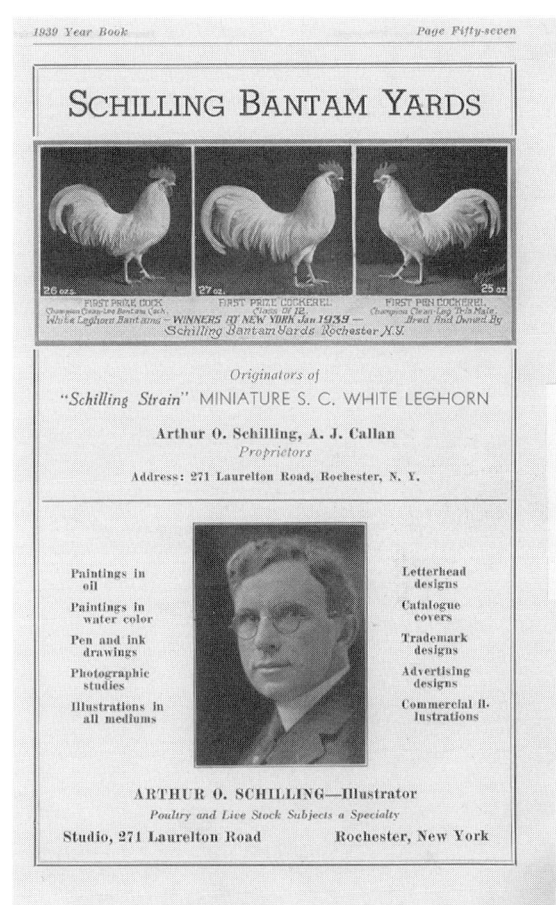

Like Arthur O. Schilling, Ross Butler was both a painter and a breeder of livestock. A painting by Schilling hangs in the Ross Butler Studio.

Ideal Types of the farm animals. Some of the artists whose names appear prominently in these publications are Lou Burk, whose engraved pictures graced the pages of The Breeders Gazette, E.H. Dewey, Frank Whitney, Cecil Palmer, Franklane L. Sewell, Louis Paul Graham, and Louis A. Stahmer.

There were other livestock artists and illustrators whom Ross spoke of with reverence. It was taken for granted that any self-respecting student of agricultural history would certainly recognize the the names of Edwin Megargee, Edward Herbert Miner, Arthur Schilling, and George Ford Morris. In his mind they were the successful livestock artists of the day, and if his name was mentioned in the same breath as theirs, then he would be honoured.

Megargee painted the first True Type Holsteins for The Holstein-Friesien Association of America in 1922 as well as the Ideal Jersey for the American Jersey Cattle Club. Edward Herbert Miner illustrated some of the classic stock books, including Horses of The World for National Geographic. Arthur Schilling, one of the best-known livestock artists, was a master of portraying the standards of perfection of poultry. And George Ford Morris, who founded the American Animal Artists Association, was highly regarded as the successor to Rosa Bonheur as the greatest horse painter in the world.

This is the tradition of farm animal art that inspired my father in his own career.

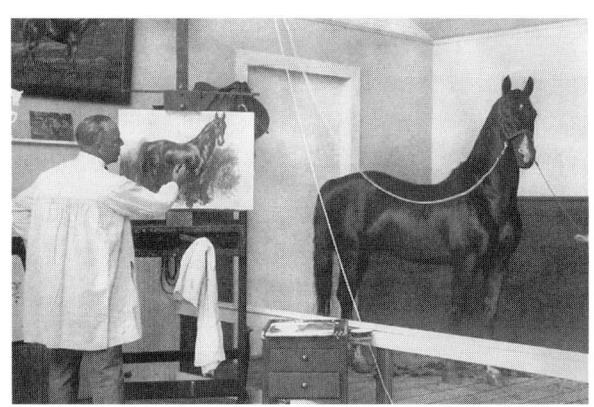

Edward Herbert Miner at work in his studio.

SAYING AN ARTIST IS SELF TAUGHT means he has no formal training, he is self motivated, driven to paint and create. This is especially true of Ross Butler. The first sketches he did were pencil studies of Jersey cows, some horses, and people. His sketch books also contain exercises from a self-study course from about 1922 which covered perspective, composition with light and shadow, character studies, and calligraphy. Many other sketches and early pictures that were stored upstairs in the barn on the farm were lost along with most of the livestock records for the bulls and Jersey cows from his cattle business days. A few pictures, including a box of cattle photographs, were salvaged but most of them were found to be in poor condition.

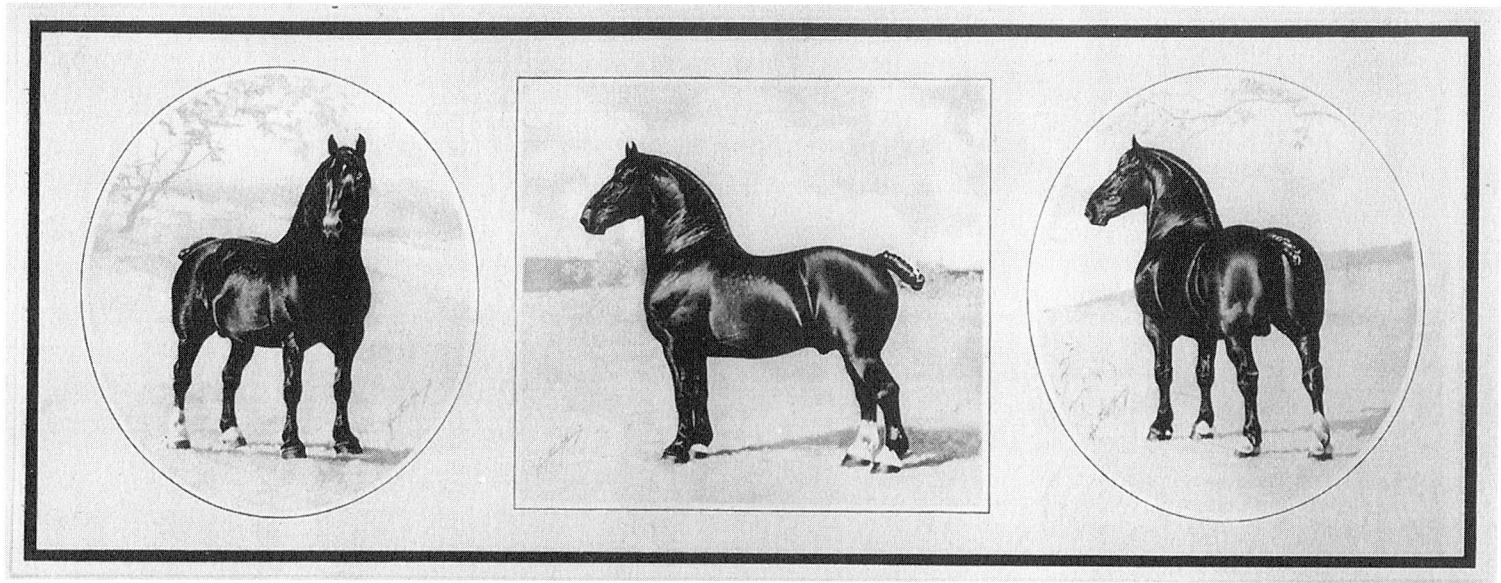

Champion Percheron "Calypso" by George Ford Morris.

Even his early drawings are meticulous and full of detail. As the skills developed, charcoal and pen & ink were used. Then tempera water colours became the medium for his creations. Several pictures display his adeptness at pastels on sandpaper. Finally, oil paints on canvas, board, and masonite would be the favoured media. The plaster casts of his clay sculptures also distinguish the finesse of careful hands. Butter sculptures, which were short lived by their very nature, remain only in photographs.

It is said that honesty and truth in art are not enough. What elevates a piece of art to a sublime level is the inherent psychological, emotional, or spiritual embodiment of the artist in the work. If this is so, then the True Type portraits are Ross' real masterpieces. Each of them shows a form that seems ready to breathe or blink or walk off the canvas. The idealized subjects are perfectly proportioned and lovingly portrayed as the epitome of man's quest for perfection in domestic animal breeding. The background landscapes, although muted, ethereal, and dreamlike, have sufficient detail to illustrate a rural setting, sometimes with a road, bridge, fence, or building indicating man's presence. Along with his theory of animal proportions, Ross's True

Types represent the accurate scientific and historical depiction of Canadian livestock breeds from an august era of the recent past. In his later and more lucrative animal pictures, he developed a more stylized background. The subjects were still accurately detailed but they seemed to be lacking in dimension or psychological perspective. This is especially so in the large format paintings with the notable exception of the *Royal Review*, which was acclaimed as a masterpiece of colour, composition, and detail.

IN LATER YEARS AS THE RIGORS OF AGE INFRINGED upon his painting, my father's creative endeavours turned to writing. He loved history and took to task the delineation of his own memoirs, the story of his ancestors, even local history. He was very proud of being a 5th generation direct descendant of Colonel John Butler, UE, one of the founding fathers of Upper Canada. In the search to understand my father's life and work, I, too, had to delve into history. And like his love of history, my search for roots has given me a broader understanding of the world around us.

Ross' life on the farm impressed upon him that the land and its animals provided food, income, and companionship — a good return for time and work invested. But more than that, he envisioned man, surrounded by the bounties of the earth and living in harmony with nature, returning to Eden. His dreams abounded with superlatives and ideals. They were full of hope for a better world and a better life. Like the pioneers who blazed new trails, sought new lands, and laboured clearing the land and tilling the soil, that enterprising spirit became the thread of the fabric woven into the culture of our country.

To those who witnessed his determination, saw his will to succeed or shared in his visions, my father was respected and accepted into that great group of doers, who, through the checkered history of our past, have made the world a better place.

— *David Butler*

1 | Of Cold Feet, a Pasture Field, and a Cow Named Daisy

ROSS BUTLER'S DIARY begins on April 23, 1907, in the Southwestern Ontario community of Norwich, where his father, David, worked as a herdsman for a prominent Ayrshire breeder:

My earliest recollections were of cold feet, a pasture field, and a cow named Daisy.

It was Ross's job every morning to fetch Daisy from the pasture field, and because shoes were only worn in summer for church and school, he went barefoot. The early morning dew was always cold and he used to warm his feet on the matted grass where the cow had lain the night. Then, grabbing her tail, Ross would allow her to pull him back to the barn where they would be greeted by neighs and grunts, quacks and clucks, a barnyard symphony of sounds.

One childhood memory which overshadowed all others occurred just before the Butler family moved from their village home to a nearby farm. One day Ross's mother asked him to take a lunch to his father who was hoeing potatoes at the new place. As usual Ross dawdled along the way, stopping to watch everything from the bees nuzzling the goldenrod to a mare and her colt grazing near the farm pond. As he was later to record in his memoirs:

It was my first journey on my own. Everything seemed so different. The trees were so big, so tall. They were like silent sentinels, their silence disturbed only by the chirp of crickets and the distant cry of a blue jay. It was a journey that would shape my future.

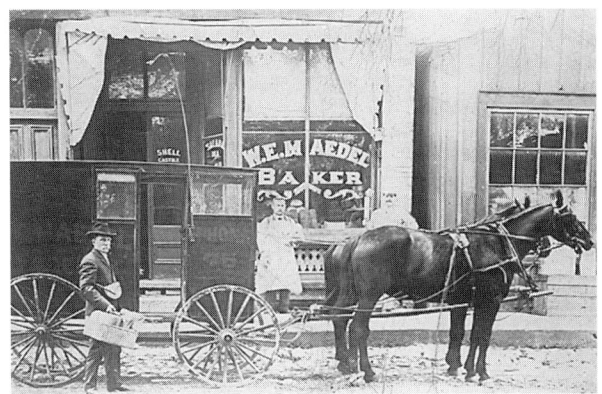

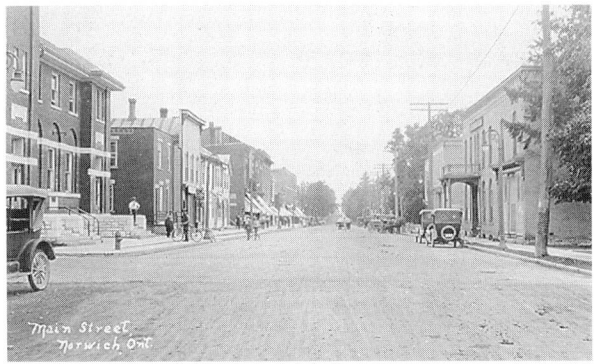

Ross Butler's father David with his team of horses and delivery wagon at Maedel Bakery on the mainstreet of Norwich in the early 1900s.

Once Ross finally arrived at his destination, father and son sat upon an old stump sharing a sandwich and talking — a rarity for the two of them. They talked of family and horses, of pastures, and cows. That summer scene would reflect itself again and again in Ross's paintings over the years.

Ross had other memories, memories that were not so pleasant — of horses being flogged when they couldn't pull their loads; a Calathumpian parade where a team of spirited bays ran away with a burning wagon; and a shivering half-tailed terrier tucked inside Ross's coat. Another memory that Ross would have preferred to have forgotten was the day he jumped into the ash pile behind Maedel's bakery in Norwich. When he saw his two older brothers, Clarence and Frank, laughing and having fun jumping into the ashes, he decided to also try it. Unfortunately, Ross didn't realize that his brothers were wearing boots. He jumped in barefoot and his feet were badly burned.

When Ross started school, a whole new world was opened up to him. His teacher found him to be quiet, respectful, and eager to learn. She soon realized that behind that gentle and quiet presence was a shy boy with a slight lisp who would rather stay inside at noon-hour and sketch than go out and play.

Seeing Ross's talent, this teacher encouraged him to draw. She even framed one of his pictures and hung it on the classroom's back wall for everyone to see. She advised Ross to "Draw things that are familiar to you." That advice was to become the foundation of a career that spanned three quarters of a century. She was not always pleased with his choice of subjects, though. One noon hour, Ross drew a chalk mural of her and her beau in a horse-drawn buggy parked in a grove of trees. He had intended to erase the mural before she returned, but two older boys had restrained him. Her thundercloud expression spoke louder than words and Ross never drew any more murals of her on the blackboard.

During the First World War Ross's father worked at many jobs to feed his family of seven children. Money was always scarce despite his work as a teamster hauling sand, gravel, and lime for construction projects in the village. David was also recognized as an astute horse trader. As Ross recalled:

We had horses of every colour, shape, size and breed in our stable . . . and every one of those horses had its own story to tell.

These stories usually came to light around the supper table, where the family gathered for their last meal of the day. One such story was of the old flea-bitten crowbait that David had bought for a few dollars from a peddler. After proper feed and care that old crowbait, which the Butler boys named "the Old Grey Dort," became their mother's favourite buggy horse. One day, while returning from the village store, two young "blades" decided to pass Mary Butler and her horse on the country road. When their younger horse drew neck and neck with Mary's horse, the old grey pulled away, leaving the astonished young men far behind. They couldn't have known that The Old Grey Dort was a retired racehorse.

One deal that was never mentioned, at least in their father's hearing, was humorously known among the family members as "the best deal he ever made." In an even-trade with two gypsies, David traded a spotted, wall-eyed, foul-tempered beast for a gentle, obedient, dappled grey circus horse which he intended to team with one of his other draft horses. Ross loved the look of that dappled grey, so he volunteered to go with this father to haul gravel from the Milldale pit near Norwich. Everything was going well until they started up the pit's incline with their loaded wagon. Suddenly, the grey's flanks started to heave and with each breath began whistling through its nostrils. It could hardly move, much less pull. David had inadvertently traded a strong, ugly horse for a beautiful, broken-winded, useless animal.

It was the proud high-stepping hackneys that Ross liked best. These were only used on holidays and Sundays, when his parents took a leisurely drive through the country to visit relatives and friends.

Flossie, my younger sister, and I would sit on the dashboard seat of the buggy and watch the world go by . . . backwards.

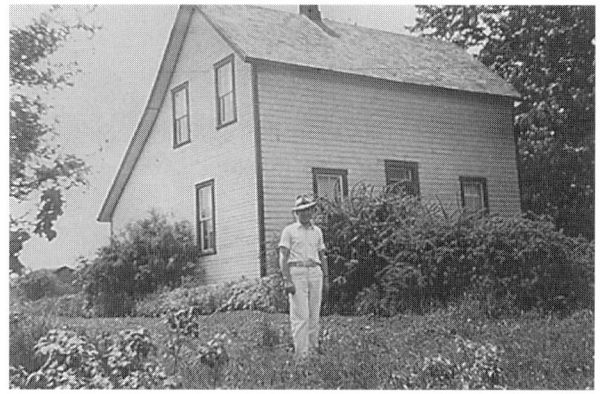

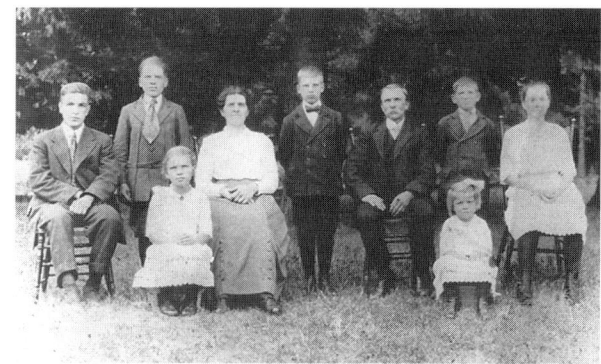

Ross Butler standing in front of the house where he was born and posing in a family portrait from 1916: (left to right) Clarence, Frank, Florence, Mary, Earl, David, Ross, Pearl (front), Lena.

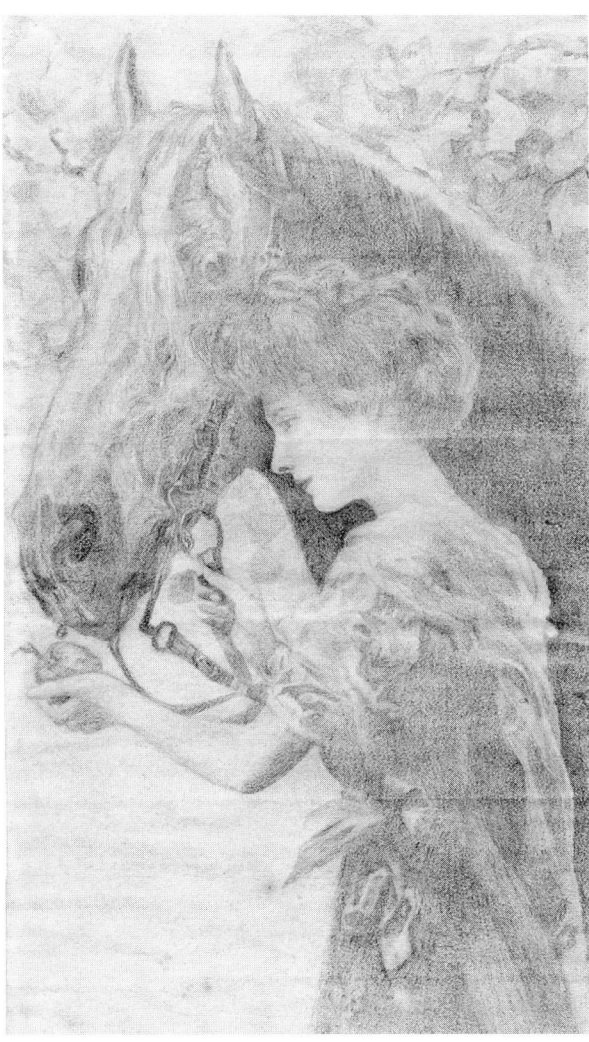

An early sketch from 1919, perhaps of his first school teacher, who encouraged him to draw.

Even in his eightieth year, Ross claimed he could still hear the swish of those buggy wheels and the rhythmic clump of the horses's hooves.

For Ross, those early years were a time of observing, learning, and dreaming — particularly dreaming. One of his jobs on the farm, when he became old enough, was hoeing potatoes, a job he hated with a passion. Of course, with a large family, there was always a lot of potatoes to hoe. One day when his father caught Ross day-dreaming instead of hoeing, he threw down his own hoe and exclaimed, "Dang it, Ross, I believe you would rather sit on a thistle than hoe it!"

With so many children the Butler household was always a hive of activity. On Saturday nights there would often be several young people in the parlour playing games or singing around the piano. Instead of participating, Ross would be off by himself sketching with paper and pencil. He did enjoy the Victrola's music, especially the records of Mozart. Years later, he would paint to the beat of that same music.

When Ross was about thirteen, the big news at the supper table was the sale of their neighbour's cow. Beryl Hanmer, the teenager next door, sold at auction Rolo Mercena De Kol, a cow he had bred and raised, for twenty-six thousand dollars. This was an unheard of price, even for a cow that had broken all the existing world Registry of Merit tests for seven, thirty and sixty days.

This sale fascinated me. What made this cow special? How was she different from all the others? Was it breeding? The feed? What? I had to find out.

When no one could give Ross a satisfactory answer, he went through the family's stack of farm magazines. Although he didn't find any concrete answers there, he did learn a lot about the different breeds of cattle: for example, which cattle produced the most milk and whose milk contained the most butterfat.

David Butler had always favoured Ayrshires — maybe because he had worked at Big John McKee's Ayrshire farm near Norwich. Ross, on the other hand, liked the fawn-coloured Jerseys with their huge brown eyes and skinny hips.

Our family's herd was like Jacob's coat in the Bible . . . multi-coloured. We had red ones, black ones, white ones, brindle and mouse coloured. And for months I badgered my father about improving the quality of our herd. I kept telling him it didn't cost more to feed a registered cow than it did to feed one with no pedigree.

David finally relented and purchased a bull and two Jersey heifers from a breeder near Eden, a hamlet south of the village of Tillsonburg. Ross was so enthusiastic about that purchase that he even volunteered to go with David to get the animals.

Bringing the animals home was far more difficult than Ross had anticipated. The day was hot and humid and the Butlers got started late. The Eden farm was five miles from the railroad station at Tillsonburg and Ross and David had to walk both ways. On the way back to the railway station, the cattle became determined to stop and graze at every patch of clover along the way . As one can imagine it took a lot of pulling and prodding to keep them moving. Things didn't get any easier once they reached the station at Tillsonburg. The train's whistle frightened the animals and it was all David and Ross could do to get the ornery beasts into the box car. During the train ride from Tillsonburg to Norwich, the cattle were able to rest and get their second wind. So, when they reached their destination, the cattle remained ornery. It was midnight before the Butler's got home.

Because Ross was the one to talk his father into buying the Jerseys, they became his responsibility, a responsibility he took very seriously. These Jerseys soon became the centre of his life. He built a stall for each animal and he printed their name above each door. He grew the best food he could for them — field peas, flax, barley, flint corn — and when the "best" food ran out, Ross hunted the barnyard and the fence lines for scrap pieces of iron which he sold to the local junk dealer. After all, *his* cows had to have the best.

Ross's feeding program paid off. The animals grew fatter and when the heifers began to produce, Ross nearly drove the family crazy at suppertime spouting their accomplishments. His obsession with the Jerseys soon overflowed into his art. He

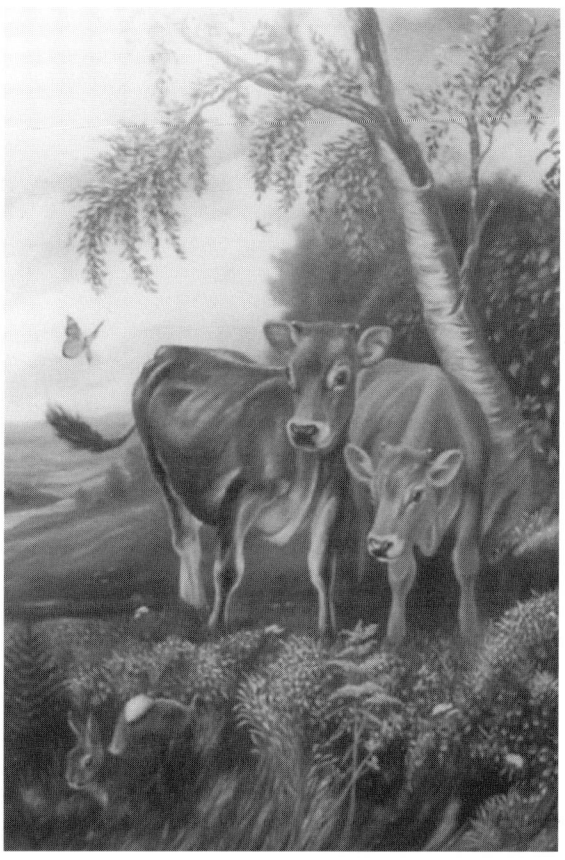

In this painting of *One Summer Afternoon* (24 x 36", oil on masonite, 1968) from memory, Ross Butler portrayed Daisy and her calf along the shore of Otter Creek.

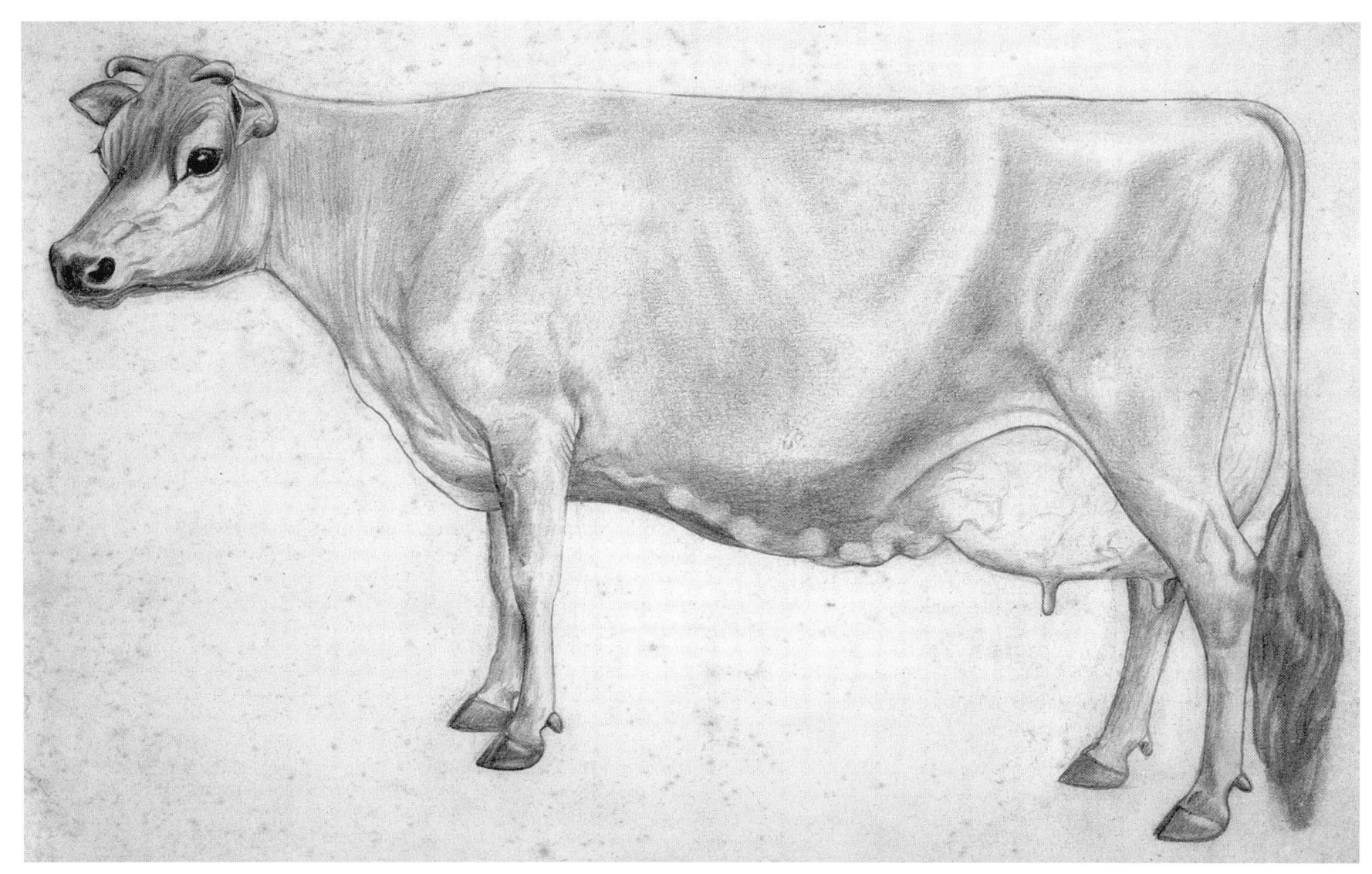

Early drawings illustrating the pedigree of the Butlers' first Jersey bull and cows.

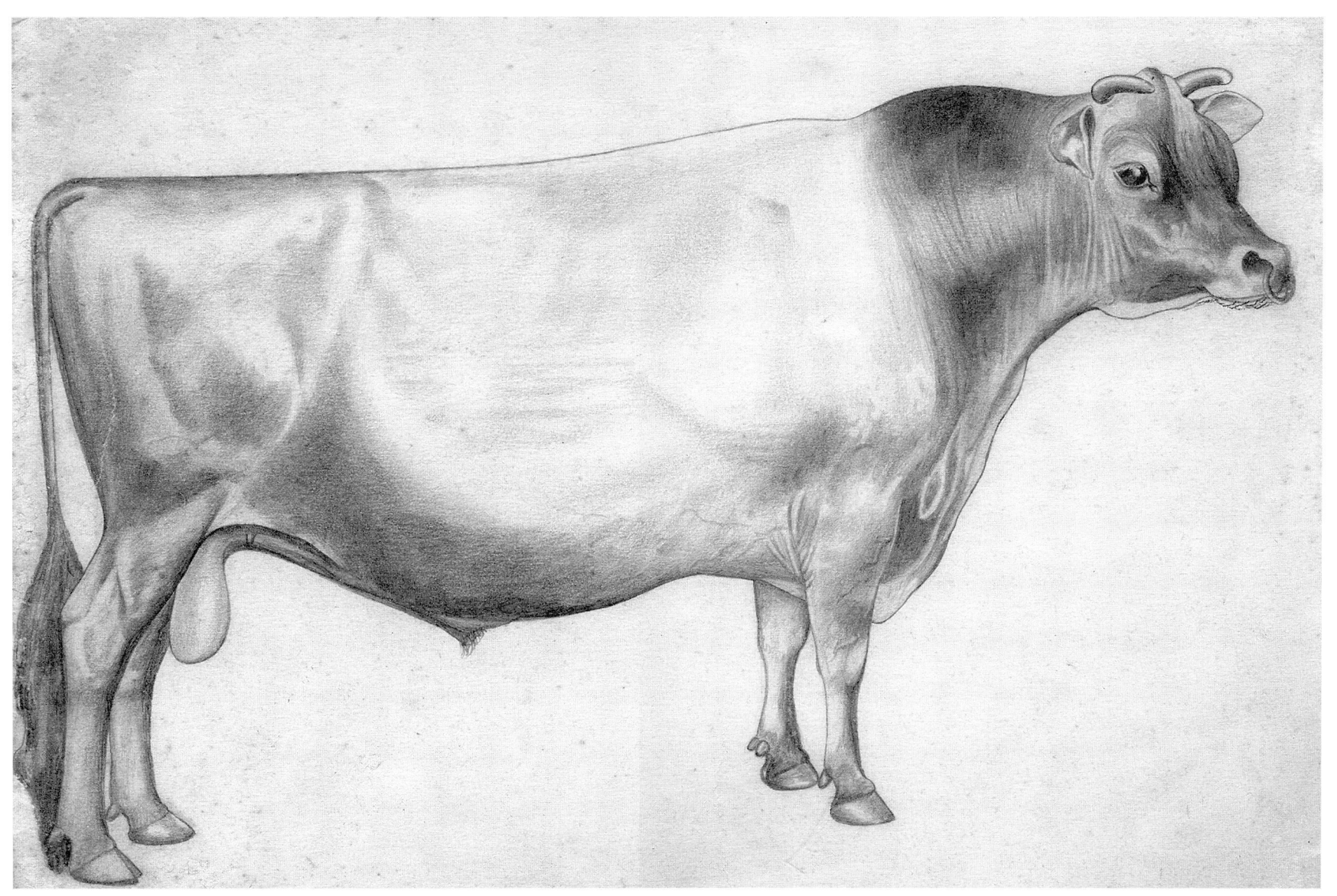

sketched them in their stalls, grazing knee-deep in clover or drinking at the water trough. He noted and recorded everything about his Jerseys. Not only did he watch them chew their cuds, but he knew exactly how many times they chewed each regurgitated wad.

Every pound of the Jerseys food was mixed and weighed. Out of curiosity, Ross measured their water intake over a twenty-four hour period and learned that his small cows required 150 pounds of water daily. He also began to record, right to the ounce, the amount of milk each Jersey produced. These charts were hung beside the animal's stall and soon they were drawing more attention than the cows.

When Ross was in his last year of public school, his Jerseys went on the Record of Performance Test (R.O.P.). They had to be milked at 7:00 a.m., 1:00 p.m., and 9:00 p.m., and the milk had to weighed and recorded.

This was my last year of public school and I had to run home every day at noon hour to milk the cows. It was an exhausting schedule and I do not recall a single milking that anyone helped me.

Ross's faith in his Jerseys was soon rewarded. One of the cows produced over seventeen thousand pounds of milk in her first two hundred and fifty days. The milk tester told Ross she was headed for a Canadian record.

While the news that the Butlers had a better-than-average cow spread quickly, Ross was still not satisfied. He wanted his cows to be recognized as the top of their breed — not just for their production, but also for their conformation and pedigree. Ross's next objective was the show ring. Only here could he prove that *his* cows were really the best.

Ross learned a lot about the show ring and how to groom an animal from his father who had groomed the Brookside Ayrshires for Big John McKee. Ross also read every magazine article he could find on the subject and soon knew how to emphasize an animal's good points and how to camouflage the bad ones. He learned how to make the cattle stand and walk for the judges. Ross also developed a few tricks of his own along the way, such as using lemon oil to make the animal's coats shine.

When it became apparent that the cattle needed to be clipped, Ross's brother Earl came to the rescue. He had found a set of hand-powered clippers which required Earl to turn the crank and Ross to operate the clippers at the end of a flexible shaft. Earl liked this clipping business so much that many years later he became a barber.

A few weeks before the fair, when Ross realized that the animals were going to need good halters and blankets and there was no money to buy such things, he was forced to improvise. He wheedled several sugar bags from his mother's cache and bleached them. With the help of his sisters, Lena and Pearl, he stitched them into blankets. Each blanket was like a made-to-measure dress, held in place by a large pearl button scrounged from Mary Butler's sewing box. For an added touch, the girls trimmed the edges of the blankets with coloured beading.

After weeks of preparation, Ross and his father were finally off to the Norwich fair. They tied their animals to the fence, and while Ross stayed to watch over the animals, David went to see if the Butler entries of turnips and mangels had won any prizes. Several fairgoers paused to look at the unusual sight of the cattle in their beaded blankets. When Ross heard one man chuckle and comment, "I'll bet that boy even sleeps with those animals," he was not sure if he should be hurt or flattered.

Ross didn't have much time to dwell on the unthoughtful comment as David returned accompanied by his former boss Big John McKee. The two men were quite a sight to see walking together: John McKee was over six feet tall and weighed over three hundred pounds; David was five feet four and tipped the scales at one hundred and ten. McKee took his time looking over the Butler animals, running his hand over the heifer's neck and the bull's flank. Then, in his booming voice, he said, "You've done a good job, Ross." When the day was over, the Butlers had two seconds and a third.

The following year, the Butlers were off to the Norfolk County Fair in Simcoe, a prestigious show with local breeders competing with breeders who had won at the Canadian National Exhibition in Toronto. Breeders like Monroe Landon from Simcoe, Colonel Cockshutt and the Papple Brothers from the Brantford area, who were dead serious about winning. For anyone to challenge their prestigious animals,

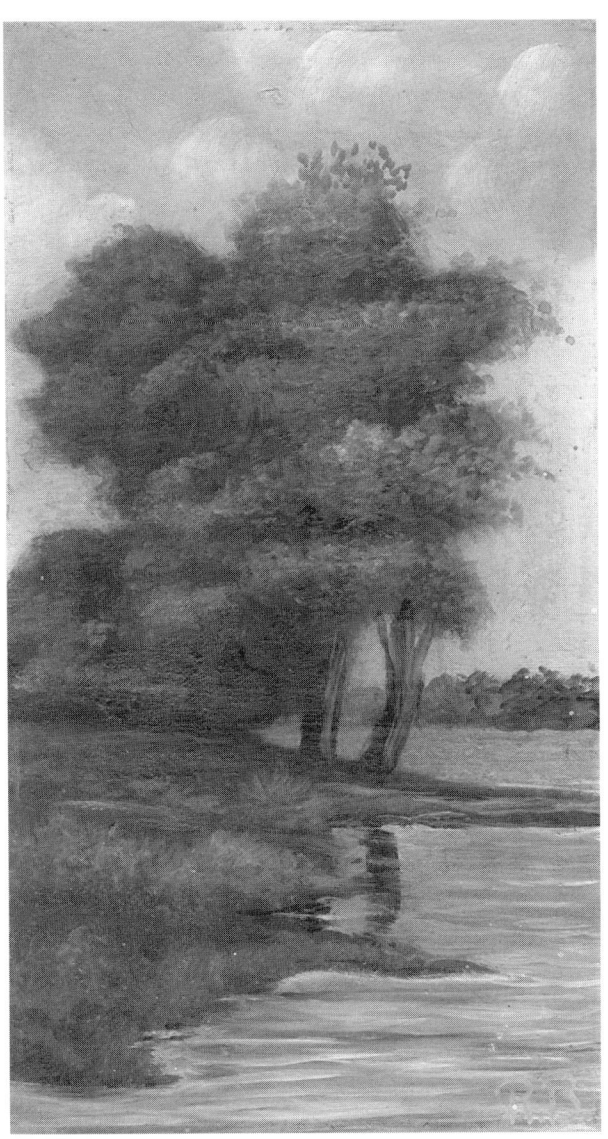

Ross Butler's first oil paintings of Otter Creek (6 x 12", oil and tempera on board, 1930s).

many of which were imported prize cattle from the Jersey Islands, was like a mere tick to be brushed aside without a thought. But Ross, too, was dead serious about winning. For months he had been preparing both his cattle and himself for this particular show. At Simcoe, he stayed by himself, watched what the others did and how they did it. When his turn came, he was ready.

My heart almost stopped beating when my Jersey decided to pause and look around. Finally, after a few whispered words from me and a gentle tug on her halter, she began to walk again. She was like a queen on parade, her head held high, her eyes alert, her steps measured and sure. I was so proud of her . . .

By the time the competition had ended, the Butlers, with their small herd of three, had won three second-place ribbons. However, they still were not taken seriously by their competitors. When one of the herdsmen was asked what had happened to his entries, the man replied, "Oh, the judge just had a bad day."

Ross was fifteen when Beryl Hanmer, the neighbour boy who had sold his cow Rolo Mercena De Kol at auction for $26,000, asked Ross to go with him to the Guelph Winter Fair. Ross's job was to stay with the cattle, help groom them for the show ring and help with the milking in a forty-eight hour milking derby.

Ross couldn't believe his luck. He had wanted to go to the Guelph Winter Fair for a long time as it was the showplace for the best in agriculture. And not only was he going, but he was also going to be paid. Ross also couldn't believe his luck when he learned that the McPhersons, whose Ayrshires were sharing the cattle car with the Hanmer's animals, hired LaVerne Rush, a schoolmate of Ross's, to help with their cattle at the fair.

Just before the train was to pull out of the station, two older boys from school came along. They asked Ross and LaVerne where they had gotten the money to buy their train tickets. The two young herdsmen said they didn't need tickets because they were working their way to the Guelph Fair.

The two older boys, who knew a bit about travel, convinced us that we needed a ticket. They said that without a ticket the conductor would throw us off the train. So every time the train stopped . . . and there were many stops as is was a slow freight . . . we dived into the mounds of hay and hid.

The train didn't arrive in Guelph until almost noon the next day. Only then did the boys realize that they had been the victims of a colossal joke.

Their humiliation was short-lived as they were quickly caught up in the excitement of the fair. Despite the noise and the confusion, Ross loved every minute. He especially liked being part of the attention as fairgoers stopped to admire the Hanmer Holsteins.

When the boys' chores were finished, they were given time off. While LaVerne headed for the midway, Ross headed for the poultry pavilion where hundreds of geese, chickens, and ducks contributed to a deafening symphony of sound. As Ross walked up and down the aisles, he was amazed at the shapes and colours of the different breeds. At home, the Butlers only had a few brown Orpingtons and some white Leghorns. Here at Guelph, there were over 6,000 birds besides the waterfowl. Over the next few days, Ross systematically explored the other pavilions which housed everything from root crops to sheep. For the boy from Norwich, it was an educational experience beyond measure.

I loved them all. . . . It gave me the privilege to live among these creatures for many days. It was the greatest thrill of my life.

When Ross returned from the fair, his family wanted him to quit school and go to work. He could learn to be a herdsman, they said, which was certainly better than a career in art. But Ross was adamant — he wanted an education and he wanted to draw.

By now I had over 300 sketches in my collection. Everything came under my observation: people, animals, birds, flowers, our chickens . . . everything that I could see, touch or smell. I have wondered if these

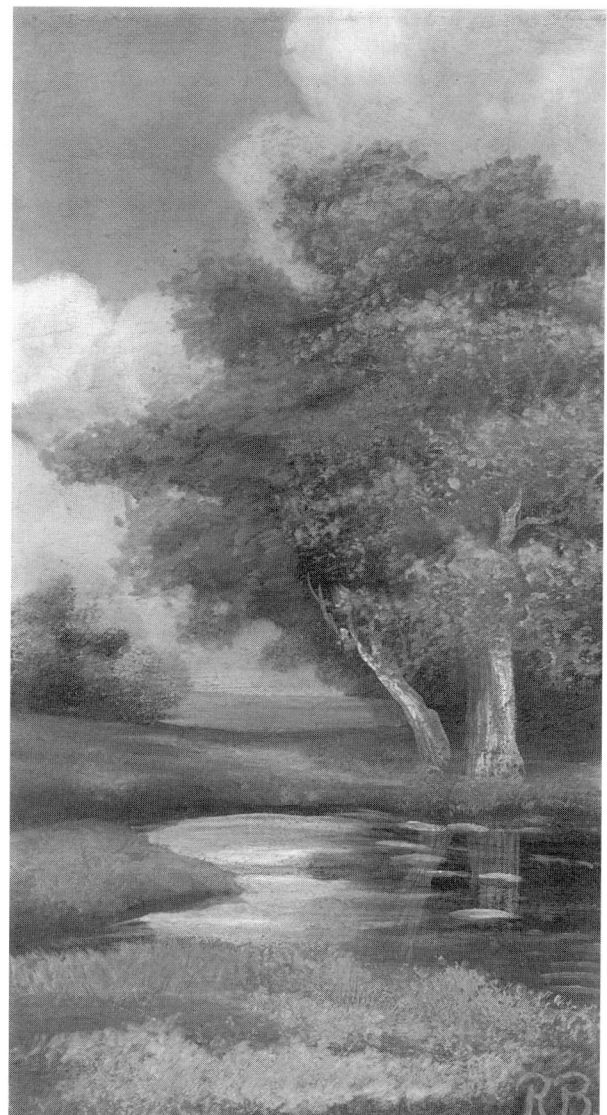

things in my environment appeared to me larger than life, or in super colour. They were so real and intimate. I found that such observation and subsequent drawing was the finest method yet invented to see and understand reality.

Even at this young age, the natural form and the intimate quality of Ross's work was already beginning to show. These qualities would become more refined over the years.

Ross's personality was changing, too. He became more social. When his brothers and sister went swimming at the "swimmin' hole" in Otter Creek, Ross went too. He loved to swim but he didn't like the clayball fights that often erupted around the pond. He had no way of knowing that one day that clay would be the core element in his sculptures. That pond also became a favourite place for the family in the wintertime. Although Ross wasn't athletic like his brothers, he loved to skate. One Sunday afternoon, while trying to imitate the figure skating skills of Fred Newton, a local celebrity, he fell and broke his collarbone. Still, he continued to skate for the next thirty years.

Despite Ross's determination to get an education, he was forced to quit during his final year of school to take over his brother's milk route. It was a gruelling job which entailed more than just milking the cows and delivering that milk to the villagers. The milk had to be strained, cooled, bottled, and loaded onto a hand-made delivery wagon. Then, with the horses harnessed and hitched to the milk wagon, the milk was peddled.

After the last quart of milk was delivered and the last empty bottle picked up, there was still more work. The coins had to be counted, the unsold milk had to be separated, and the cream made into butter. The waste milk was given to the animals. Even with his sisters' help, Ross had no time for dreaming or sketching. There was only work . . . and more work. It was a hard, never-ending job encompassing seven days-a-week and fifty-two weeks a year and Ross hated every minute of it.

After losing several customers to a rival company, David Butler sold the milk route. At about the same time a new baby named Carl appeared in the Butler family. Shortly afterward, with their older sons and daughter married and an infant boy in the family, David and Mary Butler left their farm, renting a house in nearby Woodstock, Ontario, where Ross found the freedom to be creative.

And I was free at last to begin a new life.

2 | Freedom To Create

AFTER WORKING FROM DAWN TO DUSK for almost a year, Ross Butler quickly took advantage of his new found freedom. He spent hours wandering the historic streets of Woodstock, exploring the shops and parks and admiring the beautiful girls. Anything beautiful, Ross believed was a gift of nature.

The Butlers joined a local church, as was the custom when a family moved to a new community. Ross was soon involved in a young people's group, where his polite, soft-spoken manner earned him a place of respect among his peers. When asked a question, he always gave a reasonable, well-thought, although sometimes, lengthy answer. Once a year, the church's young people's group met with other such local groups. On one such occasion when a speaker was needed, Ross was asked to give an address on the topic "The Ideals of Character in the Choice of a Life's Partner." Of course, it was a subject about which he knew nothing.

Ross was surprisingly well-read and he liked to recite the quotations of great men for inspiration. Bishop Jeremy Taylor had said, "A good wife is heaven's gift to man," while novelist Charles Reade claimed that a wife was two-thirds responsible for a man's ill-humour. With such divided opinion Ross turned to his art for help. Using a negative marking pencil, he drew caricatures of the "ideal" and "not-so-ideal" partners onto glass slides. His caricatures were projected onto a six-foot screen, which he referred to during his speech to emphasize certain points. The young people loved the presentation and Ross was besieged with invitations to do it again.

None of this put money in Ross's pocket, however. In an attempt to solve this problem, he came up with the idea of using caricatures of prominent Woodstock businessmen as an advertising ploy. The idea was to display the caricatures on the Capitol Theatre's screen before each movie. The manager of the theatre loved the idea, but was unwilling to do the leg-work to sell it to the local merchants and business people. Instead, Ross did the selling, and each week for the next six weeks several prominent people were featured on the screen. One of these was Miss Woodstock, who later became Ross's first girlfriend.

I was in heaven when I walked down the street with her on my arm. And I couldn't wait to put her face on canvas.

That painting still hangs in the Ross Butler Studio just outside Woodstock.
    Although many theatre patrons loved Ross's caricatures, his venture didn't last long. Some of the wives of his victims felt it was demeaning to have caricatures of their husbands laughed at by theatre goers. Although this venture had been short-lived, it was the first money he had earned as an artist. This venture also afforded him the opportunity to meet many of Woodstock's influential men. This would be a tremendous asset later in his up-hill climb as an artist.
    As the depression worsened, the Butlers were forced to move to a drafty old brick house at 629 Peel Street in Woodstock. Although both Ross and his father searched diligently for work, they could only find a few day jobs and some seasonal work. In this period, Ross became a factory worker, a salesman, and a herdsman at fair time for either Nesbitt's Glen Farm near Innerkip or Innes's City View Farm. Although these jobs were seasonal, and paid only a dollar or two a day, they usually included a trip to the Canadian National Exhibition or the Royal Winter Fair in Toronto. For Ross, these trips were the highlight of the year.
    When Ross was not working, he painted. Because he was a self-taught artist, he had no one to critique his work and give suggestion's for improvements. When one of his favourite pictures was rejected, he took it to a Woodstock art teacher for her opinion. She told him flatly to forget art as a career for his work wasn't good enough.

Their conversation was overheard by a student who was also in the studio. She later asked what was wrong with Butler's work and the teacher said that it was "just too different." After all, cubism and radical art were the way of the future. But Ross felt these art forms were crude and an abomination of nature.

For me, art is a beautiful thing. It is skilled and exacting work which reflects the finest in human feelings. Anything else is just a mockery of everything beautiful.

Many times during those early years, Ross felt like giving up his art, but each time his deep-seated need to paint overrode reason. At a particularly low point, he was fortunate enough to meet another artist who was also a prominent minister in the city. Both this man and his daughter, who later became Ross's receptionist, encouraged him to continue to paint, no matter what the cost. During those bad times, Ross learned to barter his art for necessities: he painted a portrait of a local tailor for an overcoat, made window signs at Woolworth's for toiletry items, and business cards in exchange for a haircut. These times were hard, but Ross used them to hone his skills.

There were a few small triumphs along the way. On one wet summer day, Ross was walking behind a group of girls who were in a hurry to get back to work following their lunch hour. He noticed that muddy water was splashing up from their heels onto the back of their legs, splattering their hose. What a shame, he thought . . . such lovely legs marred by black spots. Suddenly an idea sprang to mind. What if he could design a rubber rainboot to protect their hose?

Ross rushed home and sketched a rain shoe. Trashed it. He drew another design, trashed it too. By midnight, he finally had designed a light-weight rain boot which could be easily slipped on over a lady's shoe. A single button was used to hold the cross-over front in place.

While Ross knew it was a good design, he didn't have the money to patent the idea. Someone finally took a chance on Ross's design and lent him the money to buy the patent. Ross and his backer had their money back with interest in just a few

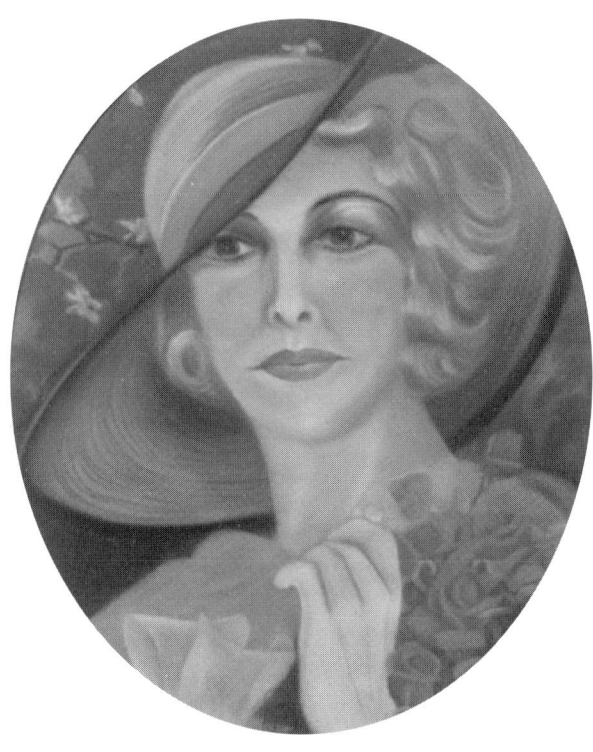

Portrait of Gertrude, Ross Butler's first girlfriend and the reigning "Miss Woodstock."

months when Ross sold the design to the Dominion Rubber Company of Kitchener for $250. Had Ross acquired royalties for his design, he undoubtedly would have been well off financially, for the company used Ross's design for many years.

At the time, Ross led a rather lonely life. His art became a means of companionship. He read to his brother Carl, who was blind, helped his father in the garden, and ran errands for his mother. He found little chance for a social life but used his artistic talents to solve this problem.

Whenever I saw a beautiful girl, I would ask her to pose for me. It was a sure fire way to seek companionship and romance.

Because Ross was a nice-looking, clean-cut young man with impeccable manners, the girls were certainly willing.

After one such portrait, Ross got the idea to hold a beauty contest sponsored by a newspaper or institution. The contest would be a fund raiser for a charity and, of course, he would paint the contestants. These paintings would be on display at the Canadian National Exhibition, where the winner would be crowned as Miss Ontario. He felt sure that such exposure to his work would bring him instant fame and fortune. The C.N.E. officials liked the idea and sponsored the contest with a prominent newspaper. For Ross, however, there was no remuneration for his idea.

Just another brainstorm that went sour.

Despite one setback after another, Ross continued to paint people in the news, for he firmly believed their success would lead to his success. When he realized there wasn't any market for these types of paintings in Woodstock, he decided to take his collection to Toronto. Early in the morning, with a painting under his arm, he would hitch a ride on a milk truck to the city. While the driver delivered his milk to the factory, Ross would make the rounds of the newspapers and magazines publishers in the

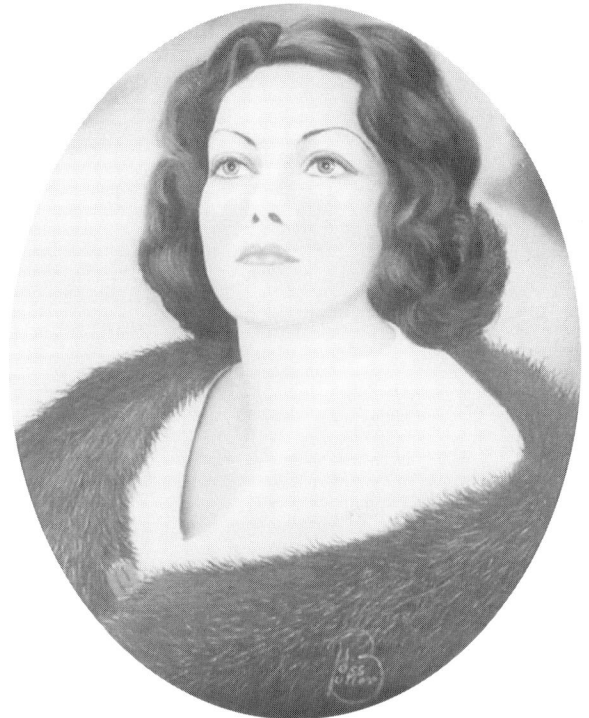

Portrait of Ida, "Miss Ontario."

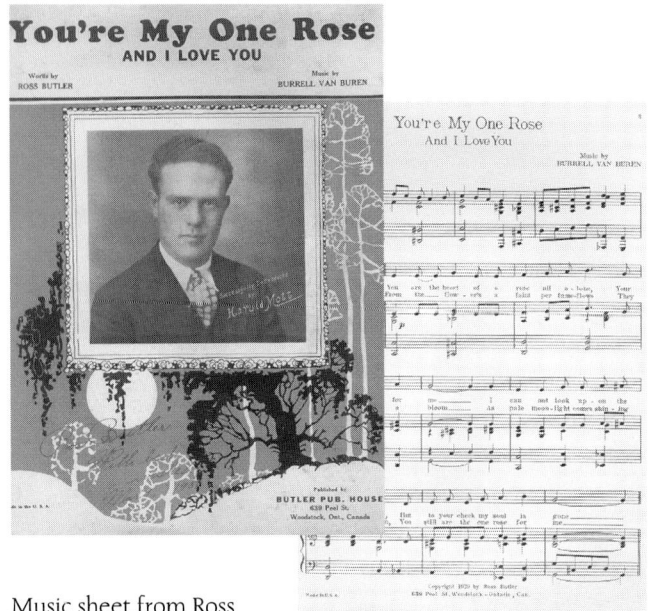

Music sheet from Ross Butler's first published song. His design for rain-shoes was patented and then sold to the Dominion Rubber Company.

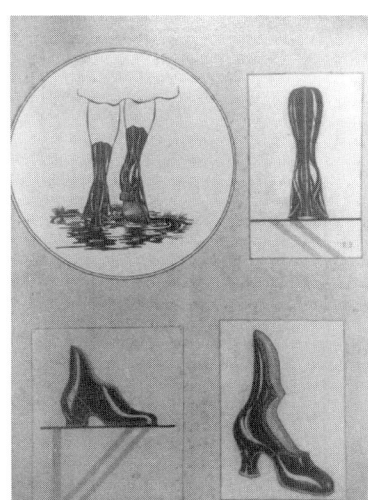

downtown core area. In the afternoon, he would hitch a ride home on the same truck — usually with the painting still under his arm. One editor became so fed up with Ross's visits that he set up an appointment for Ross with the curator of a Toronto Art Galley to evaluate his work. The curator said that while the colours were good, the drawings were poor. The editor who had made this appointment for Ross had told him just the opposite. Ross wasn't sure who to believe.

To prove his point, the curator took Ross to the upstairs of the gallery where over ten thousand dollars worth of paintings had just arrived from New York. Here, Ross saw first-hand the works of Norman Rockwell, Mead Schaeffer, Arthur William Brown, Bradshaw Crandal, and others. These successful artists had studied at the world's greatest art schools.

I got the point. He was right! I was hopelessly outclassed. And now I knew it. That day I realized I had to say good-bye to my overwhelming ambition to be an artist. It was one of the saddest days of my life.

Now disenchanted with art, Ross turned to writing haunting rapturous songs. While some of the songs were quite good, they had to be heard to become popular. So Ross bribed orchestra leader Jack Arthur to feature one of his songs at the Southside Park "Dance" Pavilion in Woodstock, for a week.

I went there every night to hear my song being played. I didn't go in. I couldn't afford the admission. I just stood in the shadows and listened.

One of Ross's songs entitled "You're My One Rose . . . and I Love You" became quite successful, selling several thousand copies of sheet music. It was first introduced on the stage at Woodstock's Capital Theatre by Harold Mott, a Norwich high-school friend of Ross's. Mott, with a beautiful baritone voice, later went on to become a choir soloist in Buffalo. "You're My One Rose" was debuted next on the stage at London's Loew's Theatre. The biggest plug came when London's Radio Station CJGC played the song again and again, always announcing the "lyrics by Ross Butler of Woodstock." This song brought Ross in contact with many musicians, singers, and publishers. Among them were the famous tenor Edward Johnson and his daughter, who years later became the wife of George Drew, the Premier of Ontario. Ross shook hands with both the famous and the not-so-famous, but everyone he met encouraged him to continue writing more lyrics.

Instead of being a poverty-stricken artist, Ross was now a poverty-stricken somebody. He scrounged together enough money to buy himself an older car, but this was more of a status symbol than a transportation necessity. He began to write articles for agricultural magazines about the techniques of farming. These articles were usually accompanied by a sketch or drawing but few were accepted. Sometimes, an editor paid Ross a dollar or two for his artwork but had someone else write the story. Still others only paid in copies of the magazines, which did little to help Ross's money situation.

When Ross was twenty-one he decided to enter the *Atlantic Monthly*'s $10,000 novel-writing contest. For a year he slaved night and day over his work *The Golden River*. However, when the manuscript was completed, he realized that he didn't have the money to get it typed. So he bartered a portrait of a lawyer's assistant for the typing of his manuscript. When his novel didn't win the contest, Ross was devastated. His only consolation was that a fellow Canadian, Maza de La Roche, had won the contest with *Jalna of Whiteoaks*. He had been so absorbed in his writing that he had neglected everything else, including his health, his painting, and the need to find work. He had survived during this time by borrowing money from his friends, but now when they saw him coming, they crossed to the other side of the street. He lost his car because he could not make the last two payments. At twenty-three years of age Ross Butler found himself deeply in debt without any means of support. He was bankrupt. To make matters worse, Ross was rushed to the hospital with acute appendicitis.

The only bright spot in his life occurred during this hospital stay when he fell madly in love with one of his beautiful nurses. Her portrait still hangs in the Ross

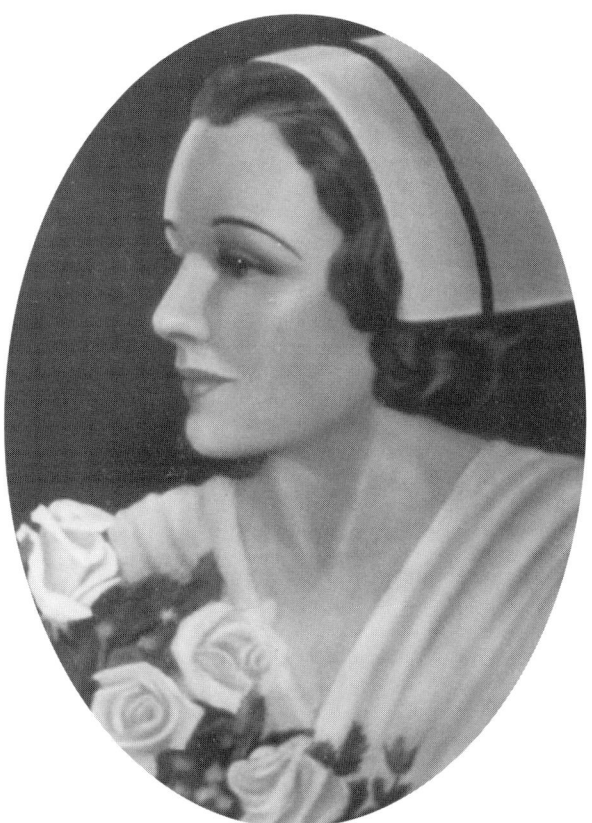

Portrait of Nurse Gladys,
painted as a tribute to her character
and her profession.

Butler Studio. When he was released from hospital, Ross became despondent. It seemed that no matter how hard he tried, he couldn't seem to get ahead. He became disillusioned and bitter. That bitterness would linger for many years. He became a loner, shunning people who were more affluent than he. His only haven was his art. It became an island to where he could escape and where hope could replace his fear.

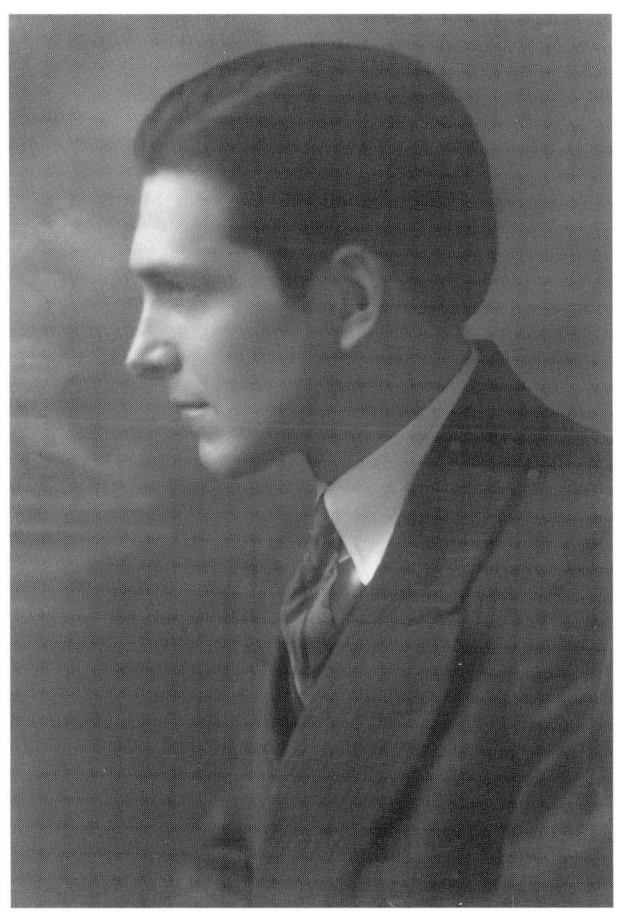

Photograph of Ross Butler as a young man.

3 | "The Greatest Animal Painter in the World"

THE SO-CALLED "DIRTY THIRTIES" began a decade of despair and depression, and Ross Butler, like many others, felt his career was on a road going to nowhere. He still searched for work, painted, and wrote, but there was still an inner feeling of defeat. However, something happened that was to forever change Ross's attitude towards life.

It was midsummer. A violent thunderstorm ripped through the county, knocking out hydro lines, tearing roofs off barns, splitting huge trees in two. Out of this violent storm came a young neighbour carrying a baby goat in his arms. He had lived alone in an old shed, surviving on the milk of the mother of this kid until she dried up. Then, he said he was going to kill and eat her. When he got her down, his knife at her throat (he was crying) the storm ripped the roof off the shed. Believing it was an omen, he grabbed up the baby goat and ran to the our place. He wanted us to feed her and keep her safe. He felt he and the mother would surely die, if not by the hand of the storm, then by circumstances.

As Ross listened to the young man's story, he had begun to realize just how fortunate he really was. Not only did he have a loving family, but also a roof over his head and plenty to eat. Ross decided to quit feeling sorry for himself and make a positive stand against the forces that ruled his life. The first step on that road was giving a certain young man and his goats food and shelter.

The next step was to head off to the C.N.E. as a herdsman for a local breeder. There Ross heard that the Canadian Jersey Association was searching for a trademark emblem to represent their breed. He submitted a drawing of the horned head of a Jersey cow in a six-sided frame. When it was accepted, he was ecstatic. That winning drawing was used until Ross updated it fifty years later.

Of the two exhibitions held in Toronto, Ross loved the Royal Winter Fair best. He would browse for hours and study the animals, defining both their good points and bad ones. He would also make sketches of the animals and paint them in their true colours when he got home. Ross knew that having an animal win at the Royal Winter Fair was the height of most breeders' expectations. He decided to express those feelings in a poster for the fair, but the board turned it down. Years later, his painting entitled *Royal Review*, which depicted a march-past of animals from the breeder's barn to the final triumph, would be acclaimed by many as a masterpiece.

The following year, Ross spent the entire summer preparing a brochure for a Toronto dairy on *The Story of Milk* from the fields to the doorstep. The dairy liked the brochure, but before it was published, they gave it to a well-known advertising agency for "polishing." The agency claimed that Ross's brochure didn't stand up to high-powered advertising. For a price, and using his illustrations, they would prepare it properly. Ross, of course, couldn't afford to pay and he had to fight very hard to get even twenty dollars for his entire summer's work.

Depressed, he went back to painting portraits of celebrities. These paintings always made him feel good about himself and he hoped that some of their success would rub off on him. One of these was a large painting of King George V who would soon be celebrating his Silver Jubilee.

Ross's first real taste of success came unexpectedly and from where it was least expected — right in his own back yard. In March 1933, Ross was asked by the Holstein Friesian Association to paint Springbank Snow Countess, a Holstein cow that became famous when she broke the world record as a lifetime butterfat producer. Ross received a total of three dollars for the painting, which continues to hang today in the head office of the Holstein Friesian Association in Brantford, Ontario. When Tom Dent, the owner of Springbank Snow Countess, saw the painting, he wanted Ross to paint a second one. The price had now risen to five dollars. This second painting hangs on the wall of the recreation room in Tom Dent's son's home in Woodstock.

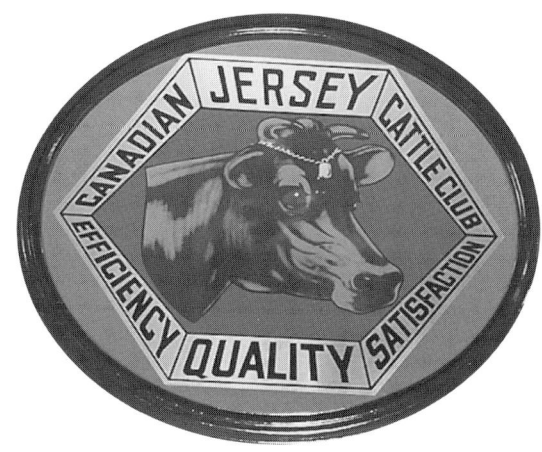

Trademark emblem created for the Canadian Jersey Cattle Club, used on milk-bottle caps, farm signs, posters, and decals.

When the Holstein Friesian Association later decided to erect a statue in honour of Springbank Snow Countess, Ross acted as a consultant on the four-thousand-dollar project. Although this statue is a symbol of the dairy industry in Oxford County, it has suffered many indignities over the years. It has been shot in the right leg, sprayed with purple paint and graffiti.

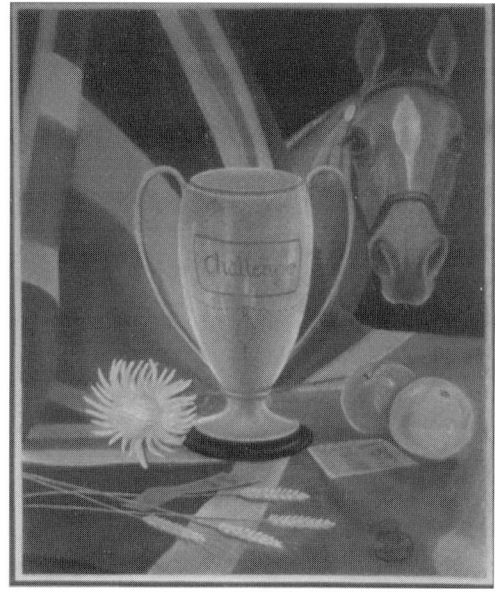

Poster designed for the Royal Winter Fair.

In Honour of
SPRINGBANK SNOW COUNTESS
81871
World Champion Lifetime Butterfat Producer
9062 lbs. butterfat and 207,505 lbs. milk in 10
lactations. Average test 4.37%
ERECTED BY THE HOLSTEIN FRIESIAN ASSOCIATION
OF CANADA, Aug 4, 1937 ON SPRINGBANK FARM
WHERE HER LIFETIME WAS SPENT IN THE SERVICE
OF HER BREEDER AND OWNER
T.R. DENT

Later that same year Ross's painting of Volunteer's April Sultan, a cow owned by the Innis family of Oxford, also made its way into the limelight. A reproduction of the painting appeared on the cover of *Farmer's Magazine*. This sale was particularly gratifying for Ross as this publication (formerly *The Ontario Farmer*) had repeatedly turned down his submissions. For the first time, it seemed to Ross that he was actually getting ahead. He painted Pontiac Dutchland DeVries, another Holstein cow that had broken the world record in her class. He sold the painting for a few dollars, but it was not enough to make him financially solvent.

Ross was in dire straights when B.H. Bull and Son of Brampton asked him to do a painting of their cow, Brampton Basilua. This Jersey cow, who weighed only 750 pounds, had created a sensation when she produced 1,311 pounds of butterfat in one

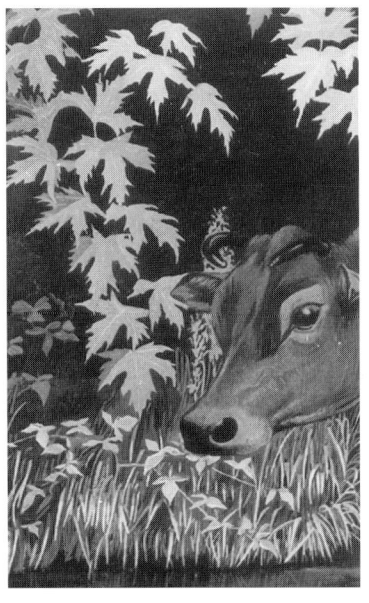

year. Ross needed a new paint brush to do the job properly but he did not have the money to buy one. Instead he wired together the bristles of several old brushes, scraped the sand off a sheet of sandpaper to use as a canvas, and hitched a ride to the Bull's Brampton farm. Sitting on the cow's manger, he completed the painting and considered it as one of his best works. Fortunately, he was not the only one to think highly of the painting. At the annual meeting of the Canadian Jersey Club, it was acclaimed "the finest painting of a Jersey cow here or abroad." It also secured Ross a commission to create the male and female ideal or "True Types" of the Jersey breed.

Ross had always believed that Jerseys were the cream of the dairy herds, and now with his new commission he had a chance to prove it. These pictures, of course, could only be composites as no one animal could have all the qualities that would make a True Type. Before he put a brush to canvas, Ross delved through the mountains of diverse materials which he had accumulated over the years. Then, armed with a comprehensive view of the "ideal" animal, he began his paintings.

Unbeknownst to Ross, his name and work as a domestic animal painter was becoming known among breeders. He was elated when Perkins Bull, a brother to B.H., was convinced that he could turn Ross into the "greatest animal painter in the world." Perkins Bull was working on a history of Peel County and he wanted Ross to paint all the famous animals of that county. This was heady praise for a young artist, but it still did not put bread on the table. After months of work and countless submissions, nothing came of it. The painting of Brampton Basilua, which had started everything, disappeared from public view and was found years later at a flea market. The finder recognized the painting and returned it to Ross for a small fee.

During this time, Ross finished his paintings of the True Type Jersey cow and bull and submitted them to the Canadian Jersey Association at their annual meeting. He would have preferred to have presented these paintings in person, but due to his financial situation, he was forced to submit them by mail. They were rejected without any explanation — Ross could not help but wonder if his association with Perkins Bull had anything to do with the situation. Disappointed, angry, bent, but not broken, Ross

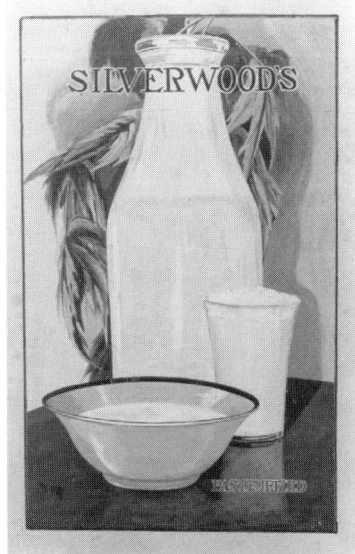

The cover and page design for *The Story of Milk*.

went back to his drawing board. With dogged determination he painted another set and submitted them to the association the following year. This time they were approved without question.

Early in 1934 Ross and his family moved again, this time to a four and a half acre holding at 742 Pavey Street on the outskirts of Woodstock. As well as a big brick house, the property also had a barn, chicken coup, orchard, and a large ploughed area for a garden. Ross's father hoped to make a little extra money with the sale of excess produce. The Butlers also purchased a remarkable milk producer, a Jersey cow whose owners were forced to part with her for financial reasons. Despite the fact that Ross had to help with the planting, hoeing, and harvesting, he loved the place. He now had a room of his own for his books and magazines. It was also a place where he could paint without disruption.

In addition to the Jersey breeders, other groups were also looking for the True Types of their breed. Ross was approached by the Ayrshire breeders, but before he would put brush to canvas, he thoroughly researched the breed. When Ross's picture of the bull was published on the cover of the *Ayrshire* magazine, the editorial read, "This is the best portrayal of any breed of livestock, yet painted. It is the nearest approach to a true type that we have yet attained." Because Ross was desperately in need of money, he parted with the originals, but did keep the reproduction rights. Four years later, by bartering prints for the originals, he was able to buy them back from the Ayrshire Association.

With the money from the sale of these paintings, Ross paid some bills and bought some much-needed clothing. He hated having frayed shirt cuffs or threadbare jacket elbows, but despite these, he always looked the country gentleman. With the left-over money, he purchased a used Dodge car for seventy-five dollars. Now with his own transportation, he was able to travel to different farms to see and paint animals in their own environment.

Many farmers wanted a painting of their "special" cow or bull, and Ross was gaining a reputation as a man who knew cattle. He supplemented his family's income

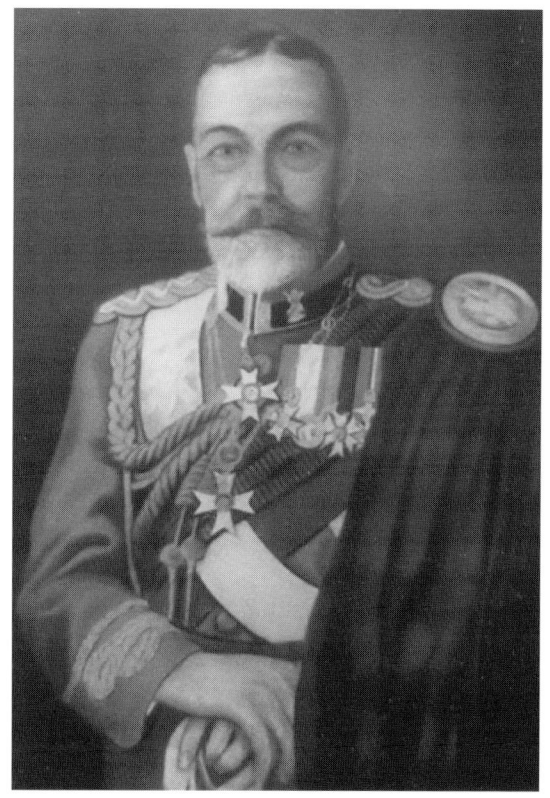

Portrait of King George V, on the occasion of his Silver Jubilee.

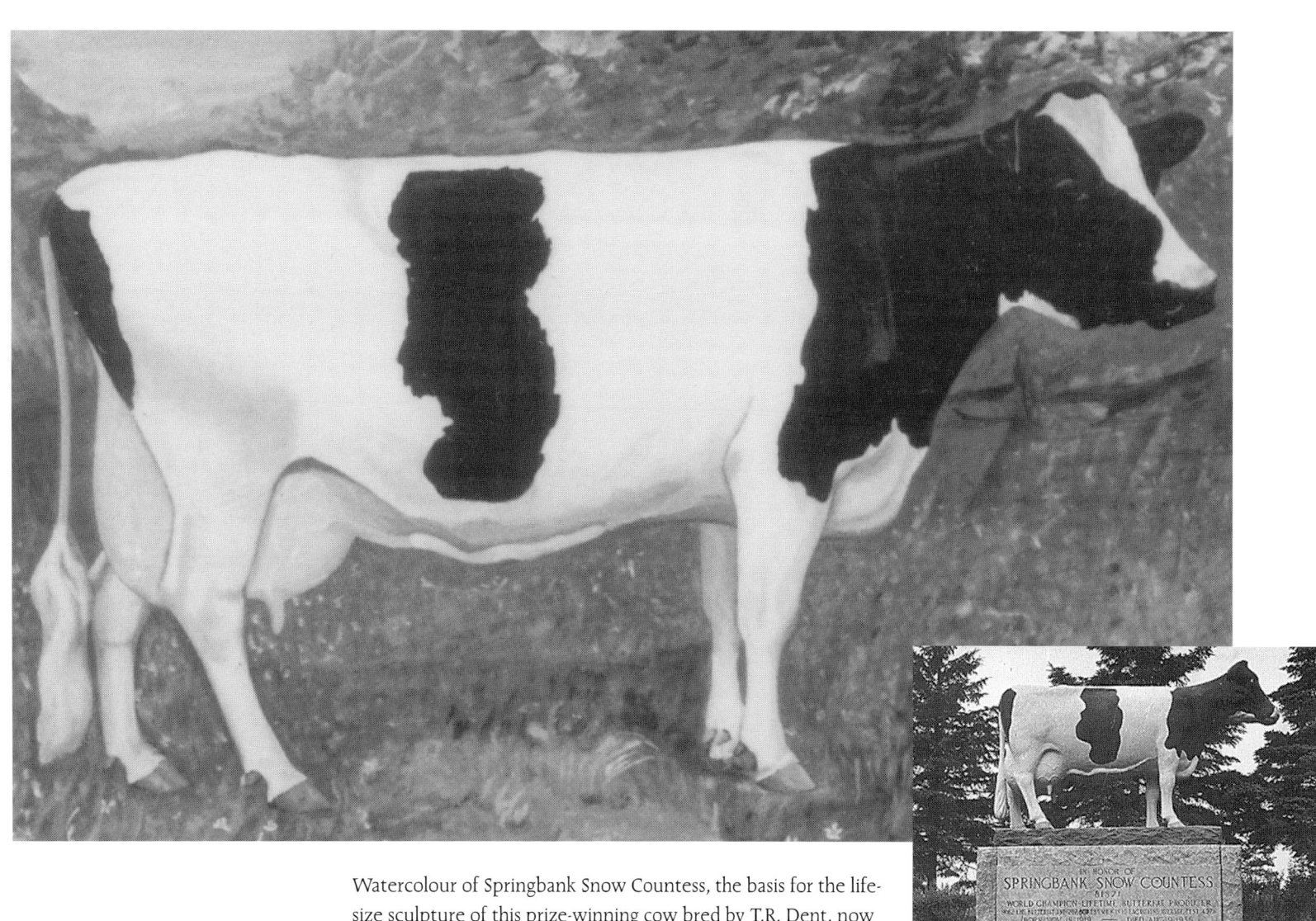

Watercolour of Springbank Snow Countess, the basis for the life-size sculpture of this prize-winning cow bred by T.R. Dent, now the symbol of Woodstock as "The Dairy Capital of Canada."

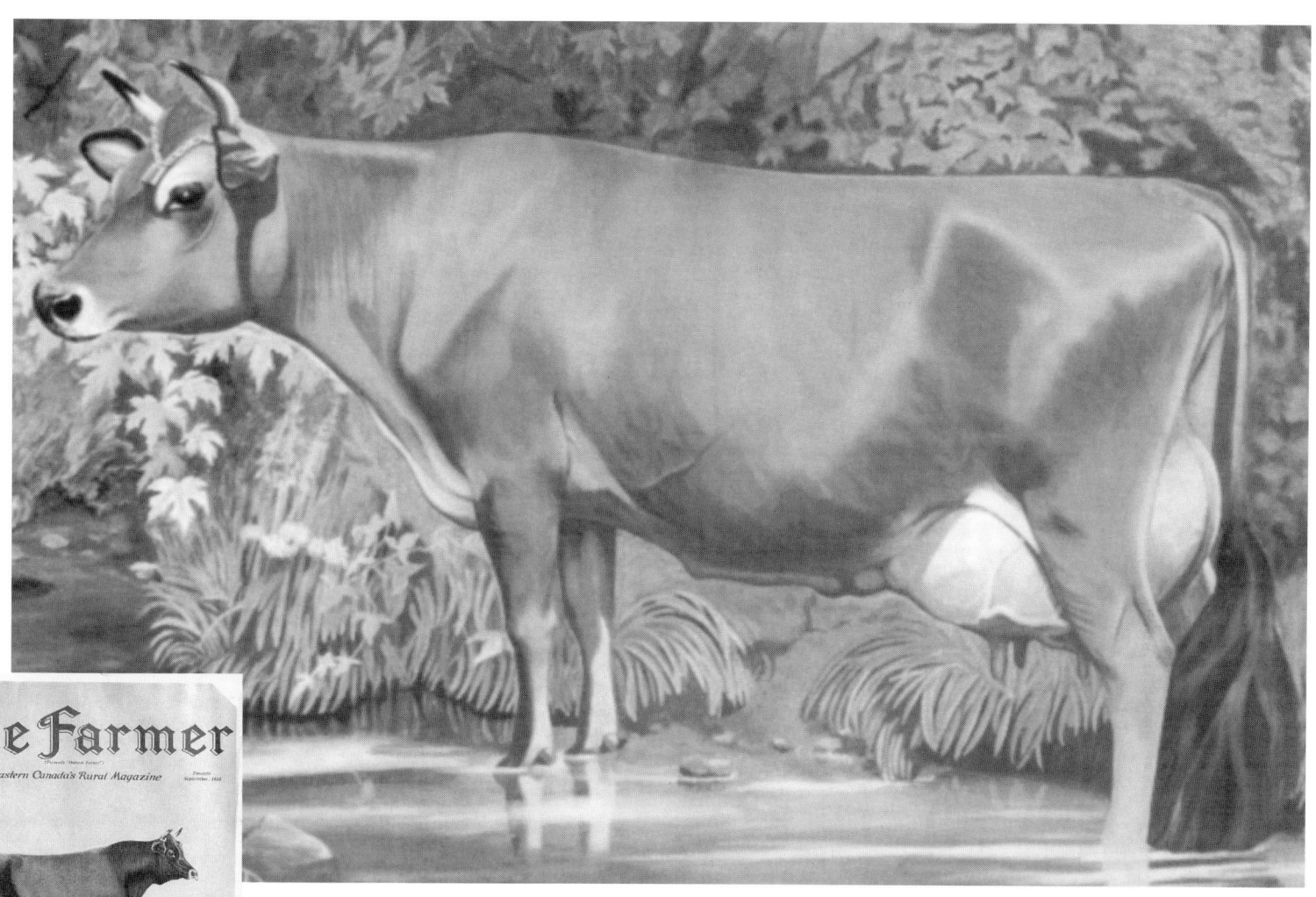

Watercolour of Brampton Basilua, published in The History of Peel County, and watercolour painting of Volunteer's April Sultan, reproduced on the cover of The Farmer.

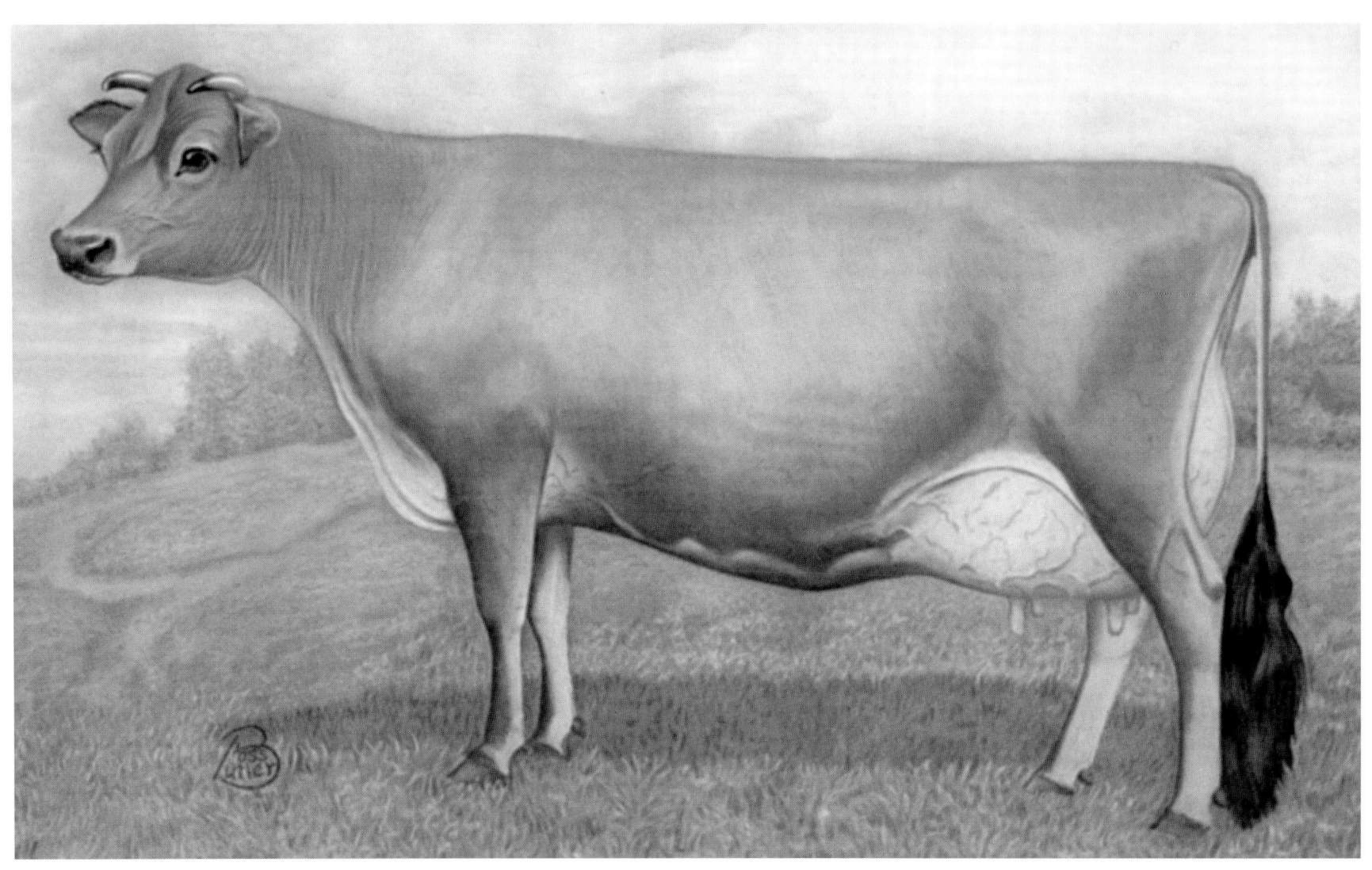

First "true type" paintings, commissioned and approved by the Canadian Jersey Club.

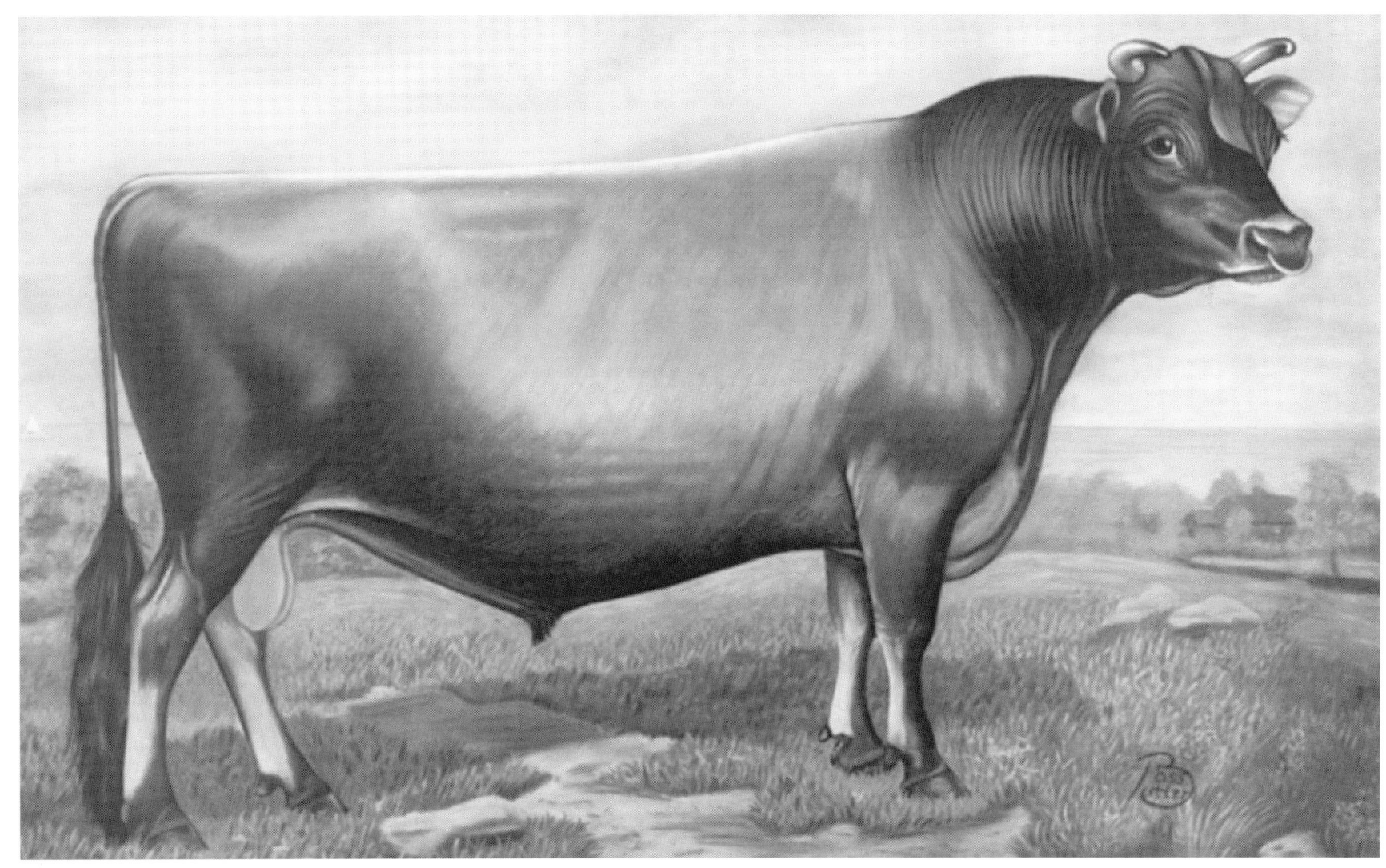

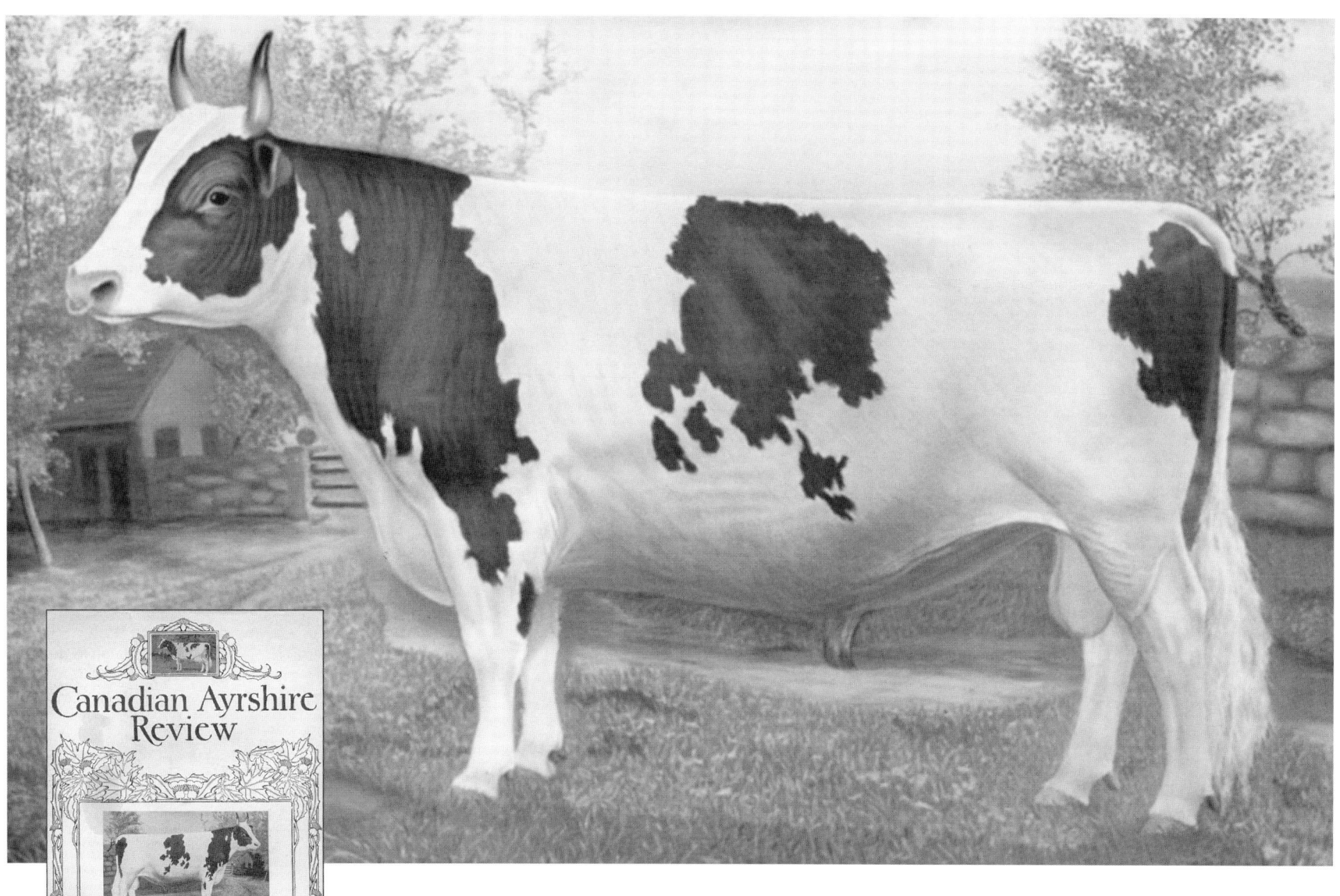

True type painting commissioned by the Ayrshire Association of Canada and reproduced on the cover of their magazine.

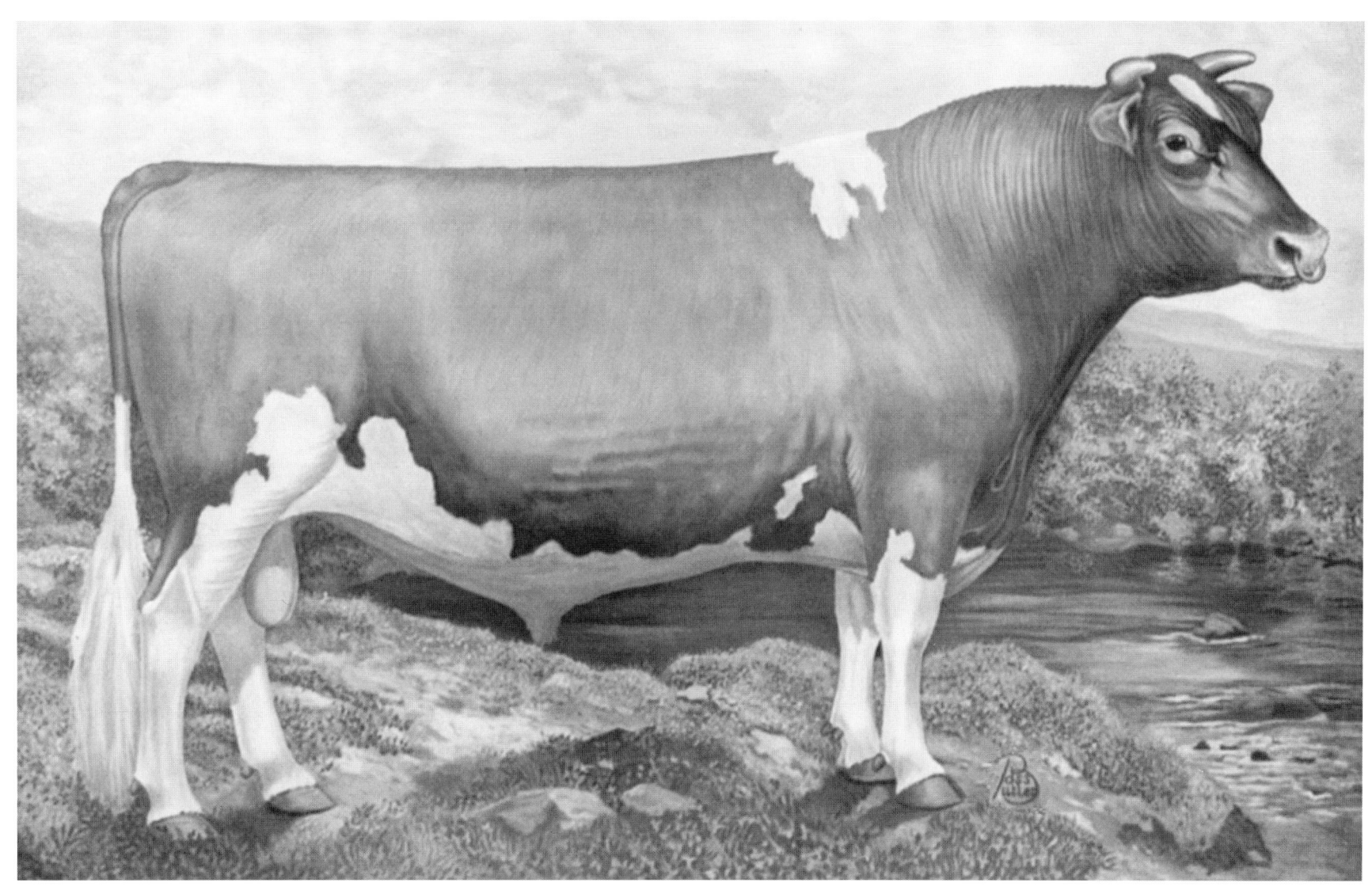

True type painting commissioned by the Guernsey Association of Canada.

by locating cows or bulls for a breeder. This netted him a small finder's commission.

About the same time, people from the Guernsey Association approached Ross about doing paintings of the ideal cow and bull for them. As he leafed through mounds of research material, he began to wonder exactly what constituted the ideal animal. Until now, he had worked with a trial and error method, often bending to what the committee's view was of the ideal animal. He did ask people in the cattle industry such as breeders and judges, as well as professors at Canada's foremost agricultural college in Guelph, what they considered to be a "True Type." No one had any definite answers.

During his research, Ross became intrigued by a theory developed by a man in England. The theory stated that "in order to arrive at the ideal breed, livestock breeders should draw on the wall of their barn the image of the animal they wanted. Then, keeping that image in mind, they should strive through their breeding program to make that animal a reality." In his mind, Ross drew the ideal cow, a Jersey, of course, a combination of old Daisy from his father's previous farm and their present stable of two. These animals all had special qualities, including the right colouring, the right weight, and good milk production.

One night as Ross milked the family cow he noticed that she had grown a little larger in circumference since the Butlers had purchased her. Out of curiosity, Ross measured her girth at its largest point. While painting, he later noticed that the girth of the animal at its largest point seemed to be the same as the length from the tip of the animal's nose to its tailbone. Put simply, her girth was equal to her length.

That night, while lying sleepless in bed. Ross went over his discoveries in his mind. He had learned from his father that a horse's size was determined by the height at the animal's withers as expressed by so many hands high. Would this same measurement apply to a cow? The next morning, he rushed to the barn to measure the height of the cow's withers, which also equalled the height of her rump. He then noticed that her front feet stood the same distance apart from rear hooves. Mentally outlining these proportions, Ross realized that they formed a perfect square.

Over the next few months, he took more measurements and carefully recorded them. The length of the cow's head became a unit measurement. Half of the width of the head was equal to the width of the ear. However, when he tried to measure the width of her eye, which equalled the width of her nostril, the cow became down-right ornery.

When Ross took his discoveries to a professor at the University of Guelph, the man scoffed at Ross's theory. No mathematical harmony existed in animals, he claimed. Ross's theory was utter nonsense. But over the next few years, Ross continued to take measurements of many animals, including cows, bulls, horses, sheep, and goats; he even measured himself. Ross was convinced that he had stumbled upon a fundamental law of nature. This theory of proportions became a blueprint that he would follow for the rest of his life.

However, Ross continued to have other problems of a practical nature. His brother Carl was at the School for the Blind at Brantford and Mary Butler often took to her bed with severe headaches. Because medication was too expensive, she rubbed her forehead and temples with a wintergreen liniment whose smell drifted throughout the entire house. Ross wanted her to go to a specialist, but again there was simply no money for such things. No matter how hard Ross worked, there never seemed enough money to pay all of the bills.

On 28 May 1934 the Dionne Quintuplets were born at Callander, Ontario, and like the rest of the world, Ross marvelled at their birth. He spent hours that winter doing a pastel portrait of the five baby girls. As soon as the weather was favourable, he was off to Callander in an attempt to sell the painting. Instead, he was told that he would have to pay the N.E.A. News Services five thousand dollars for the right to market the print. Of course, Ross didn't have the money and this painting was added to his growing collection of un-saleables.

In 1936, as Ross struggled for recognition as a painter of celebrities, he was elated when he read in the local newspaper that the Governor General of Canada, Lord Tweedsmuir, John Buchan, was coming to Woodstock on May 6. Now he could

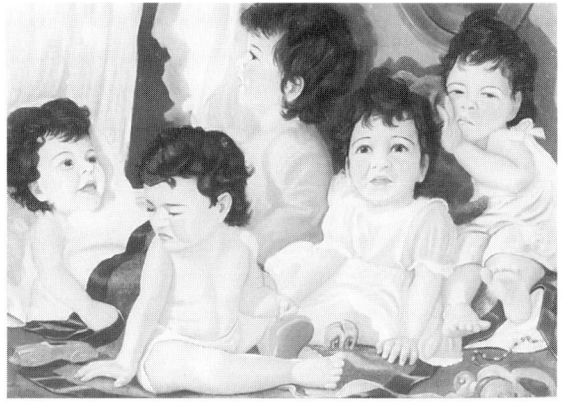

The Dionne quintuplets at two years of age.

see a celebrity up close. Buchan, besides being a celebrated statesman and orator, was a world-renowned biographer and author of historical novels. Ross had long admired his work and was determined to hear him speak.

And what a speaker he was! Never a hesitation. Never a loss for words. So confident, so self-assured . . . if only I could be more like him.

Ross continued to write for agricultural magazines and sometimes his writing contributed more to his income than his art. He became well-known and respected in agricultural circles, but at home his neighbours thought him to be aloof, haughty, even arrogant. While Ross was a loner, he was never lonely. His mind was always jumping ahead, focusing on a new idea or a better way of doing something. His interests centred around his work and his family, so few people saw the quiet, gentle man beneath the aloofness.

    Ross also had strong beliefs. He believed that the mind, if it was to be productive, had to be cultivated and fertilized.

Everything, whether it was a fine poem, a piece of art or a business, has its origin in the mind.

He became so engrossed in the subject that he developed and followed his own mind-training program and even contemplated writing a book on the training of the mind.

    He also came to believe that a healthy body leads to a healthy mind. In his early twenties he had neglected his health and had paid a heavy price for doing so. Determined never to neglect his health again, Ross developed a common sense eating program consisting of salads, fruits, cheese, and little meat. It was a program he adhered to the rest of his life. Despite the economic depression, Ross was determined to carve a life for himself that held meaning and substance.

4 | True Types

ROSS BUTLER'S NEXT PROJECT was actually conceived while he was working in his father's vegetable garden. He was hoeing potatoes and, as usual, his mind jumped to other things. Ross suddenly had the idea that all Ontario schools should have illustrated True Type paintings of the breeds of domestic animals. What an idea! Ross dropped his hoe right in the middle of the row and ran to the telephone to place a long distance call to P. M. Dewan, the Ontario Minister of Agriculture and Oxford County's member in the provincial legislature.

Dewan thought it sounded like a good idea but unfortunately it was not his department. Instead Ross would have to see the Minister of Education. Dewan assisted Ross in getting an appointment and just two weeks later, he was sitting in the Minister of Education's Toronto office. The Minister claimed that he had been looking for years to find an artist to work on such a project and was anxious for things to begin.

When Ross stated that the work could begin "right away," the minister laughed, shook Ross's hand, and said he would have a formal contract drawn up and mailed to Ross as soon as possible. In typical government style, "as soon as possible" ended up being two years, Ross recorded in his diary.

I was so happy just getting the nod to do these paintings, I didn't see the consequences. The stipulation that no money would be paid until the entire contract was completed simply never entered into it. All I could think about was the contract.

Actually the contract itself was fairly straight-forward, stipulating that each of the paintings had to be approved as the *official* type, including the American breeds. After the original paintings were approved, engravings would be made and tens-of-thousands of copies in full colour would be printed. These reproductions would be mailed to the ministry which, in turn, would distribute them to the schools. No remuneration whatsoever would be received by Ross until this first phase was complete.

Ross had been so overwhelmed by the magnitude of this contract that he hadn't stopped to think he was going to need money to finance the project. When he did realize the depth of the initial investment, he went to a bank to request a loan. Unfortunately, without a written contract or any personal collateral, Ross had nothing on which to borrow. Over the next few weeks, he talked to anyone who loaned money from London to Toronto, but no one would sponsor him. A few even laughed at his naivete.

Ross decided he needed something spectacular to make people aware of his potential as an artist. Since he had painted a portrait of King George V for the Silver Jubilee celebration, he now decided to do a painting of the Prince of Wales, the man everyone expected to be the next king. The resulting portrait was striking with rich colours, the royal robes, jewels, crown, sceptre. To display this painting and thereby gain the exposure needed to raise funds for his domestic animal project, Ross rented a booth at the Woodstock Fair's main pavilion. The portrait, which occupied the entire booth, soon became the focal point for fairgoers.

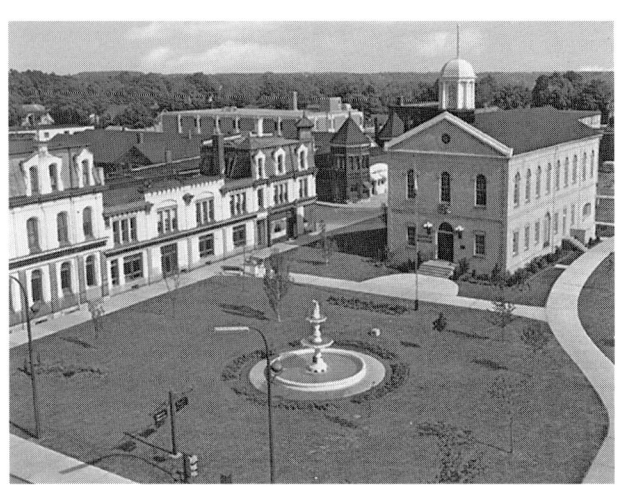

View from the Dundas Street studio across Woodstock City Hall Square.

People would stand for a moment, look at it, exclaim over it, then ask . . . who painted it? When they looked at the artist's name, they would repeat Ross Butler. Then, as if a light suddenly went on in their brain, they would ask, "Is that you?"

When Ross assured them that he was indeed the artist, the fairgoers would shake their heads, possibly in disbelief, and move on to the next booth, the Illbury Fur display manned by Alfred Searles. During slow periods, the two men talked. Alf was an outgoing person with a good sense of humour, a complete opposite to Ross's shy and formal personality. Yet, the two men got along and the friendship that began that day at the Woodstock Fair was to last a lifetime.

Ross's bid for exposure paid off. Shortly after the fair, he found a man who listened to his plea for seed money for his project. James Carnwath, a well-known businessman and supporter of the arts, understood Ross's need for money and agreed to help him. Carnwath arranged a meeting between Ross and three of his influential friends, Woodstock Mayor Ben Parker, Charles Tatham, publisher of the *Sentinel Review*, and contractor James Vance. All three men listened carefully as Ross outlined his verbal contract. He concluded by saying that the contract would be lost without financial support.

After some discussion, the men agreed to supply funds for the completion of the first phase of the work. In exchange for the two-thousand dollars which they would make immediately available to Ross, they would receive fifty percent of the net receipts. As soon as the written contract was received, they would form a company to handle the business. The agreement was all very straightforward, but they, too, had overlooked that things are not always done quickly by the government. It was two years and an election later before Ross's written contract arrived.

Ross's new backers thought he needed a proper studio, preferably one located downtown, where he could display his paintings. They recommended a seven-room, second-floor apartment-studio on Dundas Street overlooking Woodstock's City Hall Square. This suite of rooms had once been occupied by Dr. Donald Sutherland, the former Minister of Defence in the Federal Government. It was a prestigious location and Ross couldn't wait to move in.

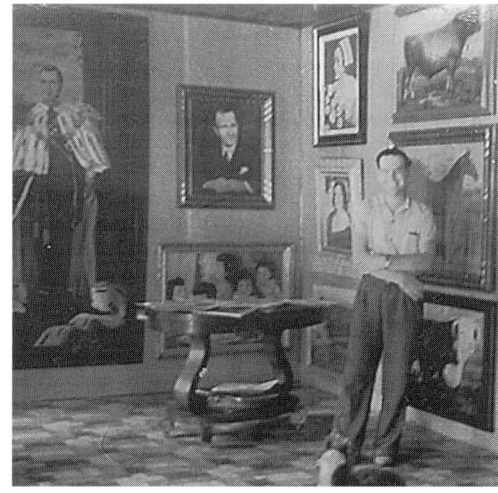

This painting of King Edward VIII hanging in Ross Butler's Dundas Street studio was later "gored" by a bull at his Pavey Street barn studio.

For the first time in my life I had a place of my own and a space for everything . . . and I had a studio with a southern exposure and natural light, a place where I could paint to my heart's content.

This suite was ideally suited for the artist. At the head of the stair was a small room suitable for a receptionist-secretary and at the back a smaller room which could accommodate a cot and a hot plate. Next to the main studio there were display rooms for Ross's paintings and sketches and a work area where he could do his framing. His sponsors advised him well.

Unfortunately, Ross soon had so many demands on him that he didn't have time to paint. Being men of influence, his sponsors soon had him in the public eye. He was asked to speak at the Rotary Club, the Lion's Club, and other prestigious organizations in the city. The men who heard Ross speak then brought their wives and daughters to his studio to see his paintings. Almost overnight, Ross became a celebrity. He had waited years for this chance and now revelled in the attention.

The press loved him as well because there was always someone important visiting his studio. The Federal Minister of Agriculture and the Minister of Trade and Commerce came from Ottawa. Through their interest, the government delegated George Rothwell, head of the Dominion Services Branch, to work with Ross. From Toronto came the Deputy Minister of Education, the Minister of Agriculture, and the Chief Inspector of Schools. Ross's studio became a mecca of officialdom.

Ross's social life changed as well. It had become a habit for Ross and Alf Searles to go skating at the local arena on Saturday nights. On one particular Saturday night, 14 February 1936, Ross saw a pretty lady skating alone. He shadowed her around the rink several times and then casually skated up beside her and locked her arm over his. He told her she was pretty. She said that he had an awful line. They kept skating, and it wasn't until six blustery years of courtship that Ruby Mae Leuszler became Mrs. Ross Butler. That same Valentine's night, Alf Searles met the woman who was to become his wife — only it didn't take them six years to make up their minds.

As the depression worsened, Ross seemed to be the only one getting ahead. People who had once accused him of being haughty and aloof now knocked on his door looking for work. Printers, engravers, insurance men, and tradesmen of all kinds offered him everything from picture frames to car deals.

Breed committees assembled in his studio to view his paintings. In all, there were twenty-six breed type committees and many of these men stayed overnight in Woodstock. They also visited area farms and Ross became their official escort. What Ross had expected to be a simple procedure had now become time-consuming and costly. A breed committee was supposed to come to the studio, recommend changes if necessary, give their approval and leave. However, this did not happen. The committees often debated the changes for hours and lingered for days waiting for Ross to complete the changes. Once the committee approved the paintings, they reported to their parent association, who would issue a letter stating that Ross' paintings were ideal types of that particular breed.

In Ross's handshake contract, the Minister of Education had stated the True Types had to include the American types of the breeds as well. Some associations in the United States already had paintings of their True Types and were not interested in Ross's idea of the best of their breeds. Often, it took months for Ross to get the Americans to agree that Ross's paintings were satisfactory.

Then, there were the Shorthorn breeders. They had been considering the standardization of their breed for over a year, but there was a steadily widening cleavage between two factions — the strictly beef versus the dual purpose or milking Shorthorn producers. The two groups simply could not agree with each other. Often these disagreements became long and violent and Ross felt like he was in a boxing arena. He knew his paintings of the Shorthorns were good, but no matter what he did, the committee could not agree on the True Types. Ross decided that in a controlled environment, without a flask of whisky at their elbow, these men could reach an agreement. His studio became that controlled environment and, finally, after painting two pairs, one of the beef Shorthorn cow and bull and one of the dual purpose cow and bull, the committee gave their approval.

All of these delays were costly. Ross's funds began to run dangerously low. His expenses were high and included rent for the studio, his secretary's salary, and his clothes budget. He was in the public eye and he was determined to be well-dressed. Of course, his old car was not in keeping with his new position either, so he traded it

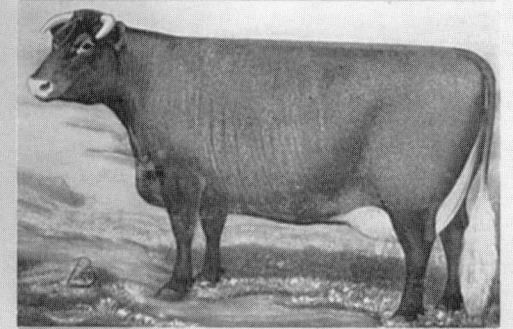

in on another. When his expenses finally surpassed his budget, he called an emergency meeting of his sponsors. They were appalled that in less than two years he had gone through their initial investment of two thousand dollars. They also had reason to be upset because Ross's written contract from the Minister of Education still had not arrived. Maybe, they said, there was never going to be a contract. His sponsors had lost faith in him, and understandably so. They walked out.

Ross was absolutely stunned. He had never expected them to withdraw their support; he had not asked for much more money, just a little to tide him over. He was so close to realizing his dream. He could not understand how they could do this to him. They built him up, gave him a good life, and then suddenly took it away. Slowly, Ross came to the realization that he had only become an investment, a commodity to be bought and sold.

I was rejected, discarded, lost . . . my self-esteem was ripped to shreds. My GRAND career was gone. I would have to give up my office-studio, move home in disgrace. People would laugh. I never felt more alone in my life . . . more abandoned.

Ross talked to Alf and to Ruby. Neither had any answers, only words of encouragement. Ross was a good artist and no one could take that away from him. Perhaps, more importantly, he had his paintings of the True Types. Most were completed and only a couple lacked the approval of their breed committees. Once these were received, Ross could proceed with the engravings and reproductions. The first phase would then be completed, but he still needed money to get to that stage.

Ross walked the streets in agony. He had no idea where he was going to get the money to continue. Even his friends crossed the street when they saw him coming. Creditors pounded on his door as word spread quickly that his backers had withdrawn their support. No one blamed them. Instead, they believed that Ross had not managed the money-part of his career very well.

The mind-training program that Ross had developed years ago came to the fore.

Ross went to his desk and took a realistic look at his financial situation. His bank statement showed that he barely had enough money for his next month's rent on the studio. Then, there were his personal responsibilities such as Carl's tuition at the School for the Blind, the taxes on the Pavey Street property, and living expenses for his family. Methodically he itemized his assets and his expenses and then tackled his correspondence. He had kept copies of his letters to and from people and organizations. He found a copy of a letter that had been written several months ago to the National Dairy Show in Columbus, Ohio. Their cattle show was being held at the same time as the first National Percheron Show and Breed Type conference, also in Columbus. He had written to both organizations, but neither had replied.

Tired from hours of analyzing his financial situation, Ross walked around his studio studying his collection. There were dozens of paintings, some finished, others almost finished. Among a group of horse paintings was one of a black Percheron, a beautiful animal that seemed to walk right off the canvas. While Ross stared at it, words from his mind training program popped into his head.

Be bold! Trust in yourself! And I knew what I was going to do. I was going to Columbus, Ohio.

5 | Percheron Paintings & Sculptures

ONCE HE HAD MADE THE DECISION to go to the National Percheron Show in Columbus, Ohio, Ross Butler had many plans to make. His new-used car would not make it to Ohio so he had to arrange for other transportation. He went to Toronto and traded his three-week old used car in on a brand new one. Well, he would worry about the payments later. If he was going to go bankrupt, he would do it in style.

Ross would also have to borrow more money. There were only a few dollars left in his bank account. He approached a local businessman from whom he had once borrowed money. Ross told him about his sponsors and his new car. The man slapped Ross on the shoulder and said, "Butler, I like your style." He handed Ross a hundred dollars.

However, money wasn't Ross's only problem. His mother was very ill and she pleaded with him not to go to Ohio. She was sure that she would die before he returned. But for once, Ross ignored her pleas. He kissed her on the cheek and with nine paintings in the backseat of his car, he set out for Windsor and the border.

Ross had forgotten that it was Sunday. The border was closed to commercial traffic and the paintings in his car were considered commercial. The customs officer said Ross would have to see a broker in the morning to get them cleared. Yet Ross was able to convince a junior official to let him pass. The truth was that Ross didn't have the one hundred dollars for the broker's fee.

Time was now of the essence and Ross drove nonstop to Columbus. Without even trying to find accommodation for himself, he went to the largest hotel in the city which was the headquarters for both the horsemen and the cattlemen associations.

I went up to the first stranger who looked like a horseman. He was wearing a Stetson. I told him that I wanted to exhibit my painting of a black Percheron for consideration in the competition for the "ideal" breed. I showed him the picture. He took one look at it and said, "Come with me." He not only found a place for me to exhibit my painting but he found me accommodation as well. Then, he introduced me to the entire staff from the association's head office in Chicago, several of whom were very pretty young women.

Ross had been lucky. This man was the National Director of the Percheron Association.

One very attractive blond from the Chicago office caught Ross's eye. She was in charge of the publicity for the Columbus show, and right from the start, there was a chemistry between the two. It soon became evident that she was determined to make this shy, gentle, Canadian with the Percheron painting the star of the show. Ross said later that he was glad he wasn't committed to anyone, otherwise the dalliance would have created problems.

The young woman had Ross's painting placed at the entrance to the auditorium so everyone who entered the show would see it. Everyone connected with the conference, including judges, college professors, and breeders glanced, stopped, and marvelled at the finely detailed black Percheron. "Where did you find a model for such a perfect animal?" they asked over and over again.

Ross told them that he had accidentally stumbled on a fundamental law of animal proportions, an unwritten law of nature. Before he knew it his painting had been moved to the front of the conference room and he was asked to explain his theory to the entire audience.

Without forewarning, and hardly knowing what to say, I borrowed a cane from the nearest person and launched into a talk about my theory of body proportions; how I used my idea in my studio to correctly gauge the measurements of an animal. I emphasized that nature had designed these animals with her own yardstick . . . that the length of the head is a unit that determines all the various proportions of the body. I said that I applied this rule to seventeen measurements, the length of the body, the length of the legs, the proportions of the quarters, the slope of the shoulder and the width of the body in three vital places. I told them that my painting of the Percheron horse had the balance, symmetry and proportions of the ideal type of the breed.

Ross's theory caught the attention of several college professors. They later congratulated him on his discovery of this relatively unexplored law of nature. The artists in attendance were not so pleased. They resented this Canadian who had somehow taken over their domain. George Ford Morris, considered by many to be the foremost painter of horses in the United States, just glowered down at Ross from his six-foot height.

Later that same afternoon, the Percheron True Type committee asked Ross to paint the True Types of the breed. They also wanted him to create three-dimensional models for their next national show to be held in California in two years time. Ross was ecstatic about the offer, but he didn't have the faintest idea of how to go about making miniature Percheron models. He knew absolutely nothing about sculpting.

Ross's continued to have more success at Columbus, Ohio. Several of his paintings were on display in the cattle breeder's building and a few even sold for a good price. More importantly, were the contacts that Ross made. Foremost was his new friendship with Benjamin Hill, the President of the U.S. National Dairy Association. Hill, a recognized authority on the history and development of Guernseys, had written a book on the breed and Ross was anxious to secure a copy for his own library. It had always been Ross's policy to thoroughly research a breed before he painted it. Unfortunately, in Canada, there was little on the Guernsey breed so Hill's book would be a valuable research tool.

Ross also had the privilege of meeting Alvin Sanders, an agriculture writer covering the Columbus show. Sanders complimented Ross by saying that truly Ross brought the animals to life on canvas. It was quite an honour as Sanders was considered one of the top American agriculture journalists. Over dinner, one evening, Sanders told Ross about a book he had written on Percherons. The book was now out of print, but when Ross showed interest, Sanders said he would find him a copy. Several months later, Sanders mailed Ross the original proof copy complete with corrections and marginal notes.

At Columbus, Ross's days and nights were filled with excitement, but he couldn't wait to get home. He had left Woodstock a failure, but he was coming home a success, though outside his personal friends, no one knew or cared about his successes. One of the first things Ross did when he returned from Ohio was hang his Percheron stallion painting in a place of honour. He covered the painting with glass to afford it some extra protection, but forty years later this "protection" would be the ruination of the picture. The humidity that was created inside the frame had caused the paint to stick to the glass.

When Ruby heard the exciting news of Ross's success in Ohio, she was very happy for him and secretly hoped that he would now concentrate on her and marriage. Unfortunately for Ruby, his concentration did go into high gear, but in another direction, the creation of three-dimension models.

Before he got too involved with the sculptures, Ross's written contract from the Minister of Education arrived from Toronto, more then two years after their handshake contract had been made. Ross completed the order and mailed it to the ministry for distribution. The terms of the contract were such that Ross still owned the originals, the engravings, and all the rights to the pictures. He could use them again and again. While the government had been very slow in sending his written contract, a cheque to cover his work, followed shortly after the delivery of the reproductions. Ross was now able to able to pay some of his creditors in full and those he couldn't pay in full, he paid as much as he could. For a while at least, he was free of the horror of seeing the sheriff at his door with an order to seize his paintings.

As usual, Ross was off to the Royal Winter Fair that November. He still loved the excitement of the show ring and could always be found close by either sketching or drawing a prize-winning animal. In the 25 November 1936 issue of the *Family Herald and Weekly Star*, there was a feature article entitled "At The Royal." The article contained a

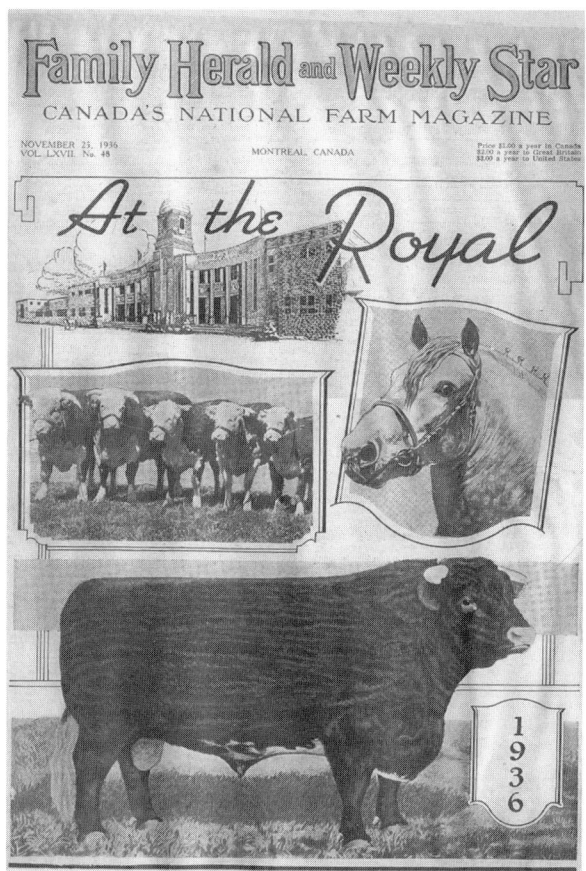

Ross Butler was "heralded" as Canada's foremost painter of livestock in this issue of *Canada's National Farm Magazine.*

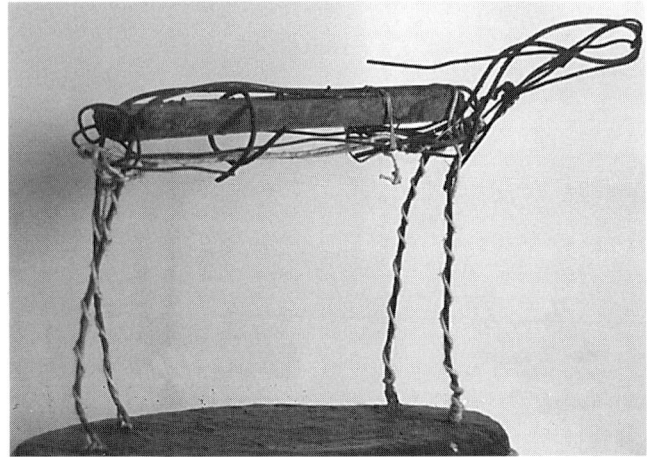

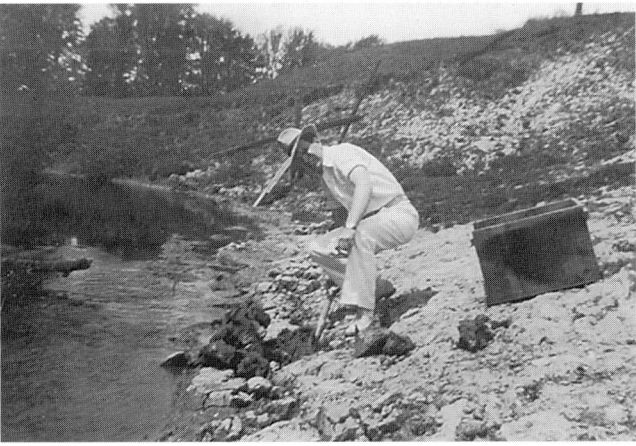

Digging clay on the banks of Otter Creek to sculpt on wood and wire frames.

picture of Ross sketching a grand champion Jersey cow with a caption describing him as Canada's foremost painter of domestic animals. This exposure in a national farm magazine brought numerous commissions and requests for prints.

Ross now faced the immediate problem of creating three-dimensional models for the Percheron Association. He didn't know anything about sculpting, but he believed the same theory of proportions would apply. The real question was what material should be used as a sculpting base. His mind skipped back to the old swimming hole on his father's farm in Norwich and the deposits of soft blue clay that he and his brothers and friends had used in their mud fights. He remembered that the clay had easily moulded into a ball. Why not try it as a sculpting material?

Ross immediately was off to Norwich where he dug up several bushels of clay, completely forgetting that he and Ruby were supposed to spend the afternoon together. When he examined the clay back at the studio, he was disappointed to find it was riddled with straw, manure, pebbles, and other impurities. Frustrated, he threw a glob down on his work table and a piece of manure flew out. He slammed it again and this time a pebble became dislodged. He started to laugh, realizing that he would have to beat the impurities out of the clay — and that's exactly what he did . . . beat the impurities out of the clay with an old baseball bat. For the next several days, he pounded the clay until it was purified. Then, he kneaded it until the texture was plastic in consistency and would roll into a rope. When he was finished, this rope was strong enough that he could whirl it around his head and it would not break.

The next step, of course, was to create a frame for the model which was to be one quarter the size of a Percheron horse. This was fashioned out of wood and wire and anchored to a sturdy oval-shaped wooden base. Ross plastered the moist clay over this frame and left it overnight to dry. The next morning, much to Ross's chagrin, most of the clay had cracked and fallen off the frame and he was forced to start over again. That night he wrapped the sculpture in wet towels and the shrinkage of the clay became only one of the difficulties he encountered.

When he was almost finished plastering the frame with clay, it collapsed under its own weight. The wire Ross had used for the legs simply would not support the structure. Something stronger was needed; iron rods became the answer. After endless hours of trial and error, he arrived at a finished product complete with hair, mane, tail, and hooves. Even the eyes and nostrils were clearly defined.

It was now time to call the True Type Percheron committee to approve the model. This approval was needed before a mould and cast could be made. Four committee men came to approve the model, Ellis MacFarland, the Secretary-Manager of the U. S. National Percheron Association, Warden Spitler, president of the American Percheron Association, Professor Curtis, the Dean of Agriculture from Ames University in Iowa, and George Dix from Ohio. All were experts on the breed. The men inspected the paintings and sculptures, and while some changes were needed, they were relatively minor. For example, the mare's mane needed to be thicker, the curve of the stallion's rump needed to be softened, and a hoof needed to be rounded more. For the sculptures, more clay had to be added to the chest, but lessened on the belly. This often threw the symmetry of the animal out of proportion. One simple change took hours to perfect. After four days of Ross's meticulous work, the committee approved both the sculptures and paintings of the stallion and mare.

Before a mould could be made, Ross shellacked each sculpture and dried it with a blow torch. He then covered each sculpture with cheesecloth. Because Ross had not been able to find a tool and die maker in Woodstock who would be able to do this delicate job, he went to an established firm in Toronto. Great care had to be taken in the making of the mould because the original model was destroyed in the process. Years later, he would learn to save his meticulously-created models by covering them with a rubberized skin before the die was cast, but now it was a one-shot deal.

Since the models were in his upstairs studio, he had to take them down the stairs to his newly purchased pick-up truck, where they were placed in a specially built crate and packed in sawdust. This was not an easy task as each of the models were delicate, top heavy, weighing over two hundred pounds. Once the sculptures were completed and back at his studio, Ross painted them in their natural

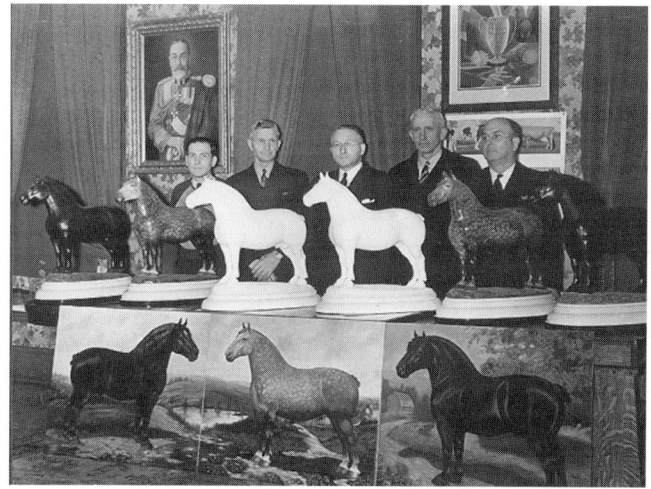

Percheron Type Committee: (l-r) Ross Butler; Worden Spittler, President of Percheron Breeders Association of America (PBA); Hon. P.M. Dewan, Minister of Agriculture of Ontario; George Dix, Executive of PBA; Ellis McFarland, Secretary-Treasurer of PBA.

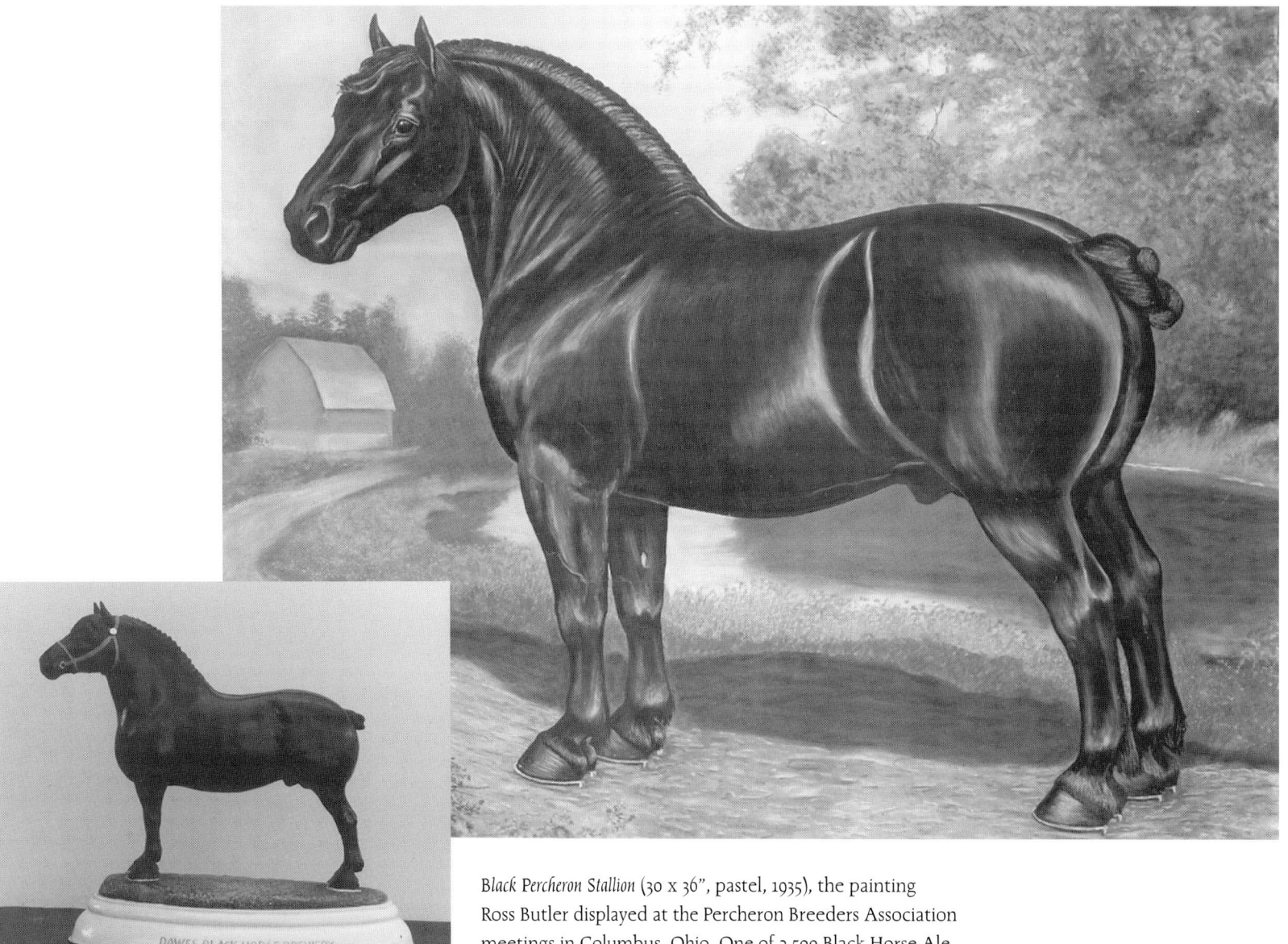

Black Percheron Stallion (30 x 36", pastel, 1935), the painting Ross Butler displayed at the Percheron Breeders Association meetings in Columbus, Ohio. One of 2,500 Black Horse Ale sculptures, commissioned by Dawes Brewery.

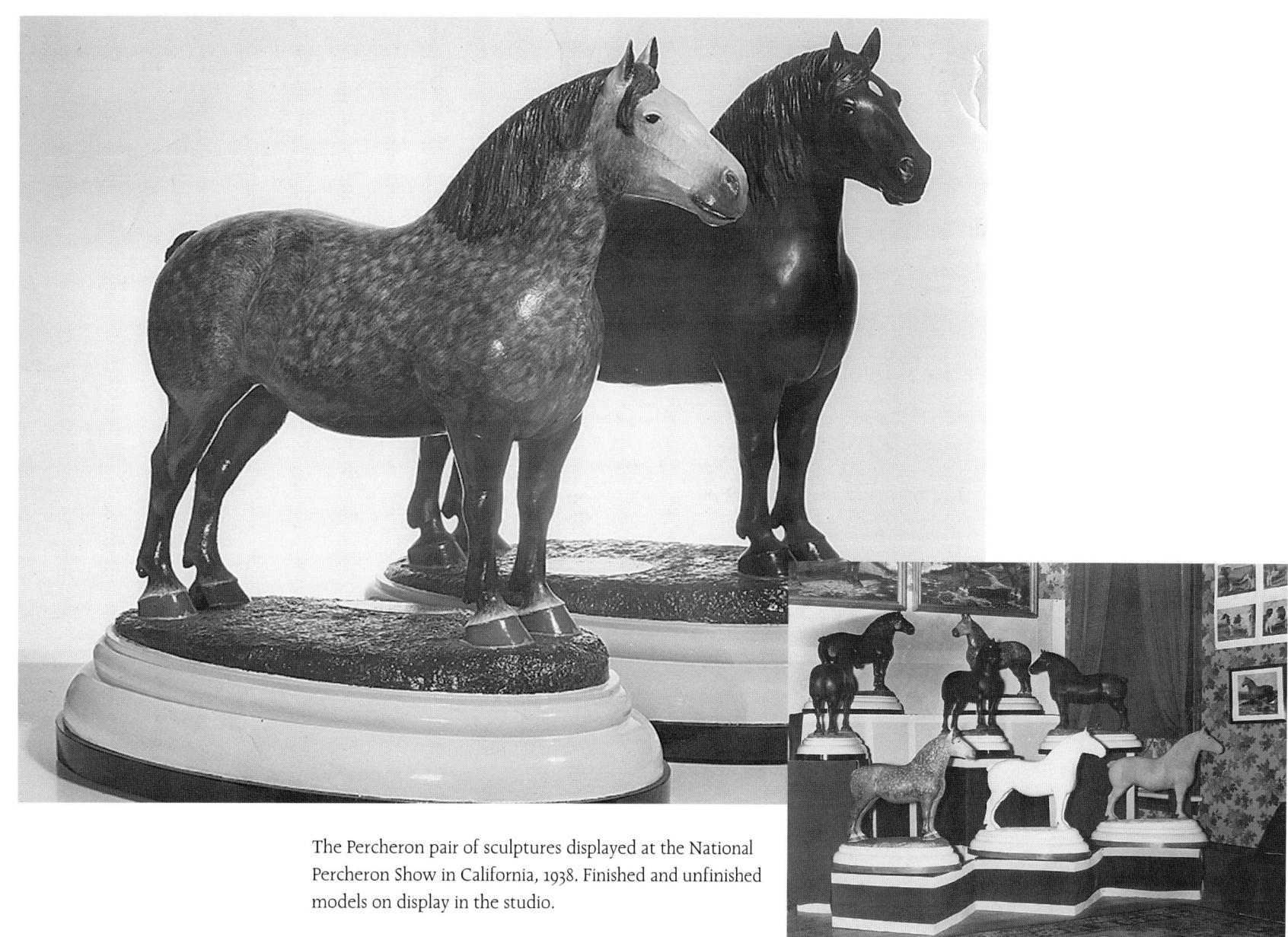

The Percheron pair of sculptures displayed at the National Percheron Show in California, 1938. Finished and unfinished models on display in the studio.

colours. It was slow, pain-staking work.

Despite the long hours Ross had put into creating the sculptures and painting ideals, he continued to write articles for different agriculture magazines. He also continued to buy "good" cows or bulls for local breeders. His work day started at six in the morning and often lasted until midnight. These long hours could only have led to a strain on Ross's lovelife. Although Ruby believed she had a claim on Ross's feelings, he didn't feel the same. Instead, he felt free to see who he wanted, when he wanted.

When Ruby was on her way home one night from work at the local Bell Telephone office, she saw that the lights were still on in Ross's studio. Deciding to surprise him, she approached his studio. However, when she got to the top of the stairs, Ruby heard laughter and a woman giggling. Furious, she raced back down the stairs to the street, climbed behind the wheel of Ross's car and began to honk the horn. She continued honking the horn until Ross finally came to the window wanting to know what she thought she was doing. Ruby told Ross that she would stop as soon as he got "that woman" out of his room. The woman finally left but not before everyone on the street knew what had happened. That incident became just another storm in their turbulent relationship.

Fortunately for Ross, his career was cruising on a more even keel. The Province of Quebec and the Quebec Club had ordered several sets of Ayrshire prints, and the Carnation Milk Company bought one hundred and twenty sets of the four dairy breeds. School and universities in the United States, were also becoming interested in his prints. Some days all Ross did was mail prints of his work. Some of them were sent to Britain, Norway, France, and South America. A few even went to Australia and New Zealand. Before the year ended, Ross's prints would cover the globe.

There were also many inquiries about his sculptures and his three-dimensional models. Finally, it seemed that his long hours were beginning to pay off.

6 | An American Celebrity

ALTHOUGH ROSS BUTLER'S PRIMARY FOCUS was now on his sculptures and paintings for the Percheron show at the Pomona Fair in Los Angeles, California, in 1938, he still had to make a living. The second phase of his contract with the Ontario Government was painting the True Types of all the draft breeds of horses. Since the American's True Type committee had given their stamp of approval to his Percherons, he felt that it would be a simple matter to get the Canadian committee to add their approval. As it turned out, it wasn't easy at all.

Before the Canadian Percheron Association's annual meeting in Toronto on 1 November 1938, Ross set up a display of Percheron paintings and sculptures. The president opened the meeting by reminding everyone that 1939 marked the 100th anniversary of the Percherons arrival in America. He felt it was a fitting tribute to have such "ideal" paintings and models of the breed on display.

Ross was introduced to the Association membership by Percheron breeder Carl Roberts, who said, "We are extremely fortunate to have the calibre of an artist such as Mr. Butler paint and sculpt our breed." Ross, then, made his presentation, revealing that the American association had already approved his paintings and sculptures. He stated that MacDonald College in Montreal and the Ontario Agriculture College at Guelph had ordered a set of the Percheron mare and stallion. It would be a nice gesture on the part of the Canadian breeders to donate a pair to the Royal Winter Fair. When Ross suggested that they could be presented to the owner of the Grand Champion Percheron, many of the members agreed. Ross then opened the floor to questions.

There were the usual questions — "Are other draft horse associations interested in having True Types made of their breed?" and "Would schools be interested in having reproductions in their classrooms?" But there was one question which seemed to be on everyone's mind: "How much is this approval going to cost us?" Ross rarely got angry but the arrogance of the person asking that particular question made him mad. Although he didn't raise his voice, he made it clear in no uncertain terms that "he" had been the one to spend hundreds of dollars to have the casts and models made. He had brought these models and paintings here at his own expense; all he was asking from the association was their *approval* that these were the True Types of the Canadian Percheron breed. He pointed out that this was costing them absolutely nothing! Ross then took his seat and there were no more questions from the members. After more than an hour of debate, their approval was finally given.

Because Ross paid his own way, attending so many events like this meeting was proving costly. To offset these costs he often wrote about the events for agricultural magazines or periodicals. Sometimes, he found himself as the subject for an article. After all, he was photogenic, approachable, and easy to interview. Either way, the publicity increased sales of his reproductions and models. Ross's financial situation improved by leaps and bounds until he was able to pay back all the money that his sponsors had invested with interest. That, alone, lifted a tremendous burden from his shoulders.

Many local people were also buying Ross's work at a good price. William Illbury, Alf Searle's employer, bought two large light horse pictures for one hundred dollars and Ruby bought a set of prints for two dollars. She said it seemed that this was the only way she could see him, although Ross did take her occasionally with him when he went to Toronto.

It was not his work that drained Ross of his energy, but the continual parade of visitors to his studio. The interruptions seemed unending, and no matter how hard he tried, he could not find a quiet time to paint. His work became sandwiched in between visitors and telephone calls, and he was afraid it was suffering. And now there was the urgency of finishing the Percheron paintings for the Pomona Show in California.

If only I could go some place where I could paint without interruption. I am so tired . . . so weary . . .

Fortunately, Alf Searles found an ideal solution when he rented a cabin trailer. He and Ross set off to find a haven of seclusion, a spot where Ross could paint "in peace the dapples on his Percheron." They found a spot quite close to Woodstock — a pasture field on Whiteman's Creek near the village of Cathcart. While Alf set up their camp, Ross got out his paints. It was so quiet and so peaceful. After all of the confusion and interruptions, it was heaven.

Usually Ross dressed immaculately, but he now enjoyed going shirtless and barefoot. When supper was over, the two men either talked or rafted along the creek, or listened to the radio. On one particular night Alf and Ross got involved in a friendly wrestling match. As they laughed and rolled over and over on the ground, Ross suddenly let out a yell. He had hit his ribs against a stone fracturing two of them.

With his ribs taped securely, Ross struggled to finish the Percheron paintings. Already two days behind schedule, Ross and Alf loaded the car with the statues and paintings and set out for California with Alf doing the driving. Despite their hurry, the two men enjoyed the prairies, the farms, and the parklands, but they were completely unprepared for the 118 degree heat of the desert. The heat made the tape around Ross's ribs itch like crazy, so they often had to stop. In an attempt to beat this heat, they decided to rest during the day and drive all night.

When they finally reached California, the first person to greet them at Pomona was the publicity chief for the Los Angeles County Fair. Ross soon found that publicity in California was an advanced science, an industry unto itself. The publicist assigned to him was also in charge of the publicity for several other celebrities, including the beautiful blonde Queen of the Fair. Because he did not know of Ross's fractured ribs, the chief had scheduled every minute of Ross's time, and Ross didn't have the heart to tell him about his ribs.

The publicity began with a series of photos of Ross working on his models, honing minor details. The photos were accompanied by interviews and both were immediately released to a chain of newspapers and farm magazines throughout United States and Canada. Because Pomona was the fourth largest fair of its kind in the

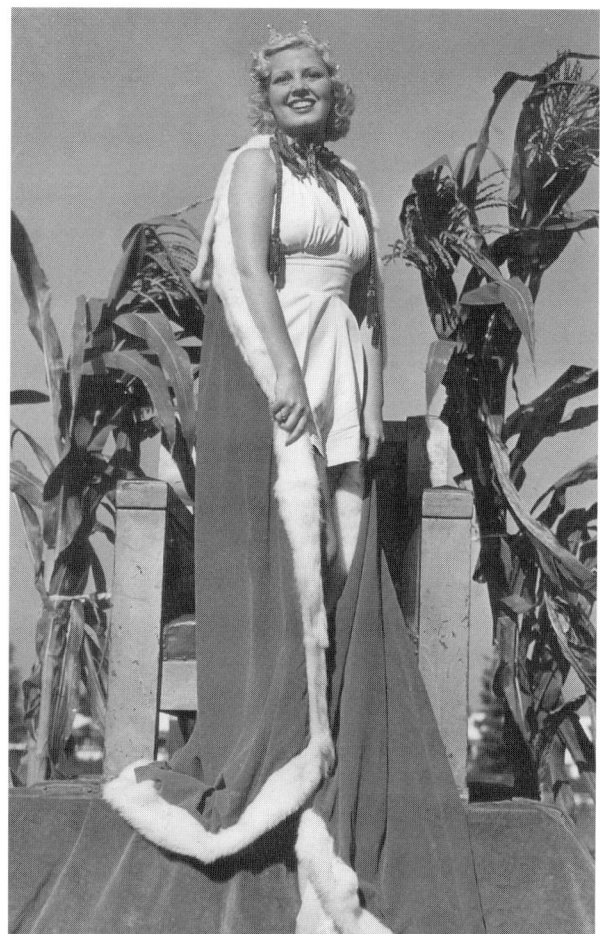

The Queen of the Los Angeles County Fair.

world, there were journalists there from Australia, New Zealand, and several European countries. Fortunately, they were all wanting interviews with Ross and photos of his work. The publicity chief estimated this blanket coverage would reach one hundred and twenty million readers around the world. This would be accompanied by a series of radio interviews, most of which were national in scope.

Ross was sometimes photographed with other well-known celebrities at a dinner or function. In one particular photo, he was with both the Governor of California and the Queen of the Fair. Whether by chance or design, the Queen's path and Ross's path often crossed. No one was more astonished than the publicity chief when she appeared on Ross's arm at the unveiling of Ross's Percheron statues and paintings.

And what an unveiling it was! Trumpets blared and when the veil was ceremoniously pulled back, Ross's models and pictures stood in a circle of light. From the speaker's podium came the words, "Ladies and gentlemen, from Canada, the world's greatest farm animal painter, Ross Butler."

Ross was choked with emotion, for he never had been so honoured or had so many prestigious people in the audience. During his speech, he spoke slowly and hesitantly until he got to his theory of proportions. Then, his shyness disappeared. Now he was on familiar ground.

Every afternoon the Percherons were paraded before the grandstand in between the judging events. The fair committee had also scheduled several races. One such race was a distance of a quarter-mile for heavy horses. Bing Crosby acted as both the official starter and commentator. It was a fun race, open to anyone. The race had to be a bare-back affair as no saddles would fit these large horses. Ross was surprised when he saw Alf Searles on the back of one of the dappled greys. While Alf didn't win the race, he performed well and finished close to the leaders.

The publicity pace was gruelling and the chief publicist decided to grant the celebrities some time off. He arranged for everyone, including Alf, to tour several of the great movie studios while the pictures were in actual production. During break time, the Canadians were introduced to the stars of the era: Myrna Loy, Clarke Gable,

George O'Brien, and several more that neither Ross or Alf had ever heard or seen.

When it was time to return to work, it was to sit at the Percheron exhibit and autograph hundreds of reproductions of the True Type mare and stallion. During these sessions, Ross talked to people about his work, explaining how he combined scientific study with art. He repeated his theory of proportions over and over, demonstrating how the length of the head was a unit which governed the rest of the animal's measurements.

However, it was a meeting with a Mr. Farrington that most touched Ross's heart. Farrington now lived in California but had once resided in Norwich. He had seen Ross's name on the Percheron display and wanted to find out if this was the same Ross Butler who had once helped him wash his car on the banks of Oxford County's Otter Creek. "Fancy!" Farrington exclaimed over and over. "David Butler's little boy here in California . . . and a celebrity, too. Who would have ever thought it?"

Ross, too, remembered that he had helped wash Farrington's car. He and his little bob-tailed terrier had been playing outside when he noticed a car parked at the bank of the creek. With his five-year-old curiosity aroused, he wandered over to see what was going on. Mr. Farrington talked to him and even let him help wash the car. As a payment for helping, he then gave Ross a short ride in the car.

Farrington was not the only one who was surprised at Ross's success in California. Neither Ross or Alf could believe all the wonderful things that had happened to them. When they picked up Ross's sister, Pearl Browning, her son, and her sister-in-law in Illinois, the two men repeated their California stories the rest of the way home.

While Ross had been in California, word of his success had filtered back to Woodstock. A few Woodstonians had even heard his name mentioned on the local radio, but it was the newspaper and agriculture publications proclaiming Ross as a truly gifted artist that brought him international acclaim.

It appeared that the home town boy had finally made it big.

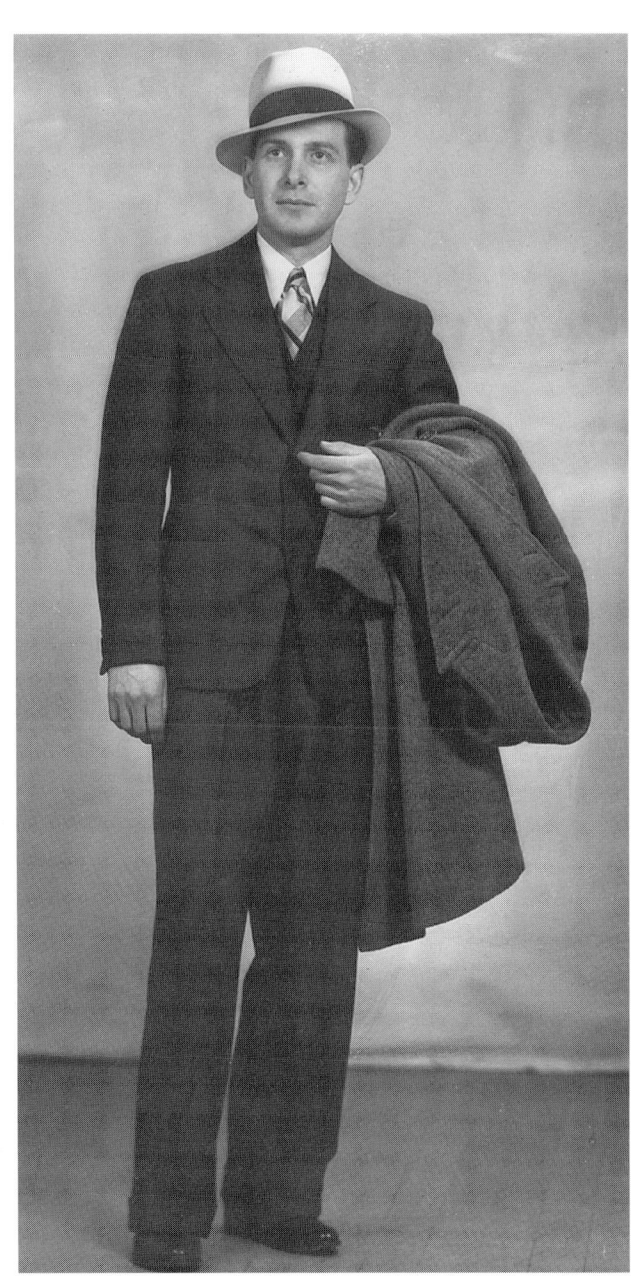

Ross Butler, California bound, 1938.

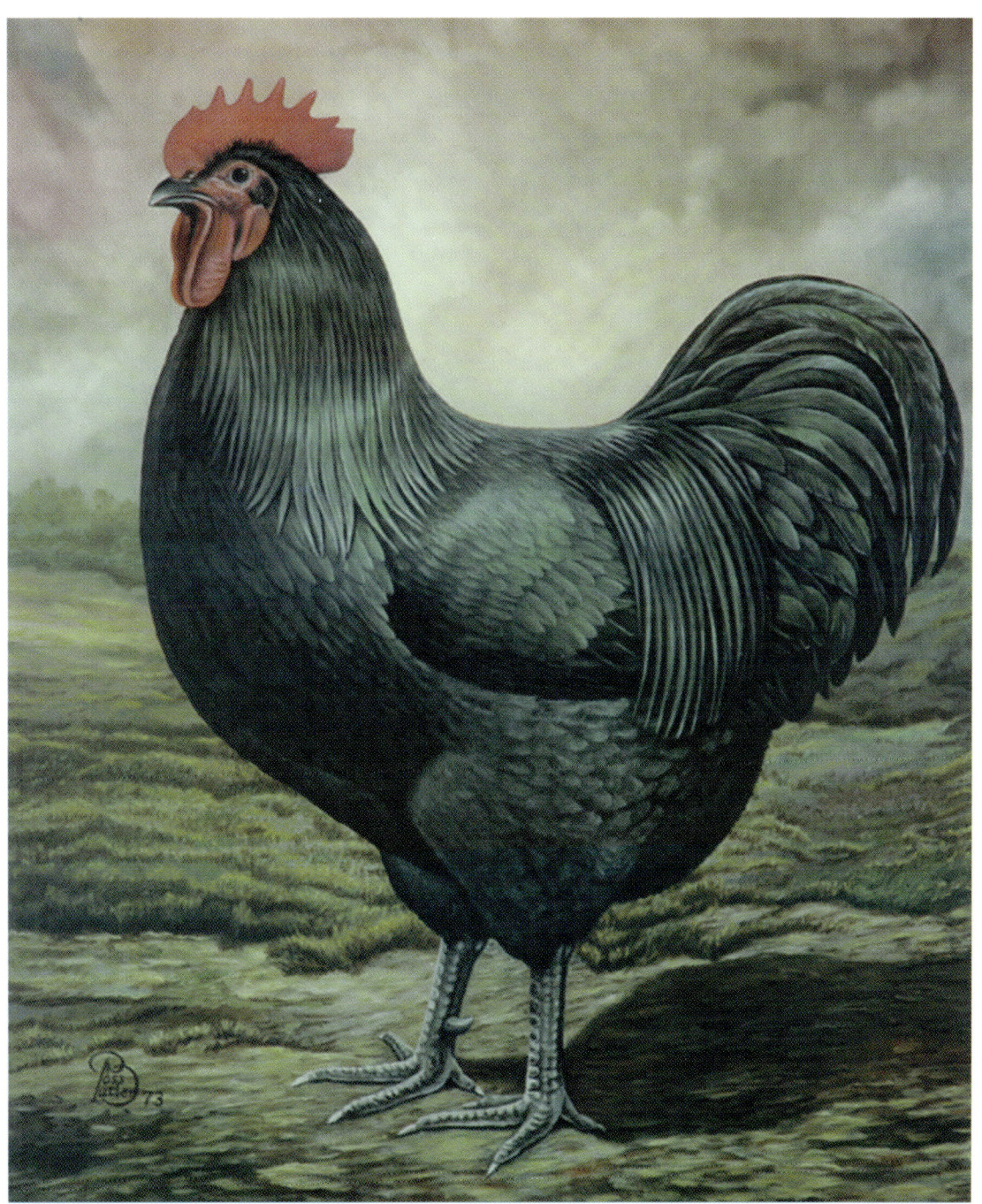

Daybreak, Black Australorp (20 x 30", oil on masonite, 1973), a breed originating in Australia from English Black Orpington stock which Ross Butler fostered through the founding of the National Australorp Club who first met in his studio.

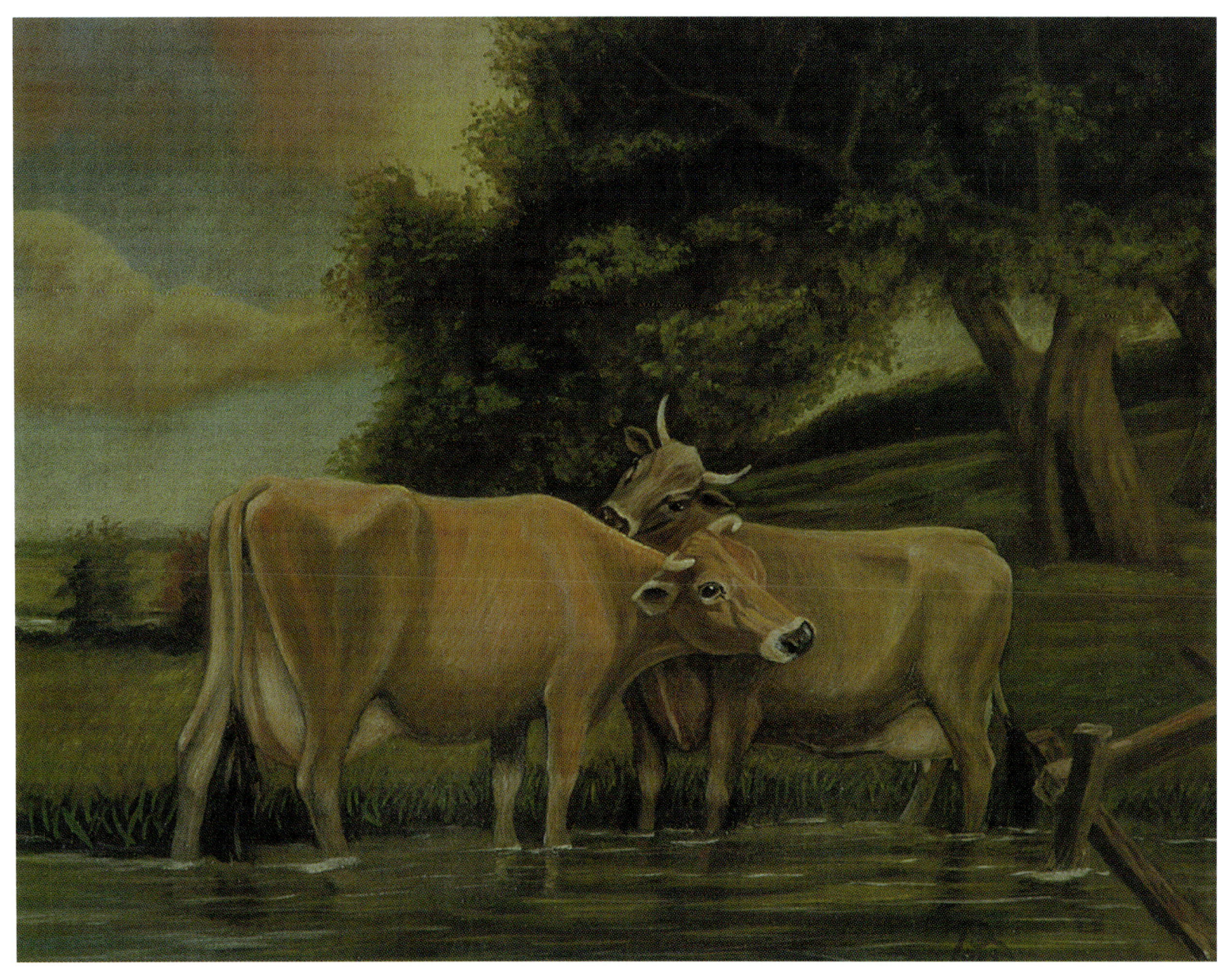

Our First Registered Jerseys in Otter Creek (16 x 20", oil on board, 1930s), portraying the two cows young Ross Butler milked so diligently three times a day for the Record of Performance (R.O.P.) test.

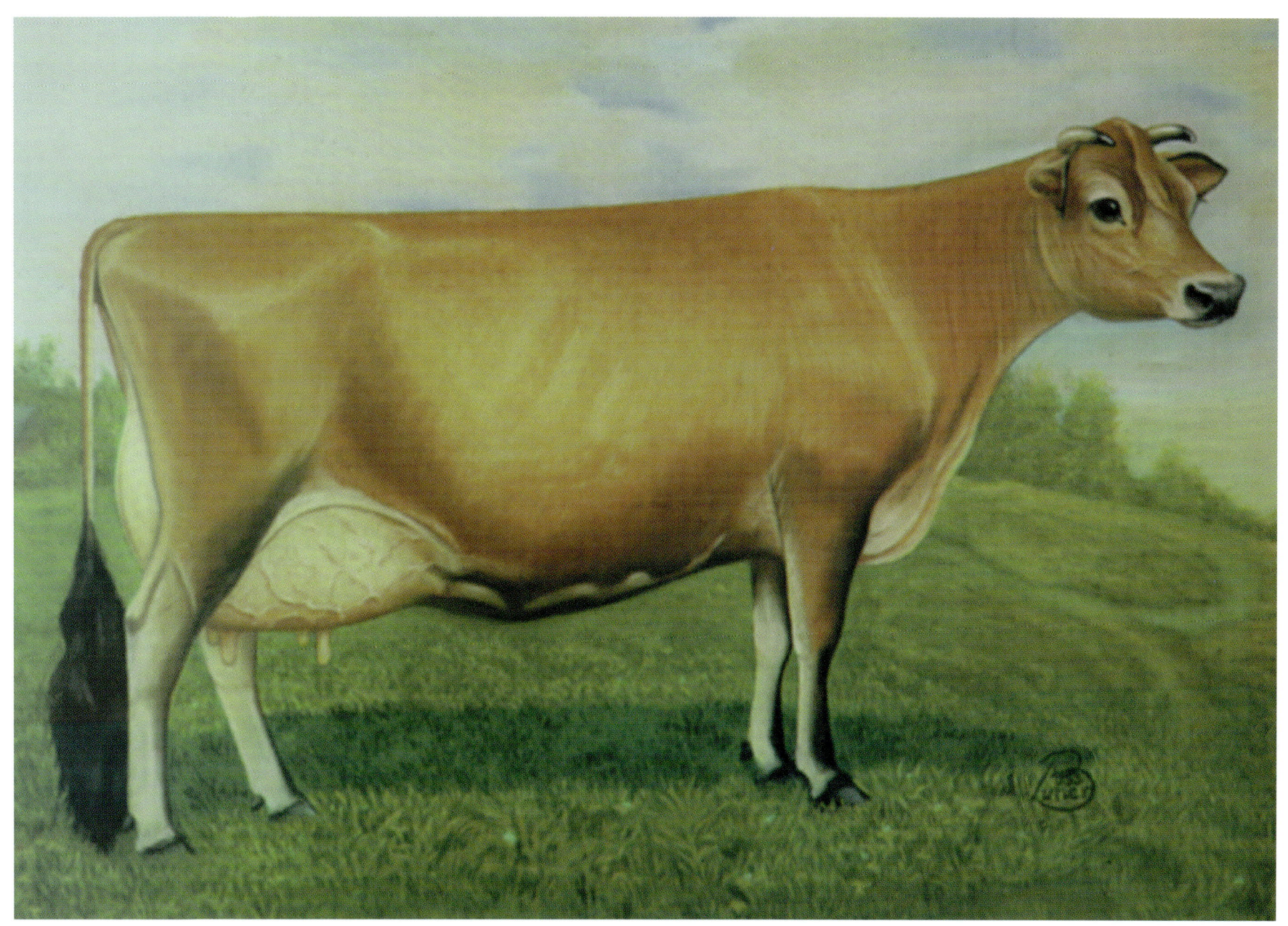

Jersey True Type (24 x 36", pastel on sandpaper, 1934), a dairy breed developed on Jersey Island and introduced to Canada in 1868 by R.H. Stephens.

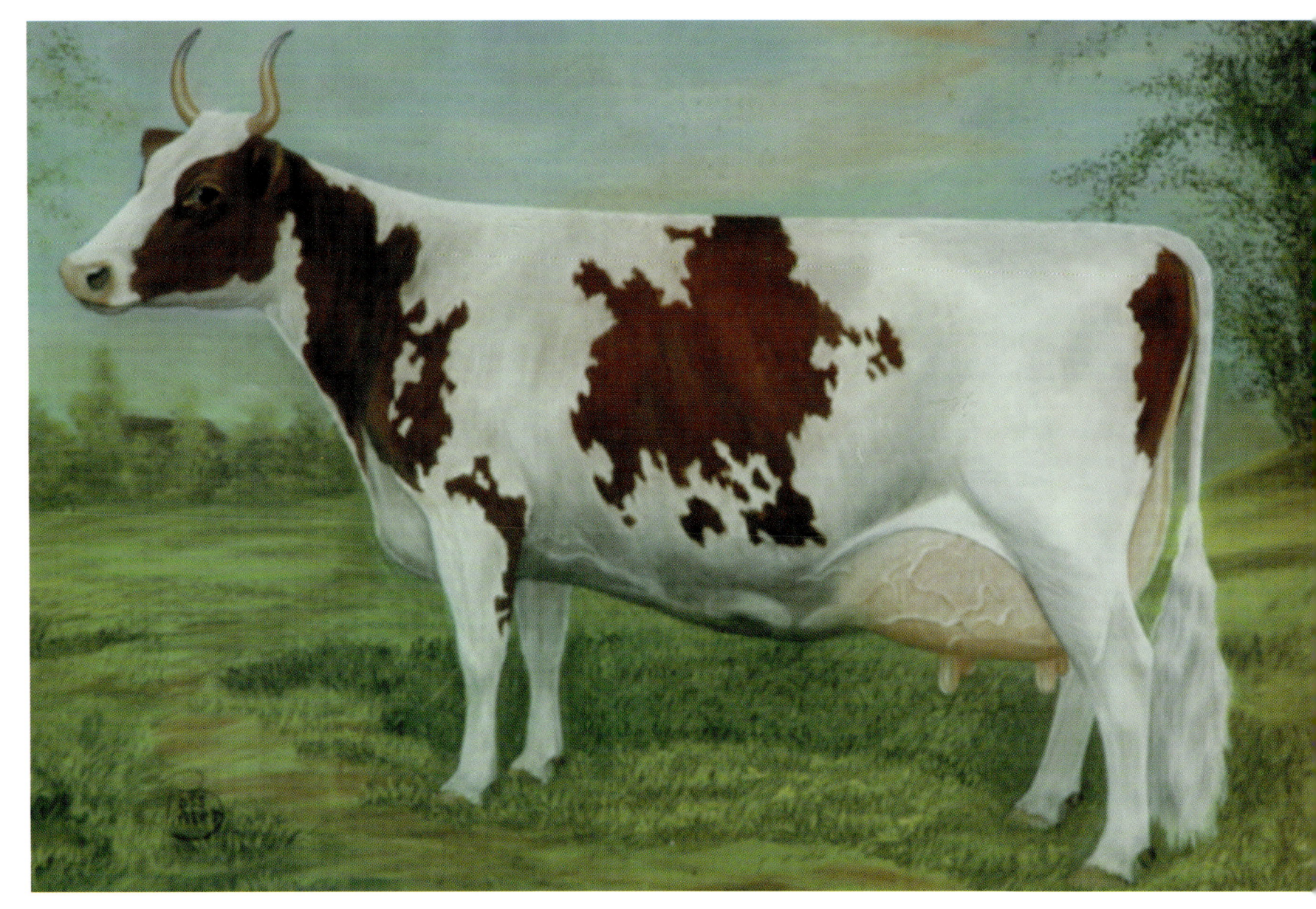

Ayrshire True Type (24 x 36", pastel on sandpaper, 1934), a breed originating in the County of Ayr in Scotland and introduced to Canada by Lord Dalhousie, Governor General of the Province of Canada, in 1821.

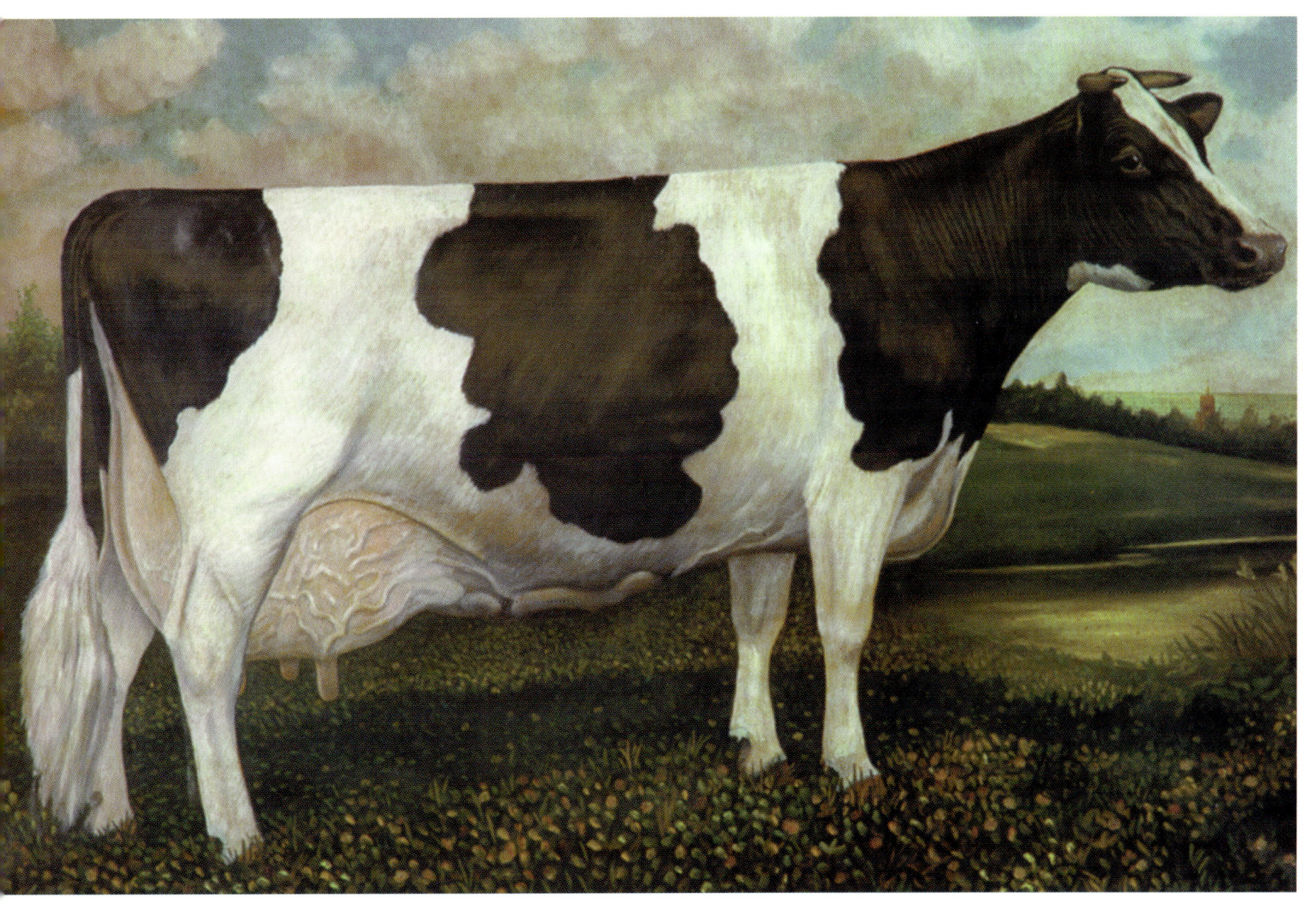

Holstein True Type (24 x 36", oil on canvas, 1935), bred in the Province of Friesland in Holland and introduced to Canada in 1881.

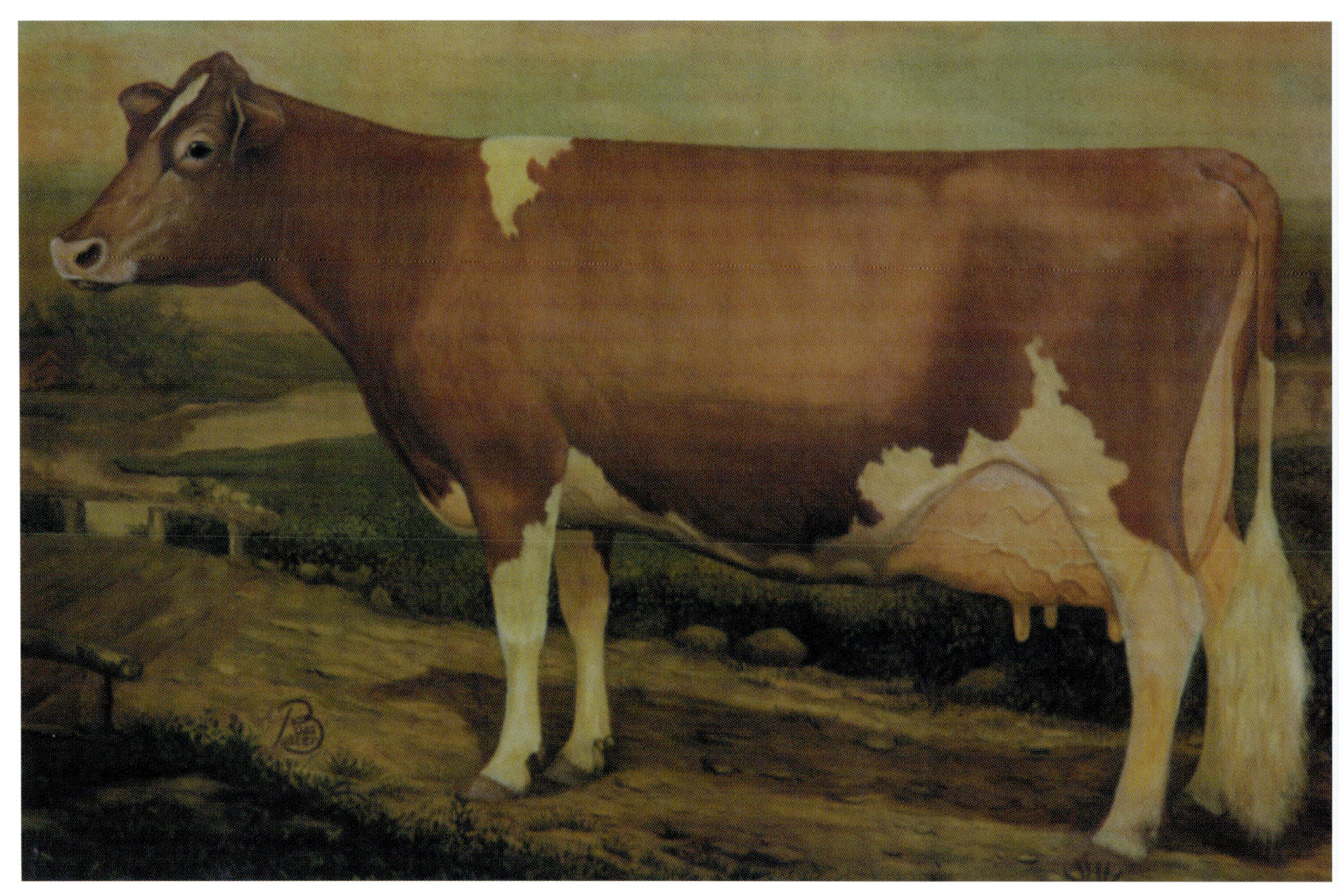

Guernsey True Type (24 x 36", oil on canvas, 1935), a breed developed on Guernsey Island and introduced to Canada by Sir John Abbott in 1876.

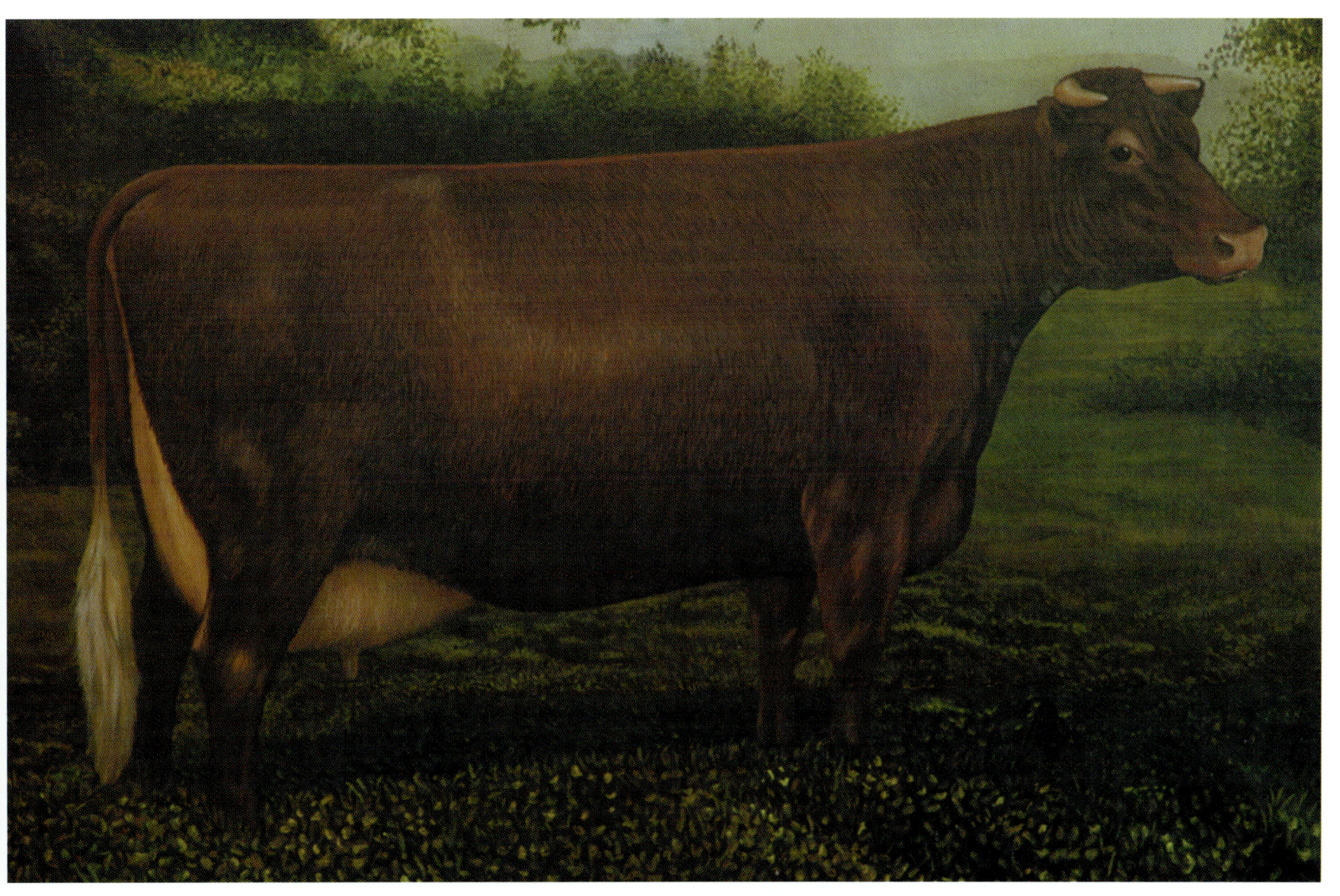

Dual-Purpose Shorthorn (24 x 36", oil on canvas, 1936), a breed originating in Durham, Northumberland, and York Counties in England and introduced to Canada in 1832.

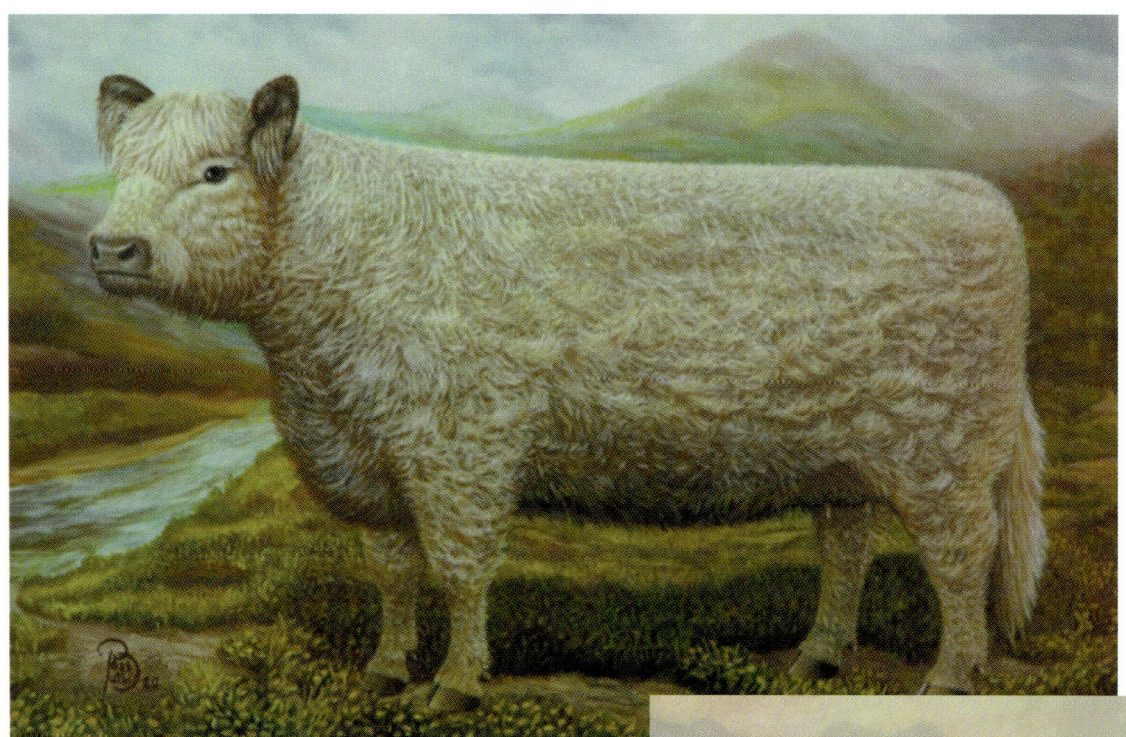

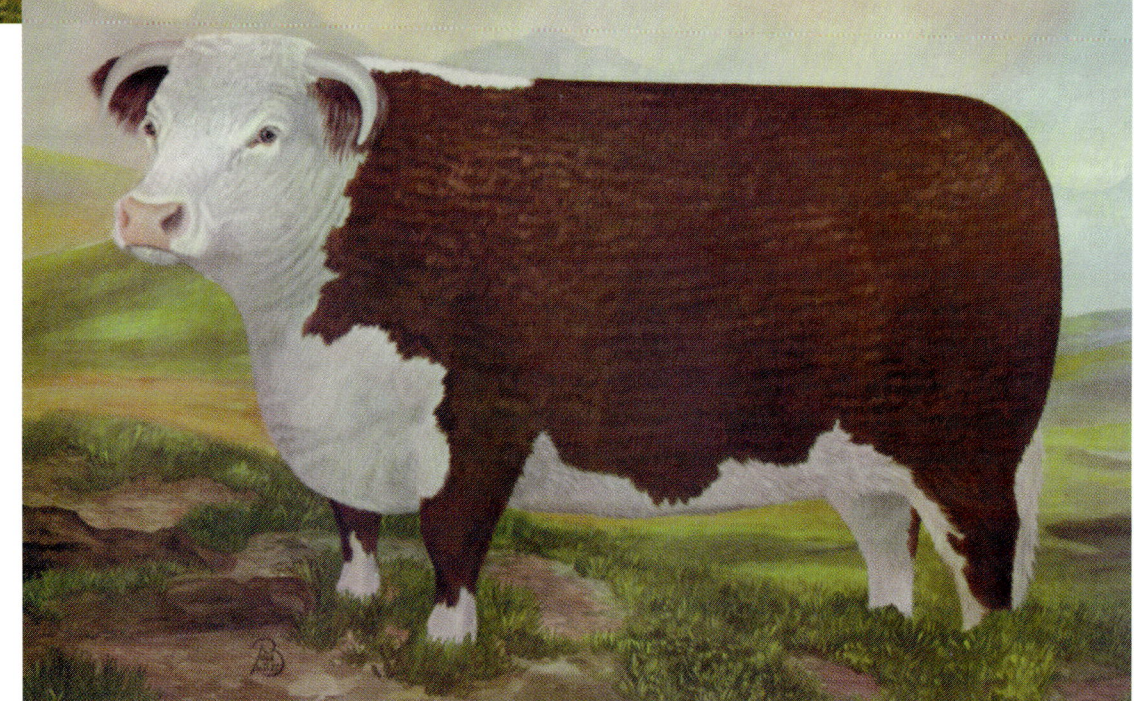

Galloway True Type (24 x 36", oil on masonite, 1980), a beef cattle breed from southwest Scotland introduced to Canada by Thomas McCrae in 1861.

Hereford True Type (24 x 36", oil on canvas, 1936), a beef cattle breed originating in Herefordshire in England and introduced to Canada by F.W. Stone in 1860.

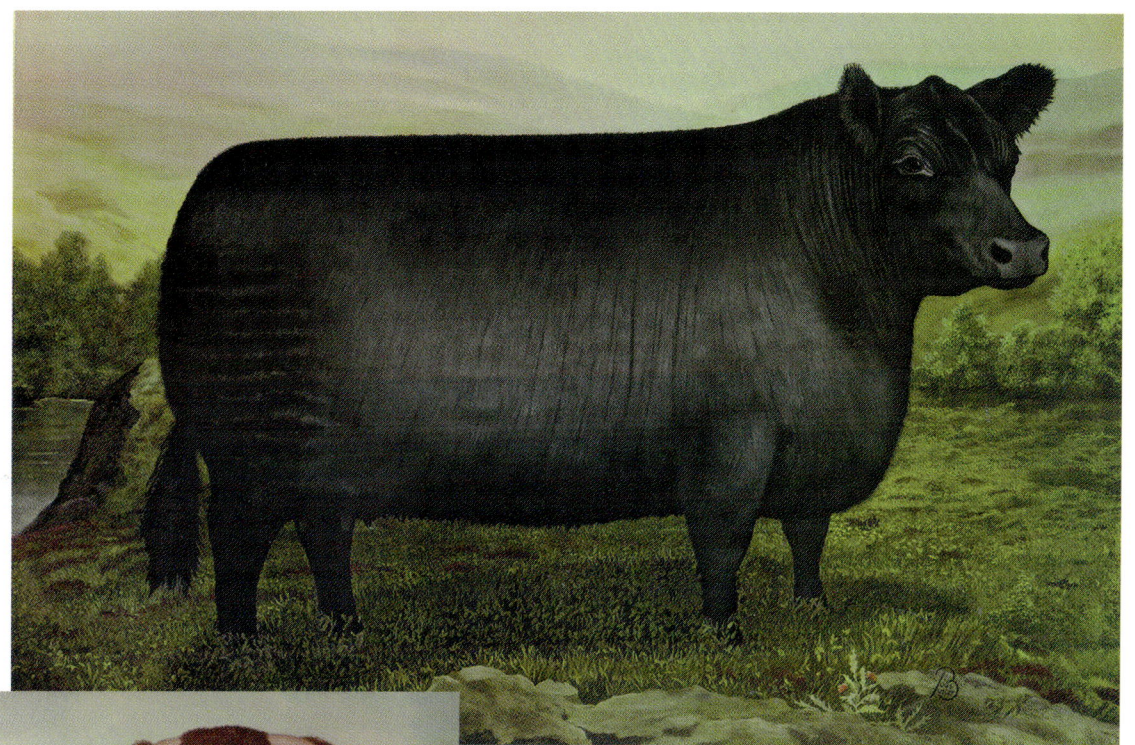

Aberdeen Angus True Type (24 x 36", oil on canvas, 1936), a beef cattle breed originating in Aberdeen and Angus Counties in Scotland and introduced to Canada by the Ontario Agricultural College in 1876.

Beef Shorthorn True Type (24 x 36", oil on canvas, 1936), a breed comprised of three sections — Beef, Lincoln Red, and Dual-Purpose — introduced to Canada from England in the 1830s.

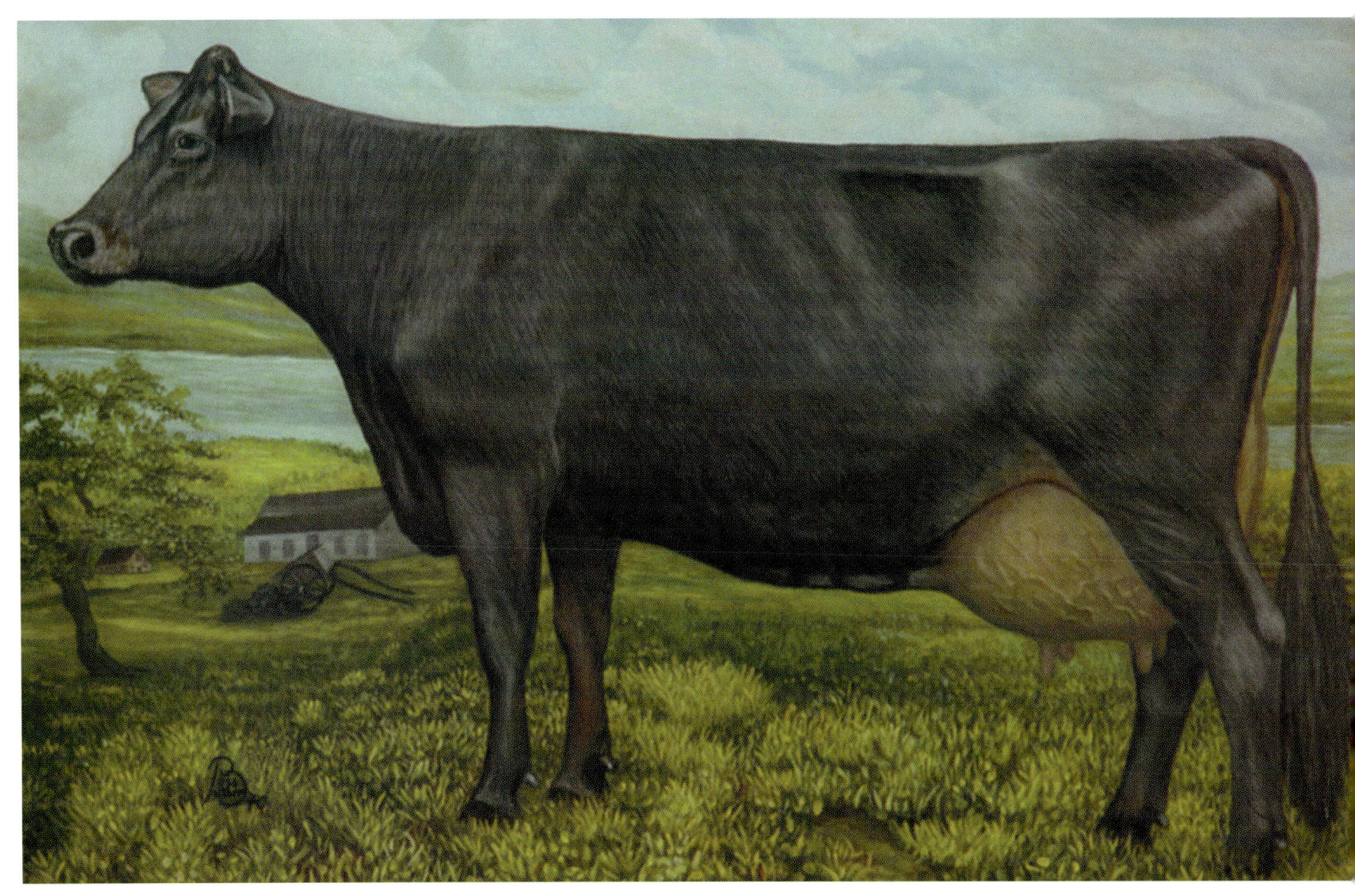

Canadian True Type (24 x 36", oil on canvas, 1940), the only dairy breed developed on the North American continent, from stock introduced from Normandy and Brittany in the 17th century by French settlers.

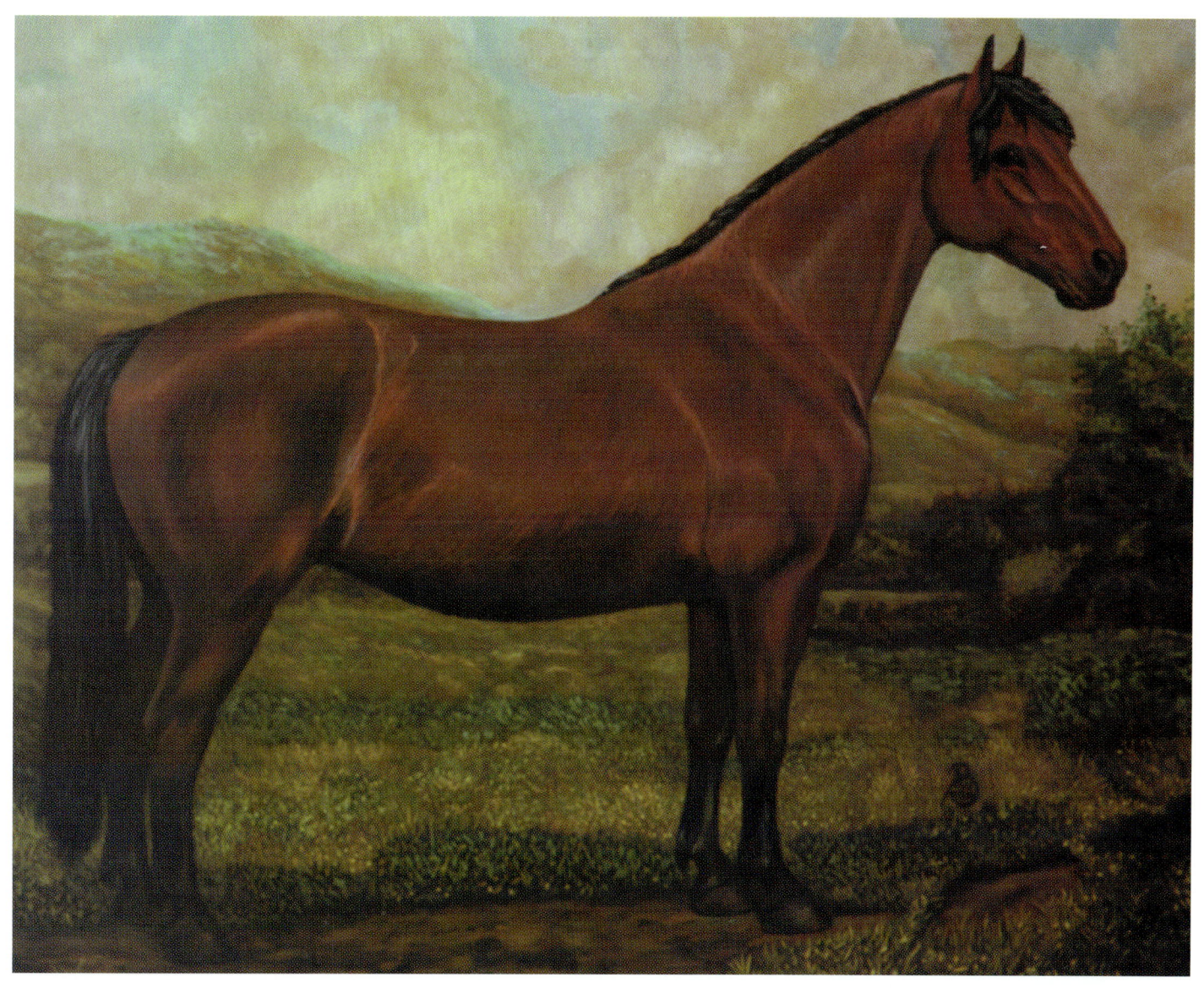

French Canadian True Type (24 x 36", oil on canvas, 1940), a breed originating in France and first introduced to Canada in 1647 by settlers of New France (Quebec).

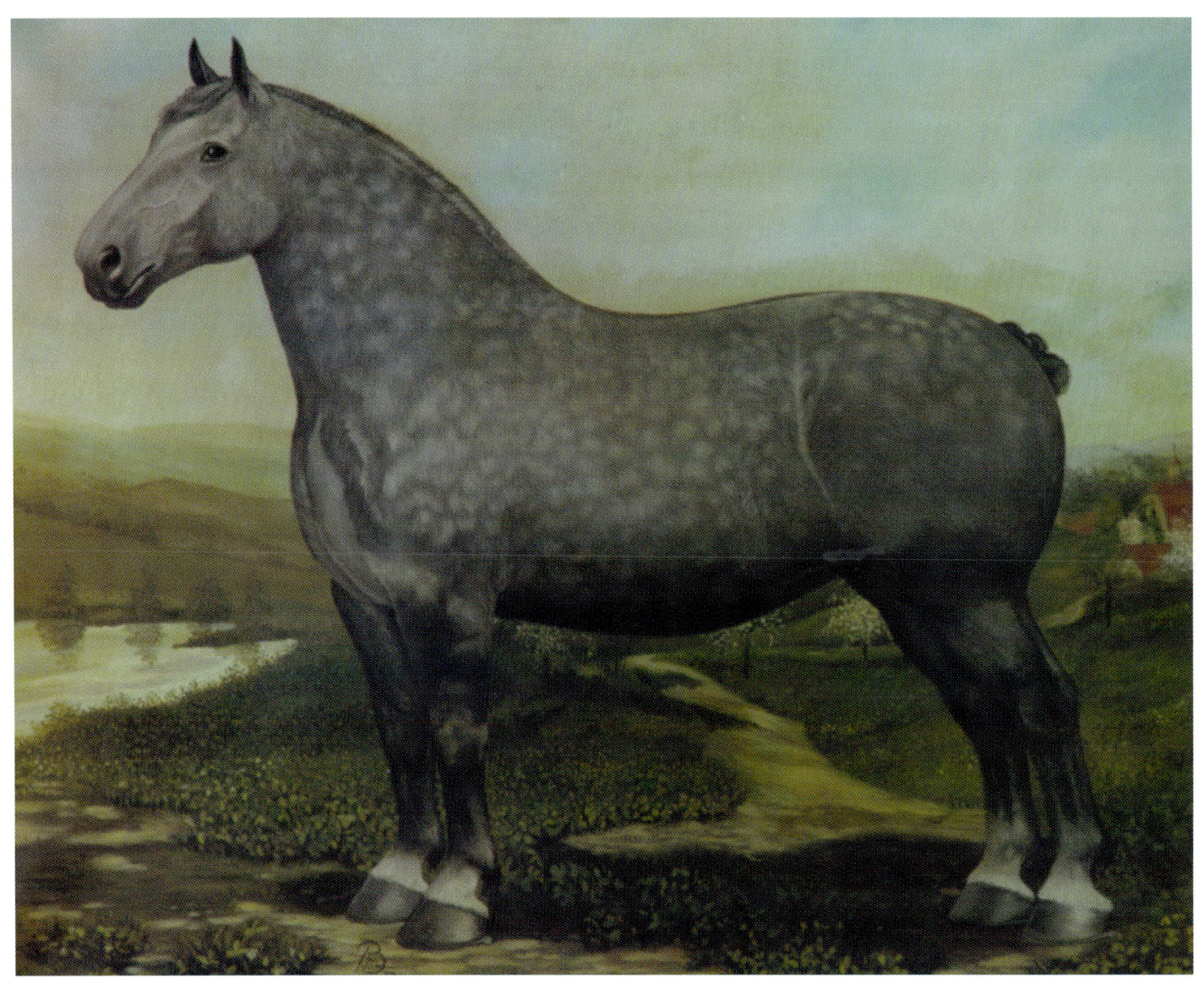

Percheron True Type (30 x 36", oil on canvas, 1938), bred in France from Arab stock and introduced to Canada in the 1840s.

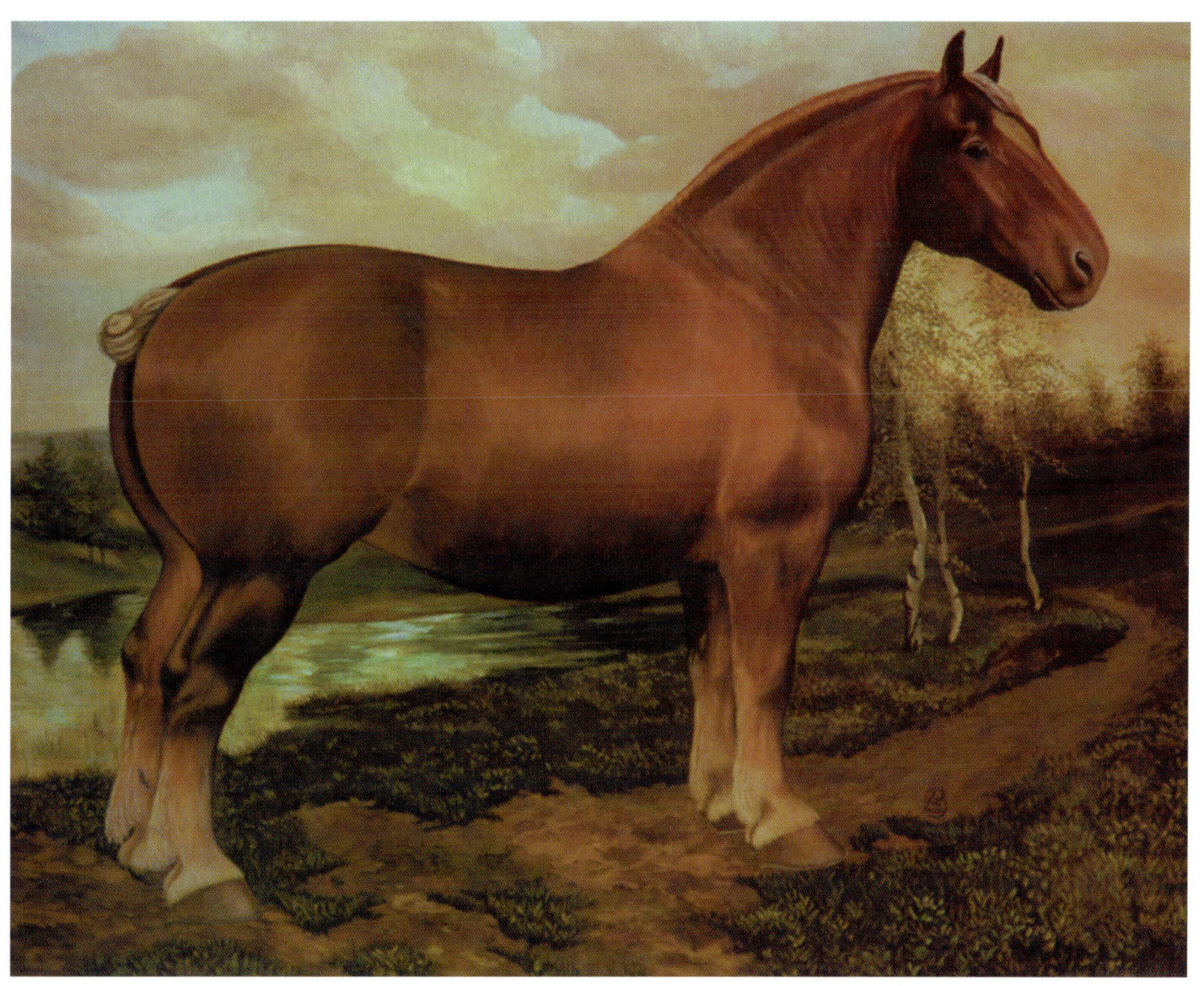

Belgian True Type (30 x 36", oil on canvas, 1938), a breed of draft horse originating in Belgium and introduced to North America in 1866.

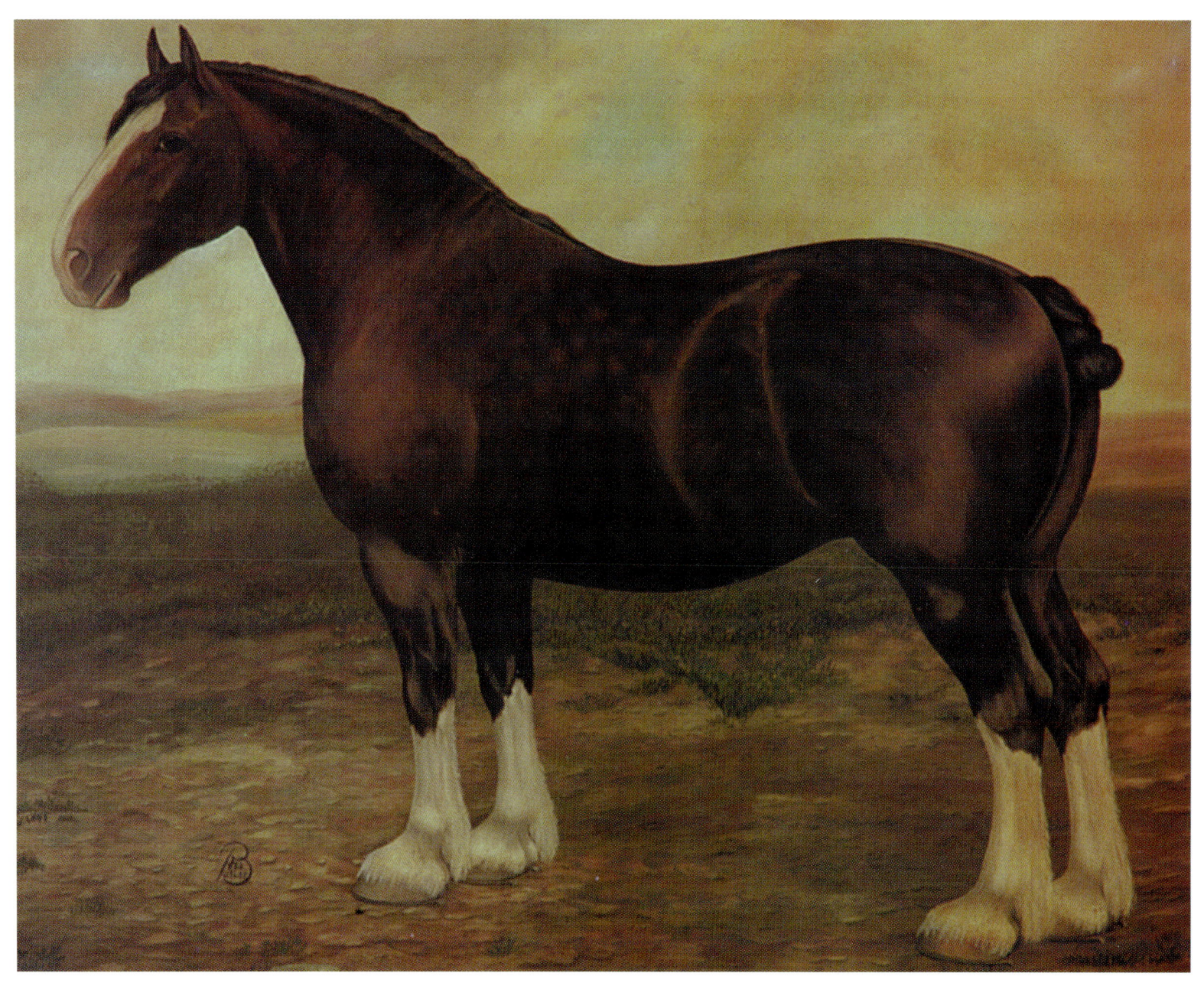

Clydesdale Mare and Horse True Types (30 x 36", oil on canvas, 1938), a breed developed from Flemish and Shire breeds in Scotland and introduced to Canada in 1840.

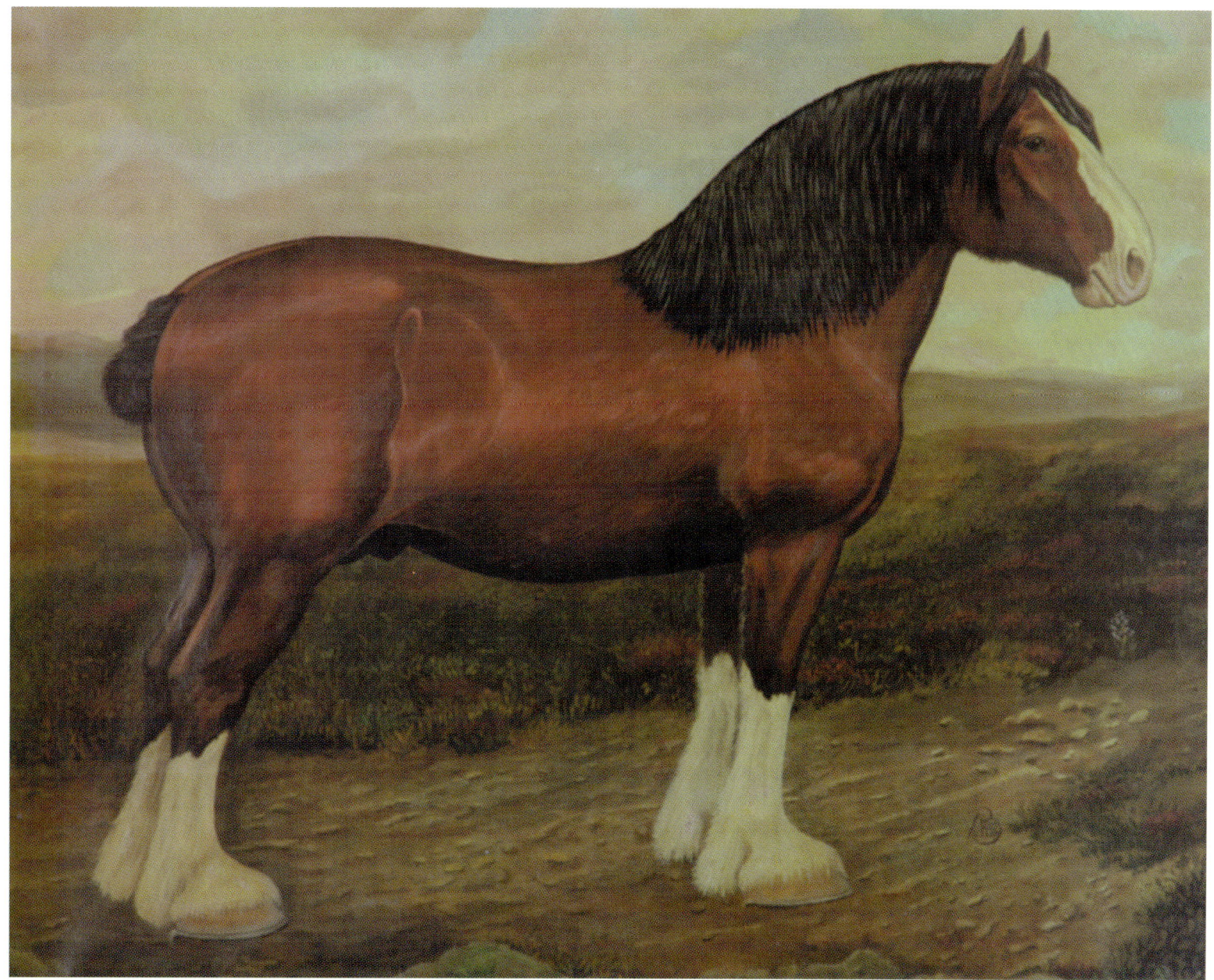

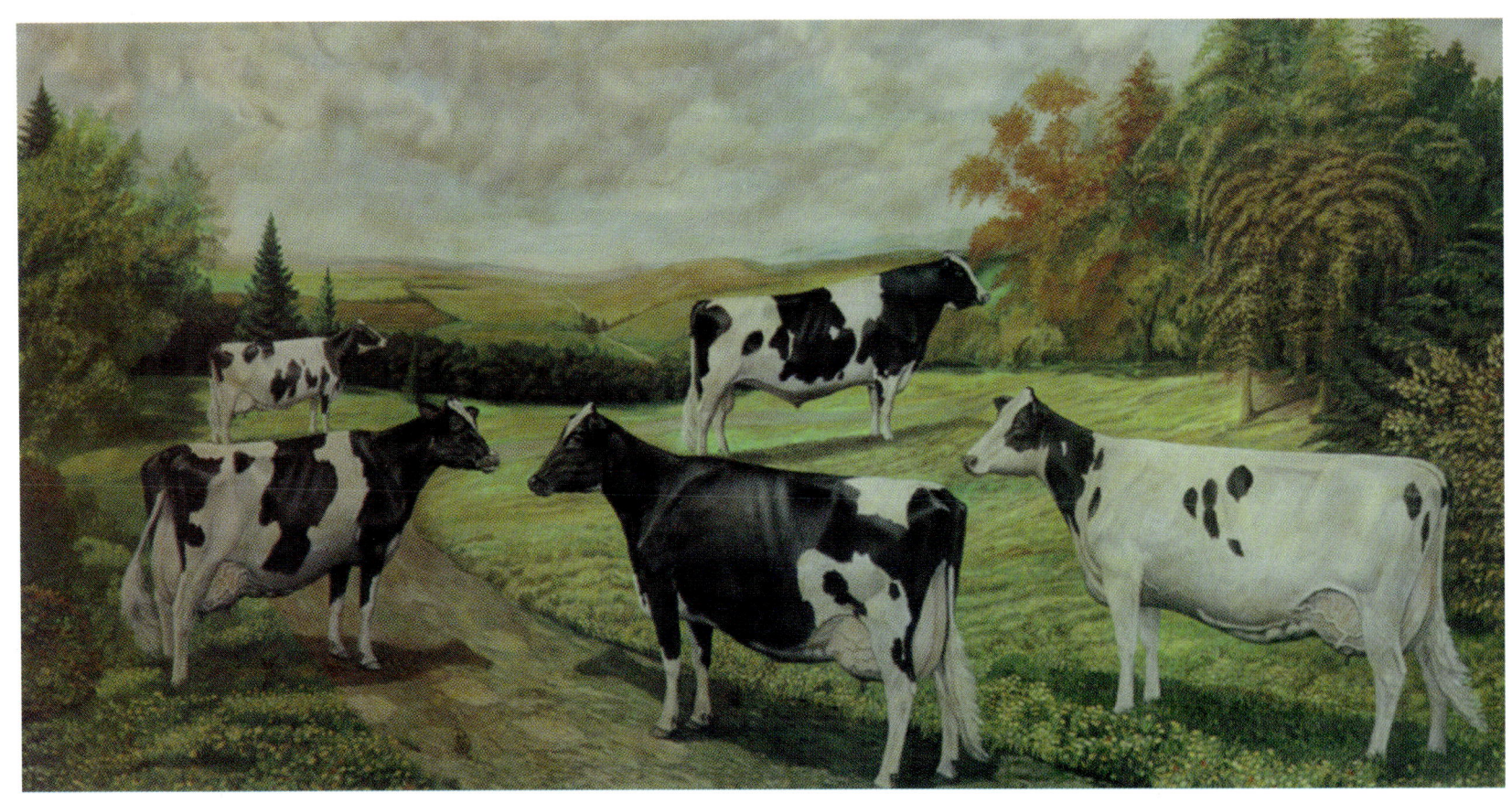

Famous Holsteins, Study of a Breed (48 x 80", oil on masonite, 1968), designed to portray with detail and accuracy the type and character of some famous Holstein cattle in Canada.

7 | Cows and Bulls Lined Up in Long Rows

THE NEW YEAR WAS A DRAMATIC ONE for Ross Butler as his career went up and down like a yoyo: he was either approaching cloud nine or hovering near the depths of despair.

One of his highs came early in the year. On 3 January 1939, Ross purchased the Butler's rented property at 742 Pavey Street for two thousand dollars with no down payment. Then with the growing interest in the agriculture industry for True Types of the breeds, Ross's True Type paintings and three-dimensional models became very popular. Several months earlier he had had a mould and cast made of a Holstein cow and bull. These models were exhibited at several conferences and shows and Ross was delighted to receive an order for 250 pair. When the purchaser asked that the models be smaller in size, Ross had to sculpt two smaller models and have two new moulds made as well. After the pouring of the plaster, each had to be hand-painted.

These made quite a sight in my studio, cows and bulls lined up in long rows, in all stages of preparation.

Ross's selling price had been based on the cost of developing the original pair. Because he had not counted on the extra time or work to develop the smaller models, he ended up with a bare bones margin of profit.

This large order had come from contacts made at a conference, but most orders came by mail. Ross decided to increase his advertising and proceeded to place ads in newspapers and national agriculture magazines. In the 25 March 1939 farm edition of the Woodstock's *Sentinel Review*, he advertised his prints: set of eight dairy breeds (Holstein, Ayrshire, Guernsey, and Jersey) $1, postpaid; single prints of horses, male and female, 50¢ postpaid.

On 22 June 1939, Ross's fortunes took a decided upward turn when he signed a contract with the *Montreal Star and Family Herald*. The contract had a *potential* value of five hundred thousand dollars, and at the time it was said that this was the largest single contract ever given to a Canadian artist. Spread over ten years, the contract called for the reproduction rights for one hundred True Type pictures in living colour, along with a two thousand word description of each breed. The *Family Herald*, Canada's national agriculture magazine, expected to circulate at least seven hundred thousand prints to farm homes and schools across the country. While it may seem that this contract would have set Ross up for life, it really was not that lucrative of a deal. The *Family Herald* advertised "a complete set of eight reproductions in full colour, on heavy coated stock, each measuring 11" x 14" for 69 cents, with postage paid." According to the agreement, Ross's profit was less than half a cent, and with the contract spread over so many years, his meagre profits were also spread over many years. Several reporters, who interviewed Ross at the time, all agreed that he seemed to be more enthused by the fact his work was going to be seen by thousands of Canadians than he was about the money involved.

Two weeks after Ross signed the contract, *The Philadelphia Inquirer*, one of the largest Sunday newspapers in America at that time, featured an article on the artist and his work. Ross was still good copy for the media. Other international magazines were quick to follow suit and articles on Ross Butler, the world's foremost painter of domestic animals, were soon spread across two continents. One American writer wrote, "Butler combines scientific knowledge with art. Having worked with, shown and judged, he has a breeder's viewpoint in evaluating an animal."

Ross had spoken at many events over the years, but one of the most prestigious was the Percheron Judges and Breeders' national conference on 17 June 1939, at Lynwood Farm in Carmel, Indiana. The conference marked the centennial anniversary of the importation of the Percheron breed to North America from France and was attended by more than three hundred stockmen. Although Ross was just one of fourteen speakers, his presentation on "How Livestock Breeders Can Use Measurements Effectively" was well received. Three American universities each ordered a Percheron mare and stallion for study purposes. These orders were followed by another order from a college in Quebec.

Several weeks later, someone from the Dawes Brewery in Montreal saw and ordered a set of Percheron models. The Brewery's logo for its Black Horse Ale was a Percheron horse. It also had a string of Percheron stallions travelling throughout the Province of Quebec with the purpose of improving the breed.

After seeing my models first hand, they commissioned me to create a new logo for them. This logo would be one-half the size of the official True Type Percheron. I was overwhelmed with joy.

Ross worked from early morning until late in the evening on the new logo as he couldn't wait to ship the model to Montreal to have it approved by the Dawes Brewery officials. There was no doubt in his mind that it would be quickly approved. When the order came, it was for two thousand five hundred black Percheron models in two different sizes. Ross's price had been calculated on only one size. Because he was afraid of potentially losing the contract if he tried to renegotiate, he let the price stand and suffered a reduced profit margin.

To fulfil the size of the order, it was necessary for Ross to secure another bank loan to cover the setup and labour costs. He certainly could not do the work all himself. As well, the models had to be distributed to every beer parlour in Canada when they were finished. For each model, packed and ready for shipment, Ross received $16.40, but his cost per unit was around the $16.00 mark. He had never thought to figure any fixed expenses into the cost such as taxes, utilities, telephone, car expenses, etc.

The models became so popular that beer parlour owners had to chain them to a wall brackets in order to keep them from being stolen. If these models are found today, they are valued from five hundred to one thousand dollars, depending on their condition.

While trying to fulfil this order, Ross's time was stretched to the limit. He no longer had time for Ruby or Alf or any of his other friends. Ross was finally persuaded to hire a manager to look after his business affairs. Maybe he could now concentrate solely on his art. While the man was from one of Woodstock's most influential families and came highly recommended, he proved to be useless as a manager. Although prospective clients were wined and dined, he came to work late and intoxicated. He also mixed up and misplaced orders and, in general, made a hash of the business part so vital to Ross's career.

Ross had no alternative but to fire the man, but he didn't go quietly. With six months still left on his one-year contract, the man threatened Butler with a lawsuit. Either Ross must buy out the contract for one thousand dollars or face the notoriety of going to court.

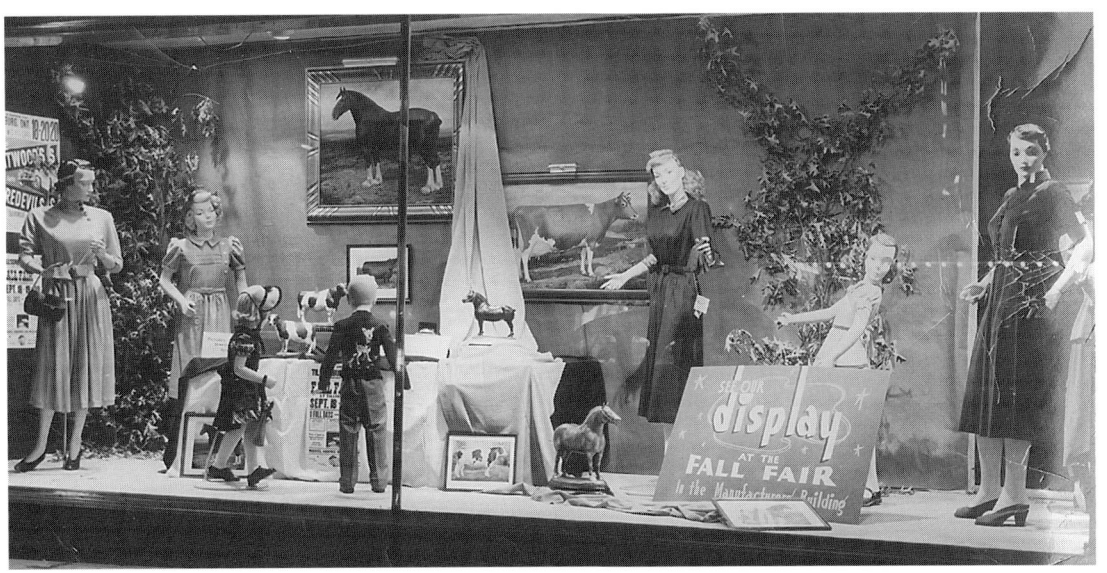

Ross Butler's art as a window display in Tillsonburg.

I paid the $1,000, but I vowed then and there that no matter the labour or the sacrifice, I would go it alone.

This experience coloured Ross's thinking for the rest of his life. There were many times over the years that he could have benefited from the expertise of a professional agent or business manager, but he would not risk being taken advantage of again.

For several months, Ross had toyed with the idea of giving up his Dundas Street studio. The rent was high and his income was often out-distanced by his expenses. He also had his family to support. He would not have dreamt of not paying for Carl's board at the Canadian Institute for the Blind at Brantford. Ross cared deeply for "Snooks", as he called him, and no matter how strapped Ross was for cash, he always brought a little present home for Carl when he returned from a trip.

One day while driving home from a day at the studio, Ross saw a small confectionary store for sale. The building was perched on the front lawn of an older home. The owner had retired and now wanted to sell it and have the building moved away. Ross and his brother Frank, who had some carpentry knowledge, later went back to have a closer look. They found it to be structurally sound and easily moveable. Ross traded a pair of Percheron models for the building and had it moved close to the main house on the Pavey Street property. Frank did the renovations plus some much-needed repairs to the main house and charged Ross a total of thirty dollars.

The acquisition of this building, its moving and renovations, had not helped Ross's financial situation. He was now eighteen thousand dollars in debt, and creditors were constantly at his door.

My creditors became so concerned about their money that they wanted me to insure my hands for $100,000. It might have been a good idea, but I simply didn't have the money.

One of the creditors demanding payment was the bank that had financed his Dawes Brewery Black Horse models. When Ross had received the money from the brewery, he had not paid back the bank loan. Instead he had used the money to pay some bills and finance another project that he was sure would make him rich.

In August 1939, Ross was forced to write to the Family Herald and ask for an advance on his contract. He was flatly turned down and he brooded about his financial situation for days. After much soul-searching, he came to the conclusion that *he* was the problem because he did not use sound business practices. His bids were

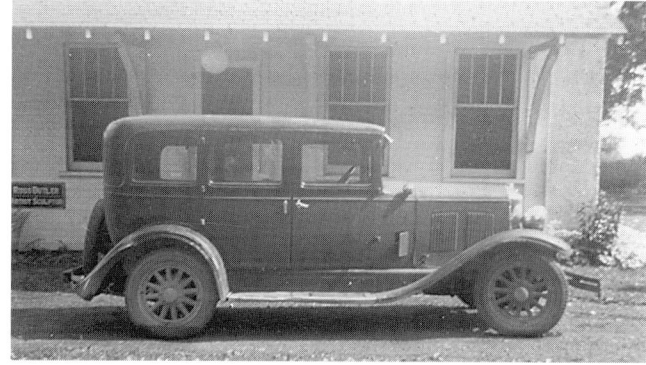

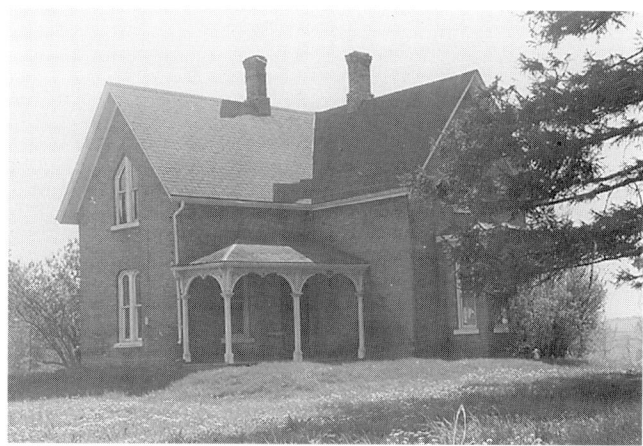

Ross Butler bartered a pair of Percheron models for this studio building (top) which was moved adjacent to his Pavey Street brick home.

often too low, he never allowed for any margin of error, and he never asked for advances on his contracts. He recognized that only he could get himself out of this financial mess, and the only way that would be accomplished was by working longer and harder.

With his resolution to work longer and harder, Ross ignored everything around him, including the news that war with Germany was imminent. He was convinced that even if war came, it would have little effect on him. After all, he was thirty-two years old and had passed the draft stage. Ross continued to concentrate solely on his work, and, somehow, managed to stave off his creditors. But the long hours began to take their toll. Although he adhered to a healthy diet of salads, cheese, and only a little meat, he was afraid that his health was going to break down again. Only his mind training saved his sanity. He badly needed a vacation, but the only way he could afford to take one was to combine it with his work at the Royal Winter Fair in November. Here he met old friends and socialized in an environment he knew and loved.

The new year, 1940, brought troubles of a different kind. Ross's oldest brother, Clarence, died of cancer, and then, without warning, the Ontario government cancelled his contract. Ross was wrong when he thought the war would not effect him; the government needed the money for the war effort. Ross was devastated. He had already completed twenty-two True Type breeds. Hundreds of hours had gone into the second phase of the contract, the True Types of the breeds of draft horses — Clydesdale, Belgian, and Percheron. Now, he would receive no remuneration whatsoever for all his hard work.

I suddenly realized all my lofty ambitions were for nought. I was back where I started, only now I was more deeply in debt . . . and I solemnly vowed never to paint commercially again.

After making this vow, Ross turned to other pursuits. He brought home a beautiful model from Toronto to meet his mother, but Mary Butler was not impressed and

PERCHERON BREEDERS TO EXHIBIT AT POMONA FAIR

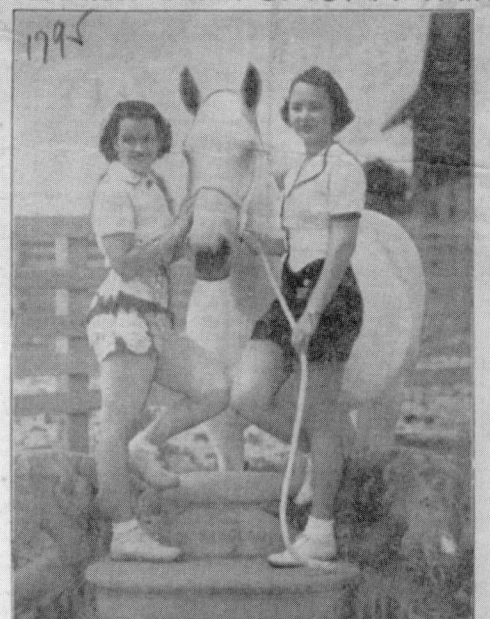

For the first time in its history the annual show of the Percheron Horse Association of America will be brought to the West and will be held in conjunction with the Los Angeles County fair at Pomona, Sept. 16 to Oct. 2. Here is California Nina, prize Percheron owned by the University of California with Lucile Hutchinson, left, and Leora Sanstad, right, of the home economics department of the university.

Giant Horses From Leading Farms of U. S. Are Entered in Competition

Promising one of the most spectacular as well as one of the most remarkable livestock exhibitions ever held in the United States, comes the announcement that Los Angeles County fair in Pomona, Sept. 16 to Oct. 2, has been selected as the place for the annual show and breeders congress of the Percheron Horse Association of America. It will be the first time that the famous event has been brought west of the Mississippi and the fact that Pomona was selected in competition with several of the largest state fairs of the nation is taken as a distinct compliment to the magnitude and importance of the exposition.

While the bulk of the entries will come from the Midwest states, every section of the United States will be represented. The association numbers thousands of leading breeders. In the roster are names of men and women who loom large in the business and professional world, such as J. O. Penney; Ely Lilly, noted drug manufacturer; Mrs. John J. Raskob; Charles J. Lynn, vice-president and general manager of the Lilly Co.; Max Dreyfus; Frank C. Rathje, president Chicago City Bank & Trust Co., and William duPont Jr. Many of these will be here in person, while all are expected to be represented in the entry list.

It requires no stretch of imagination to conjure up the picture presented by 250 to 300 of these magnificent huge draft animals, averaging over a ton apiece, on parade. Plenty of opportunity will be afforded to see the blue-blooded aristocrats in all their glory in the show ring, in the judging ring, and in harness.

In preparation for the event, which will turn the attention of the horse world to Pomona, several huge new horse barns have been built together with judging pavilion seating 5,000 and a number of other special facilities required for so great an undertaking.

The Percheron show will be accompanied by a glittering array of special events. Luncheons and banquets will round out the time between business and showing sessions. Paintings of the ideal Percheron, by Ross Butler, world's foremost animal painter, will be unveiled at a great love feast at which the "Percheron Achievement Breeder Medal" for the year will be awarded. This is the greatest honor ever to be bestowed on a pure bred livestock dealer in America.

From: The San Bernardino Telegram August 23, 1938.

$500,000 Contract for Oxford Man

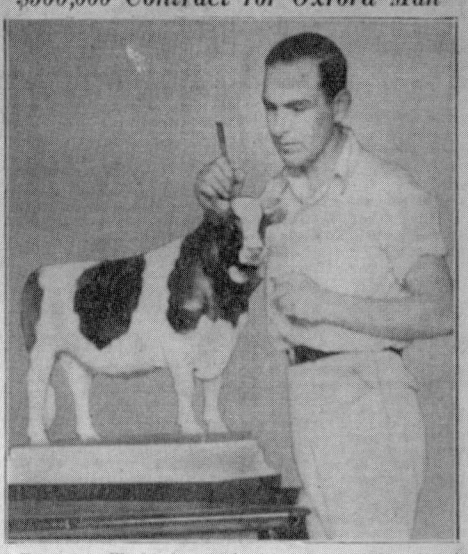

To a young Woodstock artist has come a commission which he expects will bring him $500,000 before the contract is completed. He is Ross Butler, seen here giving realistic coloring to a sculptured model, and who has become a recognized authority on Ontario dairy cattle. The contract, which he will enter into at Montreal with a farm publishing syndicate, calls for the painting of 100 pictures to illustrate all known breeds of livestock and poultry in Canada. Twenty-five breeds of poultry will be included in the list. The commission will occupy Mr. Butler's time for the next 10 years.

The London Daily Free Press, London Thur. June 22, 1939.

FARM MAGAZINE REPRODUCES FAMOUS ANIMAL PICTURES

An announcement of unusual interest appears in the current issue of the Family Herald and Weekly Star. This magazine has secured the rights to reproduce, in full colour, the now famous series of Dairy Cattle Pictures painted by Ross Butler, well-known agricultural artist. Of special interest to dairymen, breeders, junior farmers, teachers, etc., the series consists of eight paintings portraying the ideal cow and bull (approved by the breeders' associations) in the Holstein, Ayrshire, Jersey and Guernsey breeds. The pictures are 14" x 11" in size and are offered readers in sets of eight, postage paid at a nominal cost within each of all.

In making these pictures available to readers of the Family Herald and Weekly Star once more identifies itself with progressive farming. A leader in all matters pertaining to farming for over seventy years, the Family Herald has always disseminated many times more farming information .... saved and made for its readers many more dollars ... than any other magazine.

The timely offer of Ross Butler's Dairy Cattle Pictures will be welcomed by all who are interested in the fine cattle and will be hailed by another milestone in the long list of services rendered by the Family Herald to its readers.

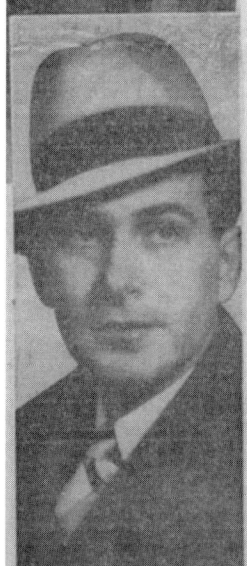

ROSS BUTLER
Artist Butler at his easel. At his back is a sample of his other type of art work —sculpturing.

An Education in Breeds

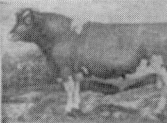

THE EIGHT FAMOUS BUTLER

Dairy Cattle PICTURES

Offered by the Family Herald and Weekly

Each beautifully coloured picture measuring 14" x 11", show ideal type cows and bulls of the Holstein, Guernsey, Jersey and Ayrshire breeds — approved by Breeders' Associations.

The Complete Set of 8 Reproductions in full color, on heavy coated stock, together with History of the Breeds, may be YOURS for only

69¢ For the 8 Pictures POST PAID

(In the Province of Quebec outside of Montreal, add 2c Sales Tax)

IMPORTANT: These pictures are available in sets of 8 only. They cannot economically be mailed unless they are in complete sets.

ORDER YOUR SET TODAY

Family Herald & Weekly Star
Montreal, P.Q.

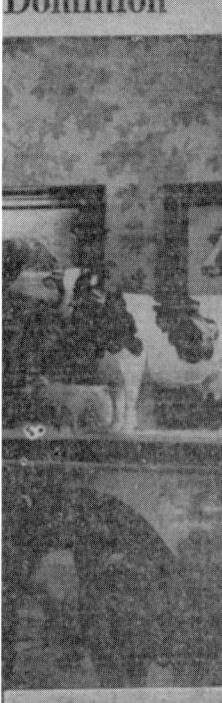

Pages from Ross Butler's scrapbooks.

immediately took to her bed with one of her sick headaches. After that, Ross concentrated on his relationship with Ruby. He traded a work of art for a pair of riding horses and he and Ruby spent many hours cantering around the area. Their friendship gradually developed into love. She became the balance in his life, a constant in his up-and-down career. She always gave Ross her support, but when she felt he was wrong about something, she told him so in no uncertain terms.

Ross's artistic career continued, albeit at a much slower pace. He had on hand some reproductions of his True Type paintings after his cancelled contract and spent some of his time mailing them across Canada. He also packed and shipped some of his models. The money trickled in.

The Quebec government asked Ross to do the True Types of their cattle and horse breeds. These French Canadian animals had come to Canada with the settlers and were truly native to Quebec. The Morgan, which many believed to be French Canadian as well, certainly originated in North America. Some of these animals were already on canvas, but, of course, Ross needed a True Type committee's approval before they could be classified as such.

When a curator from a university museum saw the models of a True Type cow and bull, he was so impressed with their perfection that he asked Ross if he thought he could make models of leaves from all the Canadian trees as well as models of all the Canadian fruits. What a wonderful idea! And Ross's visionary senses took off. In his mind's eye he could see this concept extended to industry, including lumbering, mining, and agriculture. In fact, every major industry could be portrayed with accurate realism. Ross could picture another door opening for his talents.

My artistic efforts had not been a success financially, in fact just the reverse. Therefore, I had to make a complete change. Now seemed the time.

8 | The Art of Animal Photography

OVER THE NEXT FEW YEARS, Ross Butler's life did change, both personally and professionally. In his grief at the death of his brother Clarence, he turned to Ruby who brought him comfort and understanding. Sculpting and writing were still the main focus of his artistic career, but he was developing another skill, photography.

He also took the time to collect his thoughts.

Tired and unhappy, I took a short hiatus. I drove for hours along back-country roads. I ambled along streams and sat under shade trees. The quiet and peace of the days replenished my soul.

It was during these trips that Ross began taking pictures, dozens of them with an old Brownie box camera. One day while driving along a Waterloo County road, he saw a herd of well-kept Jerseys and he decided to ask the owner if he could take some close-ups of the cattle for a magazine article that he was working on. As Ross drove up the lane, he saw the farmer running up the barn grade carrying a bag of feed under each arm. Because Ross had difficulty carrying even one bag of feed, he marvelled at this feat. The farmer, Harley Stager, laughed at Ross's astonishment and said this was only a morning workout. Stager was a wrestler and amateur boxer and farm work certainly kept him in shape.

When Ross asked him about taking pictures of his herd, Stager gave his permission, provided that Ross gave him copies of the pictures. Ross agreed to the stipulation and the slim, gentle artist shook hands with the giant with a humped nose and cauliflower ears. This handshake cemented a friendship that was to last for the rest of Ross's life.

After seeing Ross's photographs of Harley Stager's herd, several other farmers asked for pictures of their animals. Ross always obliged, but soon he found it costly to have the films developed and extra prints made. He decided that it would be cheaper to do his own developing and printing. Once Ross had his mind set upon something, he always moved quickly. He bought a book on developing film, studied it carefully, and then followed its instructions to the letter.

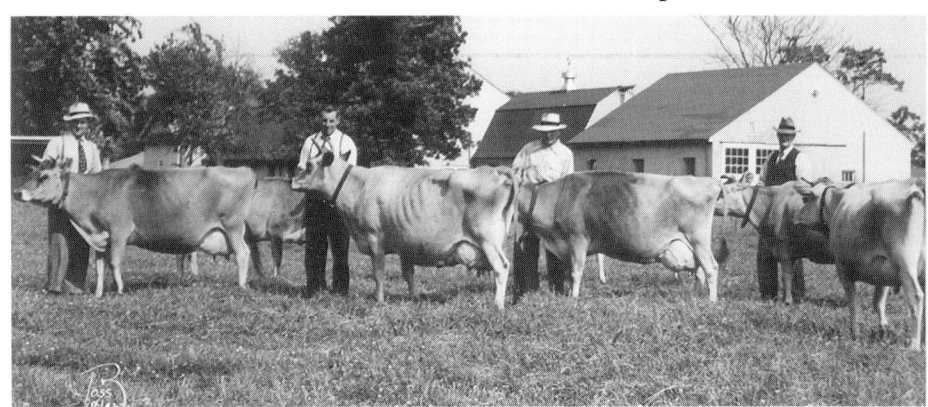

Ross Butler photograph of (l-r) Roy Roth, Harley Stager, Gus Nilson, and Wm. Henderson showing Jersey cattle at Marlu Farm, 1946.

The book had said that he would need a dark room with a sink and water. The family kitchen seemed suitable, for he could work there without interruption after his mother and Carl had retired for the night. Any stray light that would come through the windows could be easily blocked by a blanket. His next purchase was a tube of developer costing a total of five cents. Because he had decided to make his own solutions, he also needed three trays: one for the developer, one for the stop solution, and the third for a fixer. The third tray was placed next to the water faucet, the stop tray went in the middle, and the developing solution tray at the place where he would begin the process.

There was no need to rush in the developing of his films. If he made a mistake, he had the time to retrace his steps and start over again. He learned how to make negatives and how to develop them. He taught himself how to test for dark room and light leaks which would destroy his efforts. Ross bought a stop watch with an alarm and a large illuminated second hand. This watch became one of his most useful tools because he learned that everything in developing and enlarging was timed to the second. As he became more experienced, he learned to rely on his instincts during the developing process, but in the beginning, timing each step was crucial.

Ross found it a creative challenge to enlarge a picture from a small print. Before each enlargement, he would study the print under the parlour lamp. In order to find out what should be highlighted and what should be left out, he would place two L-shaped pieces of cardboard over the picture and move them around in different positions. He also experimented with different qualities of papers and with the density scale of negatives. He delved into every phase of developing and printing.

He found that large images were better if the lens was farther away from the paper. Some of the finest effects could be achieved by giving or withholding exposure from certain areas of the print. He learned the terminology of developing: adding was called burning, withholding was called dodging, and vignettes meant dropping the background and fading the subject into white. When he became more experienced, Ross began to combine two negatives into a single picture.

By trial and error he learned how to remove a spot or streak from a print. A brush dipped lightly in India ink and applied in layers worked wonders. He also added a few tricks of his own. For example, his own saliva mixed with India ink worked better.

Mounting the prints proved to be a challenge. In his early attempts, he used photographic rubber cement, but he later found that using a hot flat iron on the corners of the mounting tissue, pressed between the frame and picture, brought much better results. And he was not afraid to "doll up" a print if the need arose. After all, a little window dressing never hurt anything.

Everything was learned through trial and error, but like his paintings, his prints were outstanding. His artist's eye for detail was certainly a factor in his success. He would spend hours observing a cow, just waiting for her to move into a "perfect" position before taking her picture. Although people still dropped by his studio, they came in fewer numbers than when he was at the uptown location. On one afternoon, an acquaintance brought John and Irene Petrik, who had recently arrived from Hungary, to see Ross's paintings and sculptures. As well as being an artist herself, Irene had a remarkable knowledge of design. She was keenly interested in the material Ross used for his sculptures, and although she spoke no English, she and Ross were

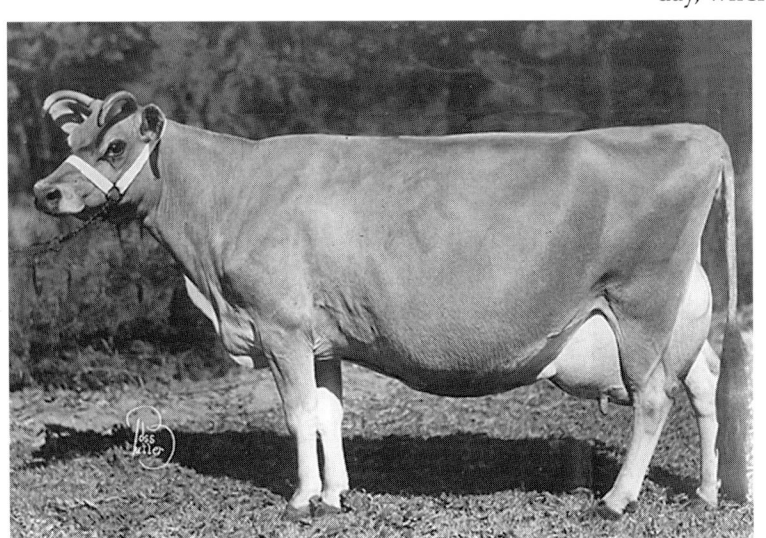

Ross Butler's photograph of Major's Sea Girl, the Jersey cow that proved his theory of animal proportion.

able to communicate quite well by using sign language. When she asked him where he got his clay for modeling, Ross took both Irene and John to Otter Creek the next day, where the Petriks dug up several bushels of clay.

A week later, Ross received a call from John asking him to come to their farm because Irene had something to show him. Lined up on wooden planks was a superbly crafted collection of flowers, ashtrays, and small art objects. However, they needed to be fired in a kiln before Irene could decorate and glaze them. Being new to Canada, the Petriks did not know of anyone who could assist them. Fortunately, Ross had a friend at the McMaster Porcelain works who could fire the pieces. With high hopes, they packed the collection in large baskets of sawdust and Ross set off.

Two weeks later, he returned with only a few pieces left intact. The rest of the pieces were distorted, cracked, or unfit for use. Simply using the clay as it came from the ground had been a failure. It obviously had to be refined before use. Ross was absolutely heart-sick. Because he felt responsible for the disaster, he bought several pounds of ceramic clay from McMaster Porcelain and gave it to Irene as compensation. In return, she painted a portrait of Ross.

While the Petriks went on to achieve worldwide success with their colourful creations, Ross continued to experimented with the clay from Otter Creek. He firmly believed that, if refined, it could equal the clays from China, Hungary, and Czechoslovakia, which were no longer available because of the war. He tested the clay's elasticity, tensile strength, and plasticity, and he fired it under varying degrees of heat. He mixed it with other compounds and its consistency improved. For example, when lime was added to the clay, its tensile strength increased, but when sulphur was added, it exploded in the kiln.

Ross became so enthusiastic about this medium that he contacted the Oxford Board of Education about starting a class in sculpting. He, of course, would teach the class. Unfortunately, the Board was not interested. Ross, reluctantly, went back to his writing and photography. To supplement his income, he continued to search for prime stock for breeders and received a finder's fee.

Late one afternoon, while driving near Oshawa, Ross and a friend saw a herd of cows for sale in a pasture field. The two men decided to climb over the fence and take a closer look at the animals. Ross paused atop the fence, took a second look, and suddenly exclaimed,

"There! She's the one! She's the cow I have been searching for . . . for years. She's beautiful. Look at her conformation . . . her colouring. I've got to have her!"

Ross's friend was not as enthusiastic. "She's too thin," he said, but that didn't deter Ross. He wanted this particular cow and price did not matter. He agreed to pay the one hundred and fifty dollars the farmer was asking. The deal was made, but in the meantime, the cow had to stay in the farmer's pasture field until Ross could arrange the money.

The young cow's name was Major's Sea Girl. She was born on 28 January 1938 and had her first calf in the spring of 1940. When Ross returned home, he researched her background and was surprised to find she was the double grand-daughter of a famous imported Jersey bull, Imperial Double Chance. The bull had been a champion in the Jersey Islands before being imported to Canada, where he also won big at both the Canadian National Exhibition and the Royal Winter Fair. Ross had good reason to remember Imperial Double Chance. His owner had once borrowed a sketch Ross had made of the bull and had never returned it. According to Judge Hugh G. Van Pelt, who had often judged the animal in the show ring, Ross's sketch was "the nearest thing to embody the ideal he had ever seen."

It took Ross three months to raise the money to buy Major's Sea Girl. However, when Ross got there the farmer had raised the price to one hundred and seventy-five dollars. After all, he contended he had fed and pastured the cow for the last three

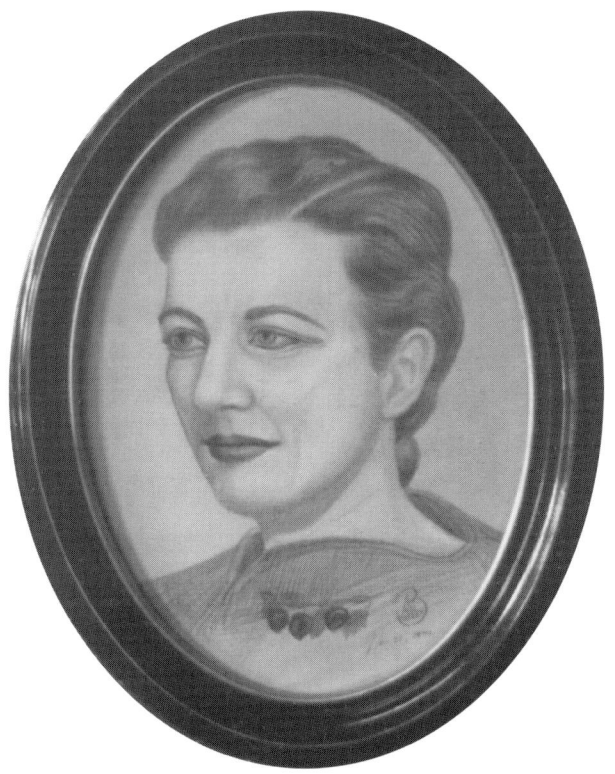

Portrait of Ruby Mae Leuszler, on the occasion of her birthday, 1940.

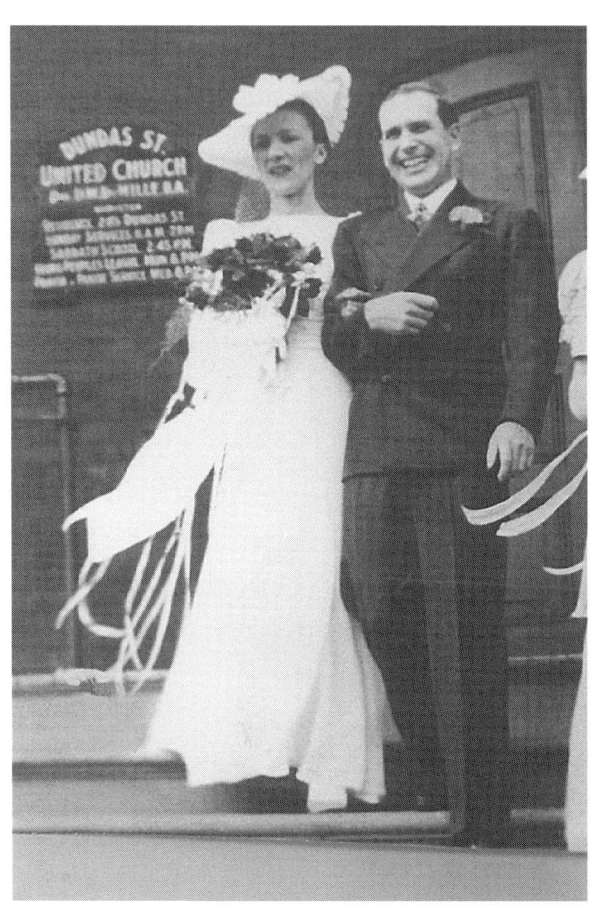

Wedding photograph of Ross and Ruby Butler.

months. Ross did have the $175 with him, but $25 of that money was for the trucker who had come with him to Oshawa. Seeing Ross's crestfallen face, the trucker said he would wait for his money, and Ross was able to buy the cow.

Major's Sea Girl was not Ross's only acquisition in 1942. On June 17, after a six-year courtship, Ross married Ruby Mae Leuszler at Dundas Street United Church in Woodstock. Although Ross and Ruby loved each other, it was not a union made in heaven. While Ross was quiet and easy-going, Ruby was hot-tempered and vocal. He was well-organized, but she was disorganized. He was a loner who was ever-ready to try something new; she was a gregarious person who wanted stability and security. Both were independent and determined. Together, they were able to build an unorthodox lifestyle, but one which suited them both. While Ross pursued his career, Ruby developed her own interests. Yet she was always there when he needed her. She was Ross's anchor to the real world.

He desperately needed that anchor when his father, David Butler, died on 12 March 1943.

I had personally nursed him for six solid months until the end. This was the most profound grief I ever had. We had grown so close those last few months. Now he was gone and I was lost.

9 | The Perfect Jersey and the Theory of Animal Proportion

THE ACQUISITION OF MAJOR'S SEA GIRL boosted Ross Butler's Jersey herd to three. He already owned Chance's Sea Girl, a direct daughter of Imperial Double Chance, and Brampton Sea Girl. With the addition of Major's Sea Girl, who Ross believed was the nearest thing to the True Type cow he had ever seen, he felt that he had the almost perfect herd. According to Ross's theory of proportion, Major's Sea Girl had all of the correct measurements.

I found that the total length of her body, from the tip of her nose to her tailsetting, was exactly the same as her girth measurement. Over and over I checked and rechecked . . . it seemed so remarkable. I found also that the height of her withers was also the same as the height at her rump. Just as interesting was the fact that her feet were also this same distance apart from the front to the rear feet. In other words, the size of her frame made a perfect square.

The length of her head, which was a unit of measurement, was duplicated in twenty-two other parts of her body. The width of her head across the eyes and forehead was duplicated twenty times. It was true that she was too thin, but with good food and care, her weight would increase and she certainly needed to be groomed. Ross polished her horns, trimmed her hooves, and oiled her coat with furniture polish, giving it a rich, golden shine.

Over the next few months, Ross measured and recorded every inch of Major's Sea Girl's anatomy. At last he had a cow who could prove his theory of proportions. Over the years many judges and breeders had scoffed at his theory, but he now had an animal who could substantiate his claims. He would prove his theory in the show ring where it counted most. Ross spent all his spare moments with Major's Sea Girl, recording every detail, including her water intake and her consumption of food. Everyone and everything else became secondary.

In his memoirs Ross documented his theory in six phases:

PHASE ONE:

The square concept: size determined by wither height which was same as the highest point of rump. More significant, feet stood the same distance apart from front to rear hooves. This formed a perfect square and framed the size of the animal. One inch in variation, up or down, equalled approx. 100 pounds difference in body weight.

PHASE TWO:

The length of the head, from the top of her poll to the nose, was duplicated 22 times throughout her body.

1. from poll to nose
2. neck length from poll to withers.
3. from withers to the break in the back.
4. from this point to the axis across the hips.
5. from hipbone to pinbone.
6. over the top of the hips from hipbone to hipbone.
7. depth of flank from hipbone to fore of udder.
8. from pinbone to stifle joint.
9. from pinbone to leg cannon.
10. from the stifle joint to point of hock.
11. from point of hock to point of toe.
12. length of tail bone above the switch.
13. when normal the length of the switch.
14. length of udder junction with body.
15. length of milk vein.
16. milk well to milk well across the floor of the chest.
17. the length of the rib cage.
18. distance from floor of chest to ground.
19. from throat to dewlap.
20. from wither to the point of shoulder.
21. body width through heart.
22. body width through stifle joints.

PHASE THREE:

Width across the head at eyes had 22 similar measurements in other parts of the body.

1. width of face across the eyes.
2. top of poll to lower corner of eyes.
3. from this eye corner to nostril.
4. from the eye to the under jaw.

5. from the chin to the throat.
6. from the clean throat to the dewlap.
7. the total dewlap itself.
8. the depth of the brisket.
9. the width of brisket.
10. the length of brisket between the front legs.
11. point of shoulder to foreleg.
12. width of forearm as it joins the body.
13. muscular development from shoulder point to wither.
14. junction of hind leg to body.
15. length of cannon from hock to body.
16. distance of pinbones apart.
17. pinbone to thurl.
18. thurl to hipbone.
19. pelvic arch to tailhead.
20. front hooves apart, center to center.
21. length of each ear.
22. ears apart joining skull.

PHASE FOUR:
One half the head width had 22 equal proportions throughout the body.
1. width of ear at widest point.
2. prominence of eye socket.
3. width of muzzle.
4. depth of muzzle.
5. length of muzzle.
6. size of knee joint.
7. hock joint.
8. width of hooves, fore and aft.
9. length of hooves, front and rear.
10. length of pasterns.
11. width of forearm above the knee.
12. width of foreleg back of knee.
13. distance of foreudder to navel.
14. sideview distance between teats.
15. distance between rear teats.
16. hipbone prominence.
17. size of pinbone.
18. depth of skin triangle above foreudder.
19. width of cannon bone above hock.
20. thickness of flank each side of udder.
21. average width of the escutcheon.
22. size of pinbone.

PHASE FIVE:
Size or width of the pupil in the eye would be the same as the opening in the nostrils, the mounting of the dewclaws on all four legs, the smallest circumference of the tail bone above the switch, the knob of the hock, and the small funnel of the teats where they join the udder. If taken in total, another 22 measurements.

These measurements based on classic design of an almost perfect animal. Variations and off-type variations found in characteristics of every animal.

PHASE SIX:
Daily and regular habits: *When fed, milked and content, cow would lie down with great ceremony, give a sigh and breathe deeply. With eyes half-closed, cud would be regurgitated, chewed a precise number of times, swallowed and process would begin again. Very little variation in the number of times each bolus was masticated.*

Each chewing movement timed with pulse visible in the neck. Habits of eating, drinking, giving milk on set pattern seemingly controlled by some inner timer.

Steps in ordinary walking were always a head length. The faster the motion, the longer the steps to a certain limit. In show ring or at home, small mincing steps are the same width as across the eye (see phase three).

With all of these measurements, Ross showed that there was a natural harmony in every animal, and with Major's Sea Girl as his model, Ross went on to prove this theory in the show ring.

Major's Sea Girl achieved greater honours than Ross had ever dreamed. Her first show ring experience came at the New Hamburg Fair where she easily won Grand Champion. She then went to Galt where a member of the famous Bagg family from Brampton fell in love with her. He said she was the greatest cow that he had ever seen. As a dry cow, Major's Sea Girl won a first at the Oxford Parish Show at Ingersoll.

Her biggest triumph came at the Ontario Championship Show in Simcoe, where all of the winners of the year came together to determine the best overall. All the big names were there, and all of the breeders believed they had the best. But they hadn't seen Ross Butler's cow. All predictions and bets were on Cosmoline, an imported cow from the Jersey Islands which had recently been sold to a new breeder for five-thousand dollars. Two men looked after her, pampering her and boasting about her achievements. She won the three-year-old class and then returned to the barn to await the championship class many believed she was sure to win.

Ross was first to show his cow in the aged cow class, then with a win moved on to the championship class.

I knew Major's Sea Girl was ready. She was right at twelve o'clock as they say in the business. Up to calving, she carried just the right amount of flesh and was filled out to perfection.

We were the first in the ring in the aged cow class and proceeded slowly around the tanbark . . . and this cow loved to be shown. She was alert, proud as a peacock, with head high, ears poised, measured steps, no fussing. I could feel the tension around the ring crowded with spectators. There was stillness, surprise. Necks craned for a better view. Many told me afterwards, they had never seen her equal. She was a masterpiece in living colour and she went right to the head of her class. In the championship contest we achieved the same success. Major's Sea Girl and I had come a long way.

During that show-ring appearance, Ross's attention was completely focused on the cow and what was happening in the ring. He did not even turn his head when someone in the crowd offered one thousand dollars for her calf, providing it was a bull. He just shook his head, not even turning to see who had made the offer. At this Simcoe show, Major's Sea Girl had competed and won against the best of the breed. Ross had also achieved his goal of proving his theory of proportions.

That night Major's Sea Girl slept in her own barn, and the next morning, she calved. Ross named her bull calf Seaboy. But he was not there to witness the event. Instead, he was on his way to the first All-American Jersey show in Columbus, Ohio. The Grand Champion of that show sold for twenty-one thousand dollars, but there was no doubt in Ross's mind that Major's Sea Girl could have beaten her. His two friends who had accompanied him on the trip completely agreed.

A few months before Major's Sea Girl's initial show ring experience, her picture had appeared in the *Jersey Bulletin*, a breed journal. Several breeders, including Bill Sweet from Oregon, had expressed interest in buying her. Sweet had expected her to be at the Columbus show, but when she was not there, he returned to Woodstock with Ross to see "this vision of perfection." He immediately offered Ross five thousand dollars for the cow. Ross hesitated, but Sweet was persistent. He promised to send Ross a prize-winning bull from his Jersey herd if Ross agreed to sell her. Ross hated to part with his "treasure" but recognized that Sweet could do more for the animal than he could, and he sold her. With Major's Sea Girl as his inspiration, Ross became interested in the formation of a Jersey Club in Oxford County. Over the years, he had researched the breed back to its origin in the Normandy and Brittany regions of northern France. From here they were taken to the Jersey Islands. Enroute to England, unscrupulous sea captains had sold the cattle to the islanders. In 1868, two bulls and fifteen cows were introduced into Canada by Harrison Stephens of St. Lambert, Quebec. The breed was later brought to Ontario.

At the inaugural meeting of the Oxford Jersey Club, Ross talked of his feelings for the breed:

The Jersey is the most refined of all cows. Although she is tiny, she produces more butterfat than any other cow. In all her features, she possesses a symmetry and rhythm like no other animal.

Ross became the club's first secretary. At his instigation, the club bought a "good" camera to take pictures of various animals and herds for advertising and publicity. When no one had the time, talent, or patience to take the pictures, Ross purchased the camera from the club and took the pictures himself.

The dairy industry was changing, and a new tool, the classification of herds, was coming into vogue for dairymen. Until then the only yardstick for classifying and judging animals had been the show ring. Classification would put all farmers on an equal footing, whether they were rich or poor, showmen or non-showmen. The new classification system became part of Oxford Jersey Club's agenda, and one of Ross's first jobs, as secretary, was contacting the local Jersey breeders.

The classification had nothing to do with the production of milk or butterfat. Instead, it was a rating of animal types. All animals over two years of age were to be classified. Each cow had to have had at least one calf to qualify for the program. The males could qualify after only fifteen months, but could not attain an excellent rating until they were at least three years old.

The classification system was broken down into several categories: general appearance (worth 30 points), dairy character (20 points), body capacity (20 points), and the mammary system with its sub ratings of fore and rear udder development (30 points). Therefore, a perfect score was rated at 100. The animals' score was broken down into six classes: excellent (90 points and over), very good (85 to 90), good plus (80 to 85), good (75 to 80), fair (70 to 75), and poor (70 points and under). After Ross had contacted all of the local Jersey breeders and had everything in place, Professor George Raithby came to supervise the Oxford program. Raithby worked at the Animal Husbandry Department at the Ontario Agriculture College in Guelph.

The first herd to be classified belonged to Geo. H. Innes, the president of the Canadian Jersey Cattle Club. Ross's herd of two (Brampton Sea Girl had died in 1944) were classified next and both of his cows were classified at "very good." Only one excellent-rated cow was found in the district, Fairmount Designs Xenia. This eleven-year-old cow was owned by Durno Innes, whose herd had the highest overall score in the county.

When Ross became president of the Oxford Jersey Club two years later, the club's treasury had a balance of fifteen dollars. He immediately set about raising funds and asked each member of the club to donate one heifer calf from their herd. Each calf would be sold at auction and the money would go into the club's coffers. In two such drives, two thousand dollars was raised.

Ross took his position in the club very seriously, and often spent more time on club business than on Ruby. Ruby had realized early in their marriage that Ross was also married to his art and that this was not going to change. She also recognized that to find happiness, she would need to develop her own interests. She became involved in different charitable organizations, worked during elections campaigns, and was there whenever anyone — relative, neighbour, or friend — needed a helping hand.

10 | Artificial Insemination

DURING THE MID-1940S, Oxford's provincial representative at Queen's Park announced that many of the buildings at the Woodstock Fairgrounds would be put up for sale. During World War II, these buildings had been leased to the Department of National Defence for their Canadian Drivers and Maintenance School. With the war ending in Europe, they would no longer be needed. Ross had been looking for a permanent home for his paintings and saw the fairgrounds as an ideal location.

In his mind's eye, he could envision the fairgrounds as the hub of the social, cultural, and agricultural life of both Woodstock and Oxford County. As well as a permanent home for Ross's work, there would also be enough space for a museum, an art gallery, a children's zoo, and a music and dramatic centre. The fairgrounds would even have a new name to go with its new image — Peace Park.

While a few shared Ross's dream for the fairgrounds, many opposed him. It seemed to be too big of a concept for most people to grasp. While speaking with people throughout the county, Ross learned that many of them were interested in the preservation of Oxford County's historical and agricultural roots. Many wanted to see a proper museum for the hundreds of artifacts and documents that were stored in two cold, poorly-lit basement rooms in the County Court House. Ross had always been interested in local history, so he decided to take up the cause. Ruby gave him her support, sharing his interest in history, antiques, family heirlooms and mementos, adding her concern for individuals. She was always giving advice or just sharing a cup of tea with someone who was lonely.

After ten months of helping to "round up assistance" for the formation of a museum, Ross was given the title of President of the Oxford Historical and Museum Society. The Society lobbied both city and county councils for space and was finally given permission to use the upper story of the Old City Hall building in Woodstock. However, renovations were needed, so fund raising became a priority. While others contacted charitable organizations and the public at large, Ross canvassed Oxford's industrial base. Their efforts paid off and the museum received over eight thousand dollars in gifts and grants. The local firemen even agreed to "nurse" old relics back to life in their spare time.

The members of the newly-formed society felt that it needed some experienced direction. Through Judge Eric C. Cross, the fledgling Oxford County museum was offered the services of three staff members of the Royal Ontario Museum plus sixty lineal feet of display cases. Cross had been the Chief of the Royal Ontario Museum's Extension Department before coming to Woodstock. Through his influence, the museum became a test case and was the first in Ontario to receive aid from the government.

Behind the scenes, there was a struggle for power. Louise Hill, a descendent of Woodstock's first doctor, Levi Hoyt Perry, became the curator of the museum. She strongly objected to Ross's friendly involvement with the Royal's staff members. In fact, she objected to almost everything Ross did, calling him an upstart who didn't know what he was doing. In her mind Ross Butler was without "pedigree," though he could trace his ancestry back to the Chief of Butlerage of Ireland, a hereditary title conferred by Henry II in 1185, and included among his immediate relatives Colonel John Butler, the famous United Empire Loyalist leader of "Butler's Rangers." By the time the Oxford Museum was officially opened by Ontario Premier Leslie Frost on 28 January 1948, Ross had already decided to resign as president.

For all my work, I received little excepting some travel expenses. This and the continual backbiting became too much and I resigned.

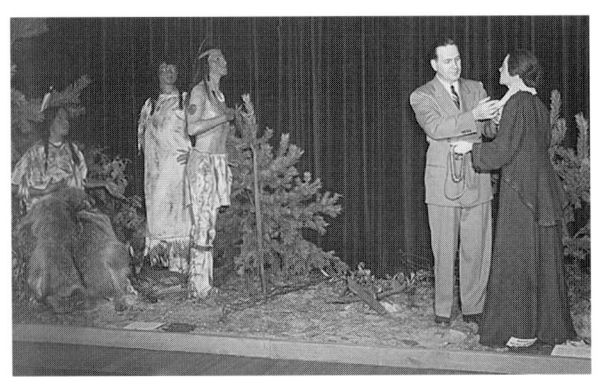

Ross Butler's diorama of the "First Settlers in Woodstock," modelled in wax for display at the opening of the Oxford Museum, 1948.

In spite of the controversy and the bad feelings, Ross was still satisfied with all that he had accomplished. His wax models of a pioneer woman stood at the entrance to the museum and several of his paintings were on display.

He continued to be involved in both the Oxford County and Ontario Jersey Clubs, but now took part in a school for judges. These schools were held at various area farms and were designed to educate future cattle judges who would work at fairs and shows. A class rating system had been developed by the schools to help judges become more consistent and accurate in their performance. Not only did Ross want to become a qualified judge, but he also wanted to write about the schools for various breed magazines.

Ross was always on the lookout for anything new. He was intrigued when his friend, Harley Stager, mentioned that a Dr. Hess, a German veterinarian who had recently come to Canada, was inseminating cows in the Waterloo area. Ross had read about this new breeding technique which was being used extensively in Europe. When Ross caught up with Dr. Hess, he was on his way to William Henderson's farm to take a semen collection. Ross went with Hess to the Henderson farm and later remarked that it was one of the most interesting days of his life. He carefully watched as Hess collected the semen and impregnated several cows. When Ross told Hess that one of his own cows was in heat, Hess gave him semen and the tools of the trade to take home and breed his cow.

Chance's Sea Girl did conceive and nine months later gave birth to a bull calf believed to be the first offspring of an artificially inseminated cow in Oxford County. The calf was promptly bought by William Henderson, the owner of the bull whose semen Ross had used.

Although Ross was extremely interested in this new breeding technique, it was several years before he became actively involved with the method. In 1947, he decided that the breeders of Oxford County could benefit from an artificial insemination program. He started an artificial insemination unit with his two good young bulls, Seaboy and Tristram Standard. Seaboy was the son of his Grand Champion,

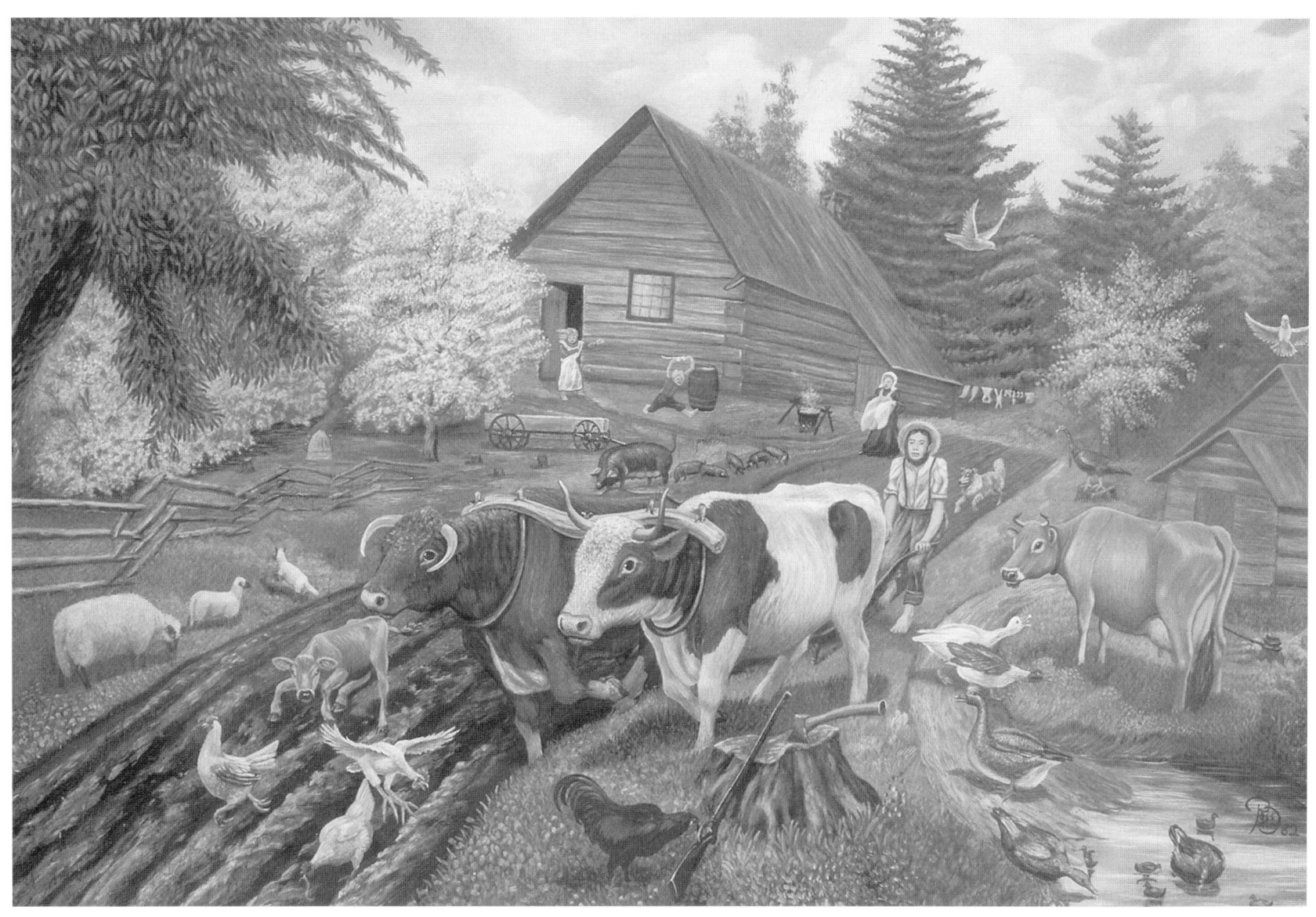

The First Settler at Woodstock (34 x 50", oil on board, 1970s), Ross Butler's whimsical painting of Zachariah Burtch and his family.

Major's Sea Girl, and Tristram Standard had been the gift from the Nash and Sweet ranch in Oregon after Sweet had purchased the cow.

Ross had never really believed in partnerships, but his limited resources forced him to enter in a co-ownership venture with Bert McGrath. The two men set up their new business, The Oxford Breeding Unit, at 334 Norwich Avenue in Woodstock, the south-east corner of Ross's Pavey Street property.

Not long after establishing their new business, Ross and Bert outlined a plan for the local Ayrshire breeders to establish a service for the Ayrshire breed. Until now, they had only serviced Jerseys, but they proposed to use the semen from two Ayrshire sires imported from United States, Woodland's Farm's Symbol and Heritage Royal Bouncer.

As more people heard about artificial insemination and it became more popular, more breeders contacted the unit. Soon the work load became too heavy for Ross and Bert, so they hired Harry Wood, a young Woodstock man who had just graduated from the Ontario Agriculture College at Guelph. Within weeks, Wood left to establish his own company as direct competition to Ross and Bert. They then hired a graduate of the University of Saskatchewan who had taken a special insemination course at Cornell University. Unfortunately, he didn't last long either and finding qualified help became a problem. Although Ross was busy travelling as a salesman, he decided to take a short course at the Ontario Agricultural College in Guelph to learn the techniques and secure a license to do the work.

Ross's days overflowed. As well as supervising the care of the bulls and making sure that they were fed scientifically for best semen results, he was off to Guelph. He was unprepared for the orders that were waiting for him each evening when he returned home. Yet after a full day, there was still more work as he had to go and inseminate cows.

When Bert decided to move on to greener pastures, Ross was left on his own. He changed the name of the business to "The Central Unit" and hired two technicians. As the business grew he secured the use of a Guernsey sire, Coldsprings B. R. Fearless. He

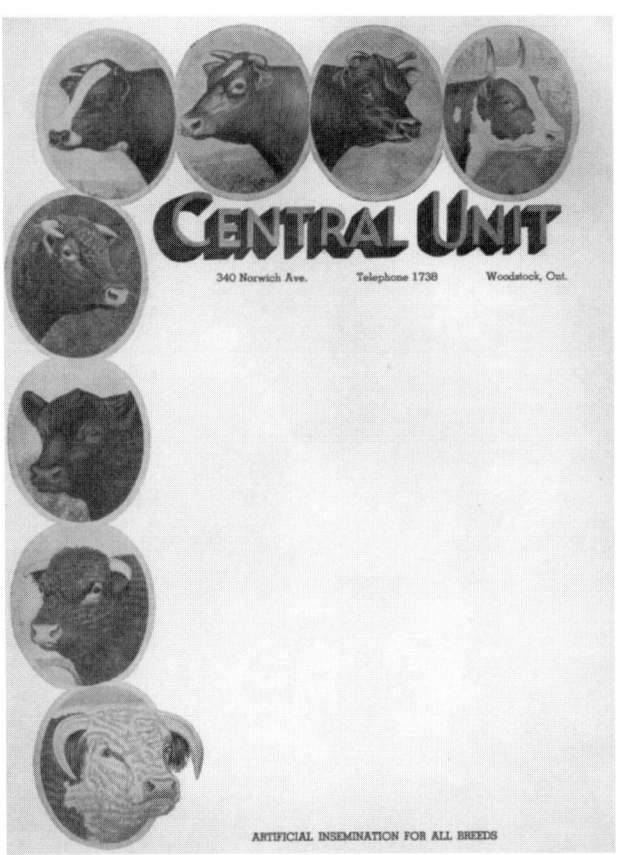

Central Unit letterhead, adorned with true type portraits.

also added two Holstein bulls to his barn. What animals he couldn't afford to buy, he leased. The business grew by leaps and bounds. As he advertised to his customers:

The most important animal in your herd is your bull. He can make or break you. My Central Unit has the best bulls and our price is reasonable: $10 per cow with two return privileges; 10 cents a mile is only charged after a breeder is twenty-five miles from the unit's base.

Ross's salesmanship had paid off financially and he was able to purchase a prefabricated barn from the old airforce base at Fingal to house the bulls. The front section of the barn became a studio to display his paintings and sculptures.

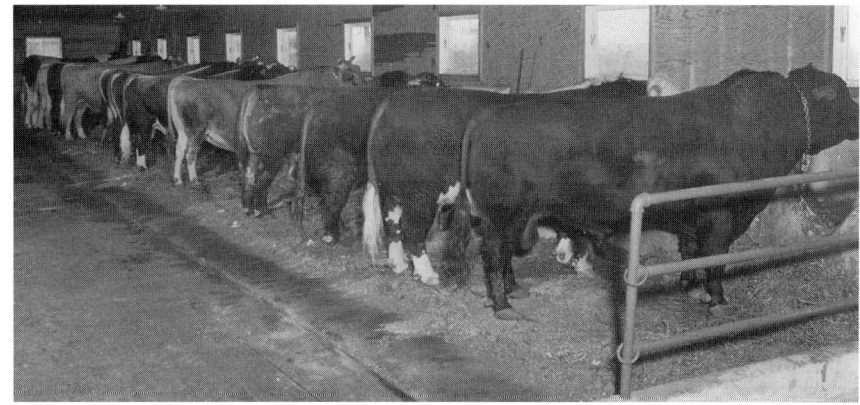

The Central Unit, 1950, the first all breed cattle insemination unit in Canada.

All went well until one particular night when two of the bulls broke loose and got into a fight. Their fight was not confined just to the stable, but spilled over into the studio. During the fight, one of the bulls ripped the ring out of his nose and was bleeding severely. When the bull shook his head with pain, his blood splattered all over Ross's painting of Edward VIII. The bull then gored the painting, but fortunately Ross was later able to fix the damage.

Agitated by the fighting, four other bulls broke loose and busted through the studio door onto the street. It was almost dark before someone noticed the bulls and called the police. The bulls loved their new found freedom and gave the police a merry chase. Several of the neighbourhood boys got into the act as well, yelling and waving their hats at the frenzied bulls who bellowed and lunged at anything that moved. To the boys, it was the next best thing to a rodeo, but to the police, it was a nightmare. By nightfall, only two of the six bulls had been corralled. Using flashlights, the police searched the ditches and elder bushes for the rest of the wayward animals. Ross finally returned home and shored up the stable with four-by-four timbers with the help of his neighbours and the police. Despite the fact that one bull was still missing, the police decided to wait until morning to continue their search. It was just too dangerous to hunt for the animal in the dark. Although Ross could never prove it, he suspected that someone had been in the barn and had deliberately left two of the pen doors open — perhaps as an attempt to ruin his business.

As his business continued to grow, Ross went to the bank to request a loan to buy more bulls and modernize his laboratory. Before the bankers would give him the money, they insisted on seeing his financial statements. Even Ross was surprised when he discovered that his business had grossed over $60,000 in a three-month period.

With his loan guaranteed Ross bought more bulls. One was Brae Mischief 6B, a Hereford bull who was a twelve-time Senior Grand Champion of Ontario. Soon the expanded laboratory became the nerve centre for sixteen full-time technicians who serviced outlets in Kent, Essex, Middlesex, Lambton, and Huron counties. At its peak, The Central Unit serviced 135 cows per day in ten Southwestern Ontario counties.

However, it was not all smooth sailing. Pressure was put on Ross to lower his fees. Other units were being organized as competition on a co-operative basis. Because they were eligible for government subsidies, they could offer cheaper rates to farmers and higher wages to their technicians. Ross's Central Unit did not qualify for these subsidies because it was privately owned, making it difficult to defend against the subsidized competition.

Ross, of course, was never content with having only a few projects on the go. He was always looking for new and interesting thing to try. And just waiting on the horizon was a new challenge that would bring him worldwide recognition.

11 | *Butter Sculptures*

WHEN ROSS BUTLER TOLD HIS WIFE RUBY that he was going to do a "butter sculpture" for The Dairy Farmers of Canada at the Canadian National Exhibition, she was very angry. She could not understand why he would agree to take on another project. Every minute of every day was already filled to overflowing. Ross had not actually considered this potential problem when Erle Kitchen, the secretary of The Dairy Farmers of Canada, had asked if he was interested in sculpting a cow from butter. Although the Ontario Cream Producer's (who came under the umbrella of the Dairy Farmers of Canada) had a new slogan — "It's Better with Butter" — they needed something more spectacular to offset the high-powered advertising and merchandising of margarine. Kitchen said butter sculpting had been done a couple of times before in the United States, but never in Canada.

Ross was sure that the same principles that applied to his clay models could be applied to butter sculpting.

I found this reversal of nature intriguing — instead of butter being made from the cow, the cow was made from butter. The whole concept was challenging.

The only major difference was that the work would have to be done in a controlled environment at the exhibition. The first stage, the building of a skeleton model, could be done at home in his studio.

Using his basic law of animal proportions, Ross created the skeleton of a Jersey cow and calf. He felt that a one-half inch steel pipe would be heavy enough for the legs, which were anchored to a two-inch thick sheet of plywood. Between the

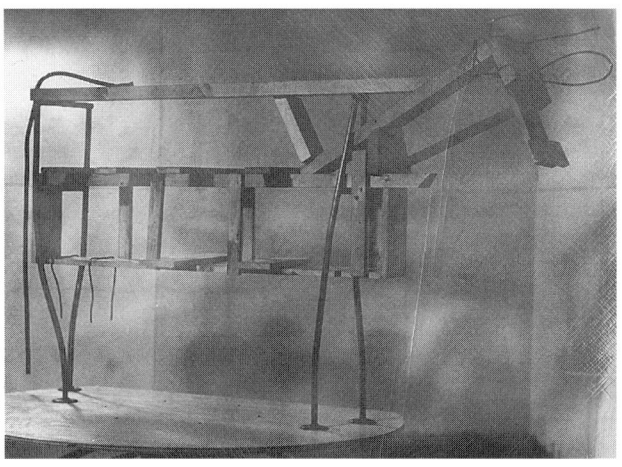

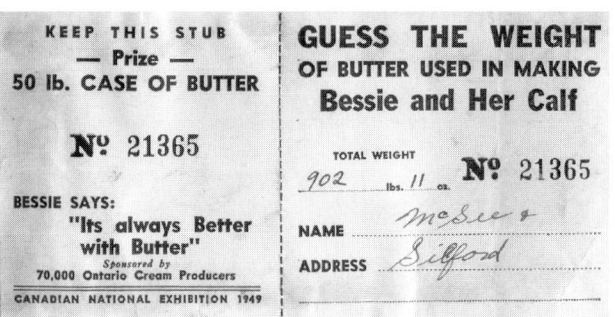

The frame for a butter sculpture, showing the strong armature needed to carry the weight of 1,000 lbs. of butter.

upright legs, he placed a plank the length of the cow. Short cross-members, which would carry the weight of the butter, were fastened onto the plank. Ross then elevated a two-by-two board for the neck and added a short piece of wood for the length of the head. Horns, ears, teats, and tail were made of copper tubing and wire and fastened to the skeleton.

Two weeks before the exhibition opened, Ross loaded the skeleton onto the back of his half-ton truck and set off for Toronto, where a specially-built glass refrigerator was waiting. Inside was stored one thousand pounds of unsalted butter to which extra yellow colouring had been added for effect. At Ross's request, the salt had been left out of the butter because he knew that it would collect moisture.

The skeleton was unloaded onto a turntable which had already been installed inside of the glass refrigerator. The turntable would be activated once the sculpture was complete. Ross felt that a revolving sculpture would attract more attention than a stationary one. Once the skeleton was secured to its revolving base, Ross began flopping handfuls of butter onto the frame. Even though he wore a heavy sweater and winter underwear, he had to emerge every hour to get his blood circulating. The temperature inside the refrigerator was forty-eight degrees Fahrenheit or lower, while the outside temperature averaged ninety degrees in the shade.

By the second day, the cow and calf had assumed their general bulk and shape. The general details of its anatomy were done on the third day. Basic characteristics — bones beneath the skin, veins, wrinkles, hair, horns, and a friendly expression — took a lot more time and a great deal of patience. Over the years Ross had learned to use innovative tools in his work. He knew that hair could be created by combing a vegetable brush through the butter, and a small knife and his fingernails were all that was needed to fashion nostrils and eyelashes.

As the butter sculpture began to take shape, people crowded around the glass cubicle, watching and murmuring. Ross found the noises and movements distracting, but he forced himself to concentrate and keep his mind focused on his work.

When he was finally finished, Ross realized that he needed something to make the sculpture stand out in relief from its background. He decided to hang a royal blue velvet stage curtain from the top of the cubicle, forming a semi-circle of deep folds behind the cow. To make the scene more authentic, he then placed flowers and ferns on a green-dyed sawdust base sprinkled over the revolving turntable.

Nine days after Ross started the actual butter sculpture, Bessie the butter cow and Buttercup were complete. While he was extremely tired, he also felt exhilarated. However, his job was not yet over. His spectacular sculpture had captured the imagination and curiosity of both the public and the media. He was now faced with numerous requests for newspaper and radio interviews. Perhaps the most trying of these was with broadcaster and writer, Gordon Sinclair: one of Sinclair's first questions was "how much money are you getting for all this?" He called Ross "Butterfingers."

The Ontario Cream Producers were elated with all of the publicity. To find out just how many people actually viewed the statue, they devised a contest where people could guess its weight. A prize of a case of butter would be given to the person who came the closest. Out of one hundred and seventeen thousand entries, only two actually guessed the weight correctly: nine hundred and two pounds, eleven ounces. There was also some negative feedback, however. Many people were concerned as to what would happen to the butter after the exhibition was over. Even before Ross began the sculpture, it had been decided that the butter would be sent back to the creamery where it would be washed, salted, and put back into the trade.

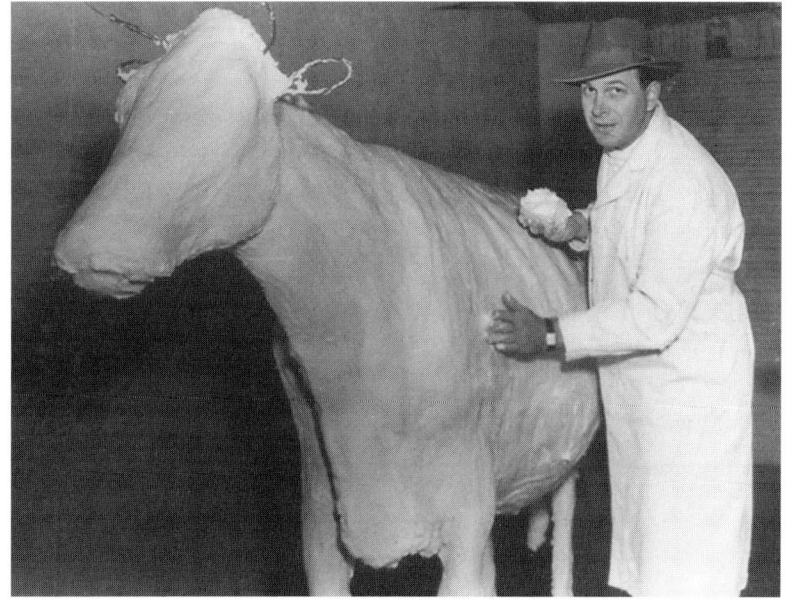

Ross "Butterfingers" Butler sculpting Bessie and Buttercup.

For Ross, the butter sculpture had been a true labour of love. Before the cow could be demolished, he made a permanent mould of her.

From an artistic point of view, the venture had been an outstanding success. Financially, it had barely been a break-even proposition. Although he was paid for his work, his artificial insemination business had suffered in the meantime. When Ruby tallied the profits, they still were no further ahead.

This didn't stop Ross when he was asked to do another butter sculpture in the fall for the Royal Winter Fair. Some people at the Cream Producers Marketing Board thought that Ross's success at the C.N.E. could not be duplicated. He proved them wrong when he used Evelyn Crone of Toronto as his model for Barbara the Milkmaid.

My butter girl earned herself quite a reputation one night when her butter shorts slipped. Whether the waist was too small or the butter was too heavy for her limbs, sometime during the night, Barbara's shorts slipped down to her knees and she required a major repair job the next morning to make her presentable.

During the next few years, Ross completed many butter statuaries, each one attaining a higher degree of perfection. Generally, the subjects were left to Ross. When figure skater Barbara Ann Scott won a gold medal in the Olympics, Ross used her as his subject. Against a background of simulated snow and ice, Ross balanced the skater on one toe in a grand swirl of butter.

The most amazing feature of this work was that the whole weight of the statue was supported on only one-half inch of contact — the toe of her skate. But I'm afraid the weight of the sculpture wasn't very flattering to Miss Scott. It weighed a lot more than Miss Scott.

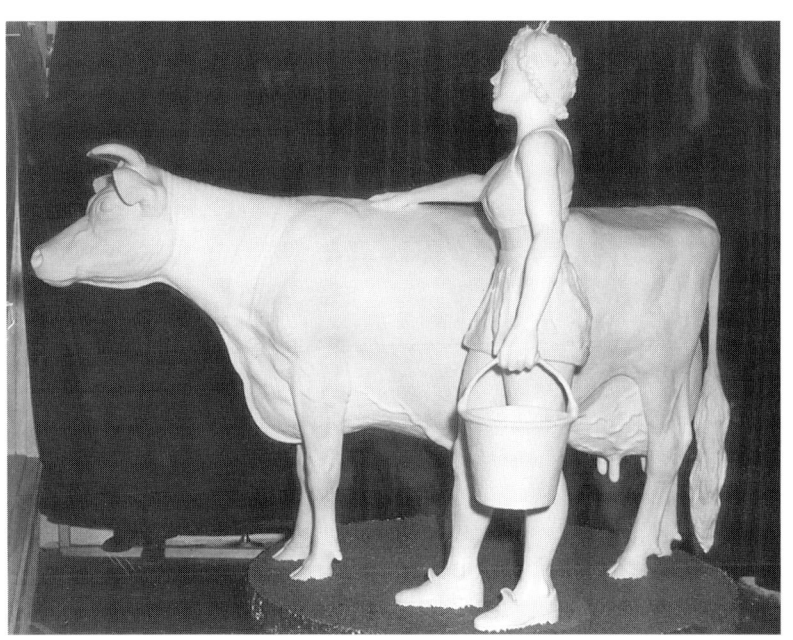

Barbara the Milkmaid.

In August 1952, Ross began what became his most famous sculpture, that of soon-to-be crowned Queen Elizabeth II on her horse, Winston. It had taken him months to secure Royal permission for the life-size model of the Queen and her horse, a sculpture that required one thousand five hundred pounds of butter and nine days to complete. Ross was well into his second day when a scout from the National Film Board saw him flopping butter onto the skeleton. The man immediately asked Ross for permission to bring a camera and crew into the cubicle to film the actual day-to-day progress of the work.

I never worked under such pressure in my life. It was like working in a zoo, people staring, pointing, asking questions. It was very distracting.

Ross's wrestler friend, Harley Stager, came to Toronto from Waterloo and immediately saw that Ross was near exhaustion from the pressure. Harley offered to drive Ross home, for he knew the artist returned to Woodstock every night. On the way to Woodstock, they talked of trivial things, including events that were happening in the area. The only exciting thing Ross knew of was a wrestling match that night at Woodstock's Perry Street arena. "Let's go," Harley suggested, and Ross was too tired to argue.

The wrestling match was just what Ross needed to relieve the pressure that he had been under. Much to his surprise, he enjoyed the rough and tumble bouts where good triumphed over evil, and he hollered with the rest of the fans when the "good guy" was being thumped. From that night, Ross Butler was an avid wrestling fan.

Because 1952 was a prelude year to Queen Elizabeth's coronation, media interest in the statue of Queen Elizabeth on her horse Winston was high. The National Film Board's film showing Ross at work on the sculpture was sent around the world. The reviews were good. Only in Britain was the work criticized. People were incensed when *The Times* reported that Ross had used fifteen thousand pounds of butter to make the sculpture and that the butter would be discarded after the exhibition. At the time, butter was still rationed in Britain. However, the paper had made a large mistake — it was not fifteen thousand but fifteen hundred pounds, and the butter would be recycled back in the butter trade. When Ross met Prince Philip that fall at the opening of the Royal Winter Fair, he assured the Prince of this fact.

After the tremendous success of Ross's butter sculpture of Queen Elizabeth on her horse, the Oxford County Breeders Association, the Woodstock and Oxford County councils, and the Board of Trade decided to honour Ross with a testimonial dinner. On 15 October 1952, over 200 people came to pay tribute to "the hometown

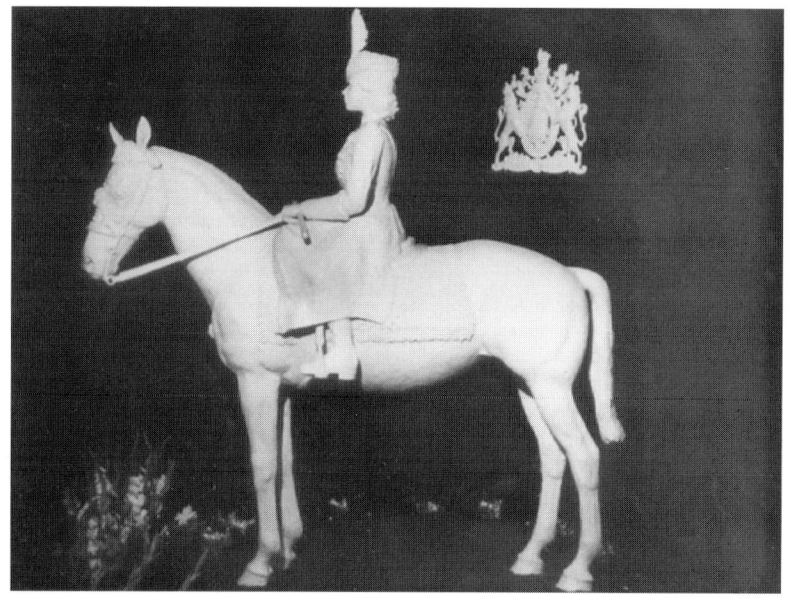

Queen Elizabeth on Winston.

boy who made good." John Arthur Carroll, Assistant Ontario Deputy Minister of Agriculture, was the guest speaker. Carroll, several men from the dairy industry, and many Woodstock dignitaries praised Ross as "one of the world's greatest authorities on proportion in artistry of domestic animals." While Ross accepted their words with a smile and a thank you, he secretly was not very impressed. Many of these men who were now spouting his praises had withdrawn their support when he needed it most. The resulting hurt and bitterness still lingered, even after all these years, and Ross strongly felt that some of these men were just paying "lip service" for the benefit of the media.

In his acknowledgement speech, Ross suggested that Canada send a million pounds of Canadian butter to England. This gift of butter would be in response to the letters from "irate British people" who had scorned the waste of butter. And such a gift, claimed Ross, would help promote the Canadian Dairy Industry abroad. He even offered to go to England to sculpt another statue.

That same year, in the period between the Canadian National Exhibition and the Royal Winter Fair, Ross had undertaken a butter sculpture of Queen Elizabeth with Prince Philip at her side for the Western Fair in London, Ontario. The work was a failure. Not only did Ross not capture their true features, but the sculptures were substandard. He was both mentally and physically exhausted and it was showing in his work.

Ross desperately needed a holiday and when someone suggested that he go to the Queen's coronation in England, he seized upon the idea. He had always wanted to see the Jersey Islands, the birthplace of his beloved Jersey cows. His enthusiasm for the trip was not shared by Ruby, however. She was concerned about where they would get the money for the trip, despite Ross's assurances that there would be enough money from the sale of The Central Unit after their bills were paid. Nevertheless, Ruby refused to make the trip.

She made it plain that she wouldn't fly, nor would she go by ship. For the life of me I couldn't figure out any other way. And so on April 23, 1953, my birthday, I set out on the greatest adventure of my life . . . alone.

12 | The Jersey Islands and the Queen of England

ALTHOUGH ROSS BUTLER had never been on board a ship before, he basked in the camaraderie of the other passengers, especially those permanently seated at the purser's table. They were a mixed group, including several military personnel, a lawyer who was going to lecture at Cambridge University, and George Gordon, the provincial member of parliament from Brant County. Another surprise was the arrival of Mr. and Mrs. Flood. Robert Flood had worked at the Glen Farm in Innerkip where Ross had been seasonally-employed years earlier. There were several others at the table, including one Scottish lady, Mrs. Hoyle, who was on her way to visit her daughter in England. She took a liking to Ross and insisted on taking him under her wing. Ross found the social life aboard the ship invigorating. There was something for everyone — games and laughter, music and dancing. It was a happy, relaxing crossing and no one seemed displeased when something happened to the *Ascania*'s twin turbine and their arrival in England was delayed by two days.

Just before the ship docked at Liverpool, Ross received a call to the ship's main office. There he was met by the vice-president of the Cunard Line and his general manager. The two men said they always liked to personally greet all of the celebrities who came aboard the ship. Ross couldn't help but be impressed. He felt at home.

As the great liner eased into her birth I had this poignant feeling of coming home. It was uncanny, especially after seven generations of domicile in the new world.

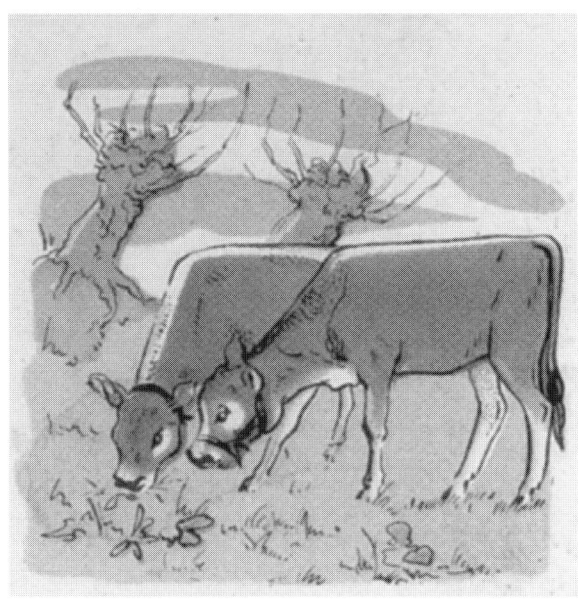

"*Jerseys* supreme among all the Dairy breeds. Beautiful conformation is allied with high production." Cartoon from a Jersey Island souvenir calendar for January 1951.

As he later boarded the train for London, Ross was pleasantly surprised to find that Mrs. Hoyle and two other ladies from the ship were his travelling companions. Mrs. Hoyle regaled them with nostalgic memories of her homeland and vowed she would show Ross 'her' England. When they parted at the station, she extended Ross an invitation to spend a few days with her and her family at their country estate in Sussex.

Tired and hungry, Ross asked a taxi driver to take him to a moderately priced hotel that had been recommended to him. The desk clerk gave him the only room available, the honeymoon suite. His first stop the next morning was at Canada House, where he applied for a pass for a press seat on the procession route. *The Sentinel Review*, Woodstock's local newspaper, had asked Ross to send back stories of the coronation and his trip. After a rigid screening by Scotland Yard and the payment of four pounds, Ross was told his pass would be issued in a few weeks by the Commonwealth Press Union. He had no idea that this pass had been precipitated by a telegram to Canada House from George Gordon whom Ross had met aboard the *Ascania*.

Ross's next stop was British Columbia House, where he met Mr. Ward, a representative of the Canadian National Exhibition in England. Ross learned that the Coronation Robes would be making a tour of Canada and it might be possible to have them on display at the exhibition. Ross had been commissioned to make a wax figure of the Queen for the C.N.E. and he asked if the robes could be available for his showing. Ward was not sure about this, but did secure Ross an interview with the management of Madame Tussaud's wax museum so he could learn more about making wax models.

Shortly after this, Ross was off to the Jersey Islands, the birthplace of his beloved Jerseys. At his Jersey Island hotel, a message had been left for him by Senator Gaudin. The next day the Senator's car and chauffeur would be waiting to take him to various farms on the island. The senator's car was right out of history, a Hillman 14 of 1919 vintage, with a fourteen horsepower motor. It was so old that many of the locals joked about the car, claiming that ten of its fourteen horses had died of old age and the remaining four were reluctantly working on their day off.

At one of Senator Gaudin's farms, Ross was surprised to meet an old friend from Oxford County, Bert McGrath, who had founded the first artificial insemination unit in Woodstock with Ross. Bert was now manager of the Senator's Jersey herd.

Ross was mesmerized by the islands where every square foot of ground was utilized. Even the grass along every path and roadway was cut for hay and some fields were already yielding crops of early tomatoes. These, Ross learned, would be barely harvested when another crop would be planted. Ross was surprised to see the Jerseys all rugged (blanketed) and tethered in long rows. These tethers, he was told, would be moved several times a day. The younger stock ran free in the fields as they did in Canada. Although there were over one thousand farms on the island, only one hundred or less of these were professionally engaged in the breeding and showing of cattle. This was mainly due to the fact that one acre of land was valued at twelve thousand dollars. Therefore, the only market for these Jerseys was overseas. Canada was one of the main importers for cows and bulls from the Jersey Islands.

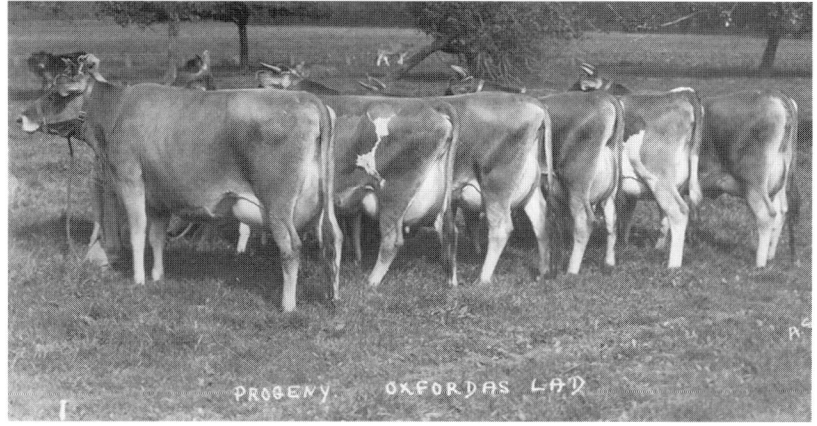
Cattle "tethered" on Jersey Island.

Fortunately for Ross, he had arrived just in time for the All-Island Parish Show, which was followed a few weeks later by the Royal Jersey Agricultural and Horticultural Society Show at Springfield. This show was over one hundred years old and its classes were huge. However, Ross's training at the judges school often resulted in him not agreeing with the judges' choices.

There was a large banquet following the Agricultural and Horticultural Society Show and Ross was asked to be the main speaker by Senator Gaudin. He spent hours preparing his speech, only to push it aside and speak from his heart. He praised the Islander's hospitality and talked about how their problems were very similar to those of the Jersey breeders in Canada. Before he closed with a toast to the Queen, Ross said he hoped to see many of the Island breeders at the World Jersey Conference being held next year at the Ontario Agriculture College in Guelph, about forty miles from his home in Woodstock.

After the banquet, Ross was invited by Lady Grasset, wife of Henry Grasset, the Lieutenant Governor of Jersey Islands, to a band concert at the Governor's home. The governor was a Canadian by birth and was very pleased to talk to a fellow Canadian. He relayed stories about the difficult war years when they had been occupied by the German army.

I was moved to actual tears by the stories of occupation. It got so bad that the people made a brew out of nettles and thistles.

The people were almost starving, Governor Grasset said, when a Red Cross ship from Canada arrived with supplies, including medicine, food, and clothing. These supplies had been donated by the Jersey Breeders of Canada. However, Grassett said that this was only one of the reasons why Canadians were held in such high regard by the island population.

Ross arrived back in London on the Sunday before the coronation. His pass to the press bleachers was waiting for him, and thanks to a chance meeting with the Veterinary Inspector of the Jersey Islands, he also had a place to stay. The inspector had arranged for Ross to stay with his son and daughter at Etham Well Hall, a residential suburb of London. They made sure that Ross had a planned itinerary for the coronation events and a detailed map to get around on the above-ground railways and buses.

In the midst of all the crowds, Ross felt very lonely and longed to see a familiar face. A little of this homesickness was probably brought on by Ruby's letters. Several of them had been waiting for him at Canada House. In each of them, she had poured out her feelings for him. Ross felt closer to her here in England than he ever had at home. On Coronation Day he took his place in the press gallery that faced Hyde Park. Beside him in the bleachers was a journalist from Sweden, in front was a

Finnish correspondent, and sitting on his left were three Italians. He knew that every nation and nationality was represented in that press gallery. Unfortunately, on such a glorious occasion, it rained. Not a gentle downpour either, but a giant cloud-burst. Then, just as the parade moved into view, the sun came out and wrapped everything in a golden glow. Banners, trumpets, and flags of every nation accompanied the marching bands. Spaced in between the bands were the horsemen, the proud Gurkas and Canada's own Royal Canadian Mounted Police.

When the Mounties rode past, I cheered to the top of my voice. I was so proud to be a Canadian that day. I waved and cheered until I was hoarse. It was a once-in-a-lifetime experience.

Just as the carriages carrying the Prime Ministers of the Commonwealth approached, it again started to rain heavily. Sir Winston Churchill with his arm out in the rain gave his famous V-sign, but the magnificent Queen Salote of Toga stole the hearts of the crowd as she rode by in an open carriage.

Next came the Queen Mother and Princess Margaret, followed by the newly-crowned Queen Elizabeth with Prince Philip at her side. After travelling thousands of miles, Ross was finally seeing the beautiful queen in an ornate coach drawn by eight white horses. The ceremony left an indelible impression in Ross's mind.

In the middle of June Ross received another letter from Ruby. She told him that she had listened to the radio broadcast of the coronation and had thought of him every minute. She had seen the film of the coronation on the television owned by Ross's sister and brother-in-law, Lena and Stewart McAlpine. The film had been flown by jet to Goose Bay, Newfoundland, on to Montreal by a second plane, and from the airport to the television station by helicopter. Ruby wrote that she was glad he had gone to England, and despite missing him terribly, she was glad she had not accompanied him. Alone, he had more freedom to go where he wanted and to see whom he pleased. "A wife tagging along beside you would have been a handicap," she wrote. While Ross had been gone, she had tried to keep busy. Among her projects,

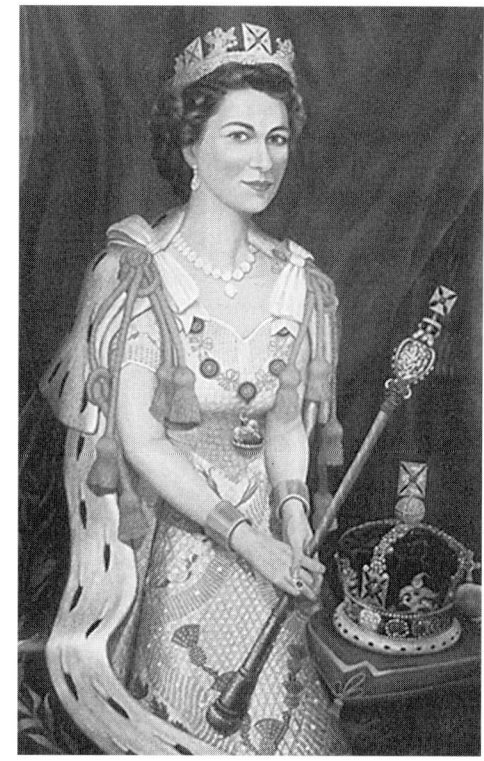

Portrait of *Queen Elizabeth* II (40 x 60", oil on canvas, 1953), on the occasion of her coronation.

she had painted the bathroom and had the shower head fixed. But finances were also getting tight because Mr. Hamilton had not paid his rent for the part of the artificial insemination barn that he used.

This last statement made Ross think about curtailing the rest of his trip. When he mentioned to Ruby that he might return before the coronation ball, she sent him a telegram: "Darling, don't miss coronation ball. I am fine. Stay until job completed. Don't worry."

With his own pocket money dwindling at an alarming rate, Ross revised his itinerary. He would have liked to have had a live audience with the Queen because he was scheduled to do a wax model of her for the Canadian National Exhibition in late August. Since officials at Canada House assured him that such an interview was impossible to obtain, Ross felt that his best bet to see the Queen close-up was at either the coronation ball or at Epsom Downs, one of the biggest events in Britain during Coronation week. Ross decided to go to Epsom Downs. On the bus to the racetrack, Ross sat beside a Mrs. Young from Australia. She was a widow and, like Ross, was alone. They decided to team up and keep each other company for the day. After placing several early bets, the pair wandered around the Royal Paddock. Ross had been advised by the officials at Canada House that he might get a close-up view of the Queen when she visited the paddock. He was told to arrive early and where to stand. Much to their amazement, the Queen passed within two yards of where they stood and Ross had several minutes in which to observe her. When the crowd shifted, Ross and Mrs. Young could then watch the races. They were jubilant when their modest bets paid off.

Following all of the coronation hoopla, Ross still had several weeks of his working holiday left. He visited the Ovaltine Farm, but thought their Jerseys were not up to the high quality of the ones he had seen in the Jersey Islands.

He attended the British Plastics Exhibition at Olympia Stadium in London. He had read a great deal about these synthetics and wanted to see if plastics could be adapted to his work. He later wrote to Ruby saying that it had been like walking into a new and magic dreamworld. Although wartime necessity had hastened the development of synthetics, Ross had not realized that so much progress had been made. Synthetics could be made in anything from wigs to automobiles, from musical instruments to glass floors. Ross found it mind-boggling.

As he roamed around the huge stadium, he came upon a demonstration that showed how flexible plastics could be made into delicate moulds. Into these plastic casts, the demonstrator then poured some material adaptable for miniature statuettes. Ross stood spellbound, for here was the secret of making an infinite variety of art objects. When he asked if wax could be poured into these casts, the demonstrator suggested plastigel, a liquid plastic with an added filler that could be used as a build-up material. Ross was told that the rubberized version of plastigel would give a soft skin effect and that colours and pigments could be added as the work progressed. When Ross asked about hair, he was taken to another exhibit and shown the applications of extruded filaments. These ranged all the way from coarse brush bristles to the finest of strands from which wigs were manufactured.

Ross realized that he could build statuaries from glass and plastic and colour them in natural tints. Adaptable to any design, these would be lighter in weight and more durable than those he presently made. They would also have the advantage of being waterproof.

Ross wanted to come back to the exhibition again and again, but time would not permit it. In her last letter, Ruby had said that some creditors were pressing her for money and reminded him that he needed to look after contract correspondence, especially his correspondence with the Canadian National Exhibition where he was to do a sculpture of a Royal Canadian Mounted Police officer on horseback.

So, reluctantly, Ross flew home a month early.

13 | Buying and Selling

WHEN ROSS BUTLER ARRIVED HOME from London, he was surprised to find Ruby waiting for him at Montreal's Dorval airport. She had driven over three hundred and fifty miles from Woodstock to meet him — and to rekindle their love, as Ross recalled.

Our leisurely trip home along the St. Lawrence was wonderful. Whether it was the impact of being home or the breathtaking scenery, the trip was like like a second honeymoon.

The honeymoon, however, was short-lived, for back in Woodstock, Ross was besieged by both work and bills. The Butlers seemed to owe everyone and there was no quick solution to their financial problems. Ross did fill several orders for reproductions of his True Types, but his contract for the wax model at the Canadian National Exhibition fell through, mainly because the Royal Robes would not arrive in time for the exhibition.

While he did complete a butter sculpture of a Mountie on horseback for the 80th anniversary of the RCMP, most of his time was spent buying and selling cattle. Breeders always claimed that he could spot a good cow in a herd without moving away from the pasture fence.

In 1954, Ross completed a butter sculpture of Roy Rogers and his horse, Trigger. One of the perks of the job was a trip to California to meet the famous pair. The expense of the trip was justified, for it was estimated that one hundred and seventy five thousand people viewed his work.

Each butter sculpture was unique, and each brought on its own problems. The only sculpture for which Ross had to submit a detailed sketch beforehand was one of Laura Secord. The Laura Secord Candy Company, who owned the Laura Secord logo, would not give their approval for a sculpture until they were sure that it would be historically accurate. The company had no need for concern, for Ross always thoroughly researched every subject — and the sculpture for Laura Secord was no different. He was fortunate to discover her milk stool and pail at the Old Fort George Museum at Niagara-on-the-Lake, Ontario. Closer to home in Ingersoll, about fifteen miles from Ross's birthplace, he also found bits of information in the historical files of the Ingersoll family. Laura was the daughter of Thomas Ingersoll, the founder of the Oxford County town which bore his name.

Once the Laura Secord Candy Company was assured of Ross's competence, they became quite helpful, allowing him to use as reference an oil painting of Laura and her cow as they began their famous journey. This painting gave Ross an insight into the style of dress of the time as well as the facial characteristics of Laura herself. The cow, of course, came from his creative mind, a combination of animal proportions and a grade cow of the period. Ross wanted the company to sponsor the construction of a permanent monument using his butter statue as a model, but after months of haggling, they finally refused.

Although Ross didn't realize it at the time, his 1955 butter sculpture of Lord Baden-Powell, the founder of the Boy Scout movement, was to be his last at the C.N.E. When he asked for more money, Ross was replaced by William Clements. Clements completed several butter sculptures over the years, but none of them achieved the success of Ross's Queen Elizabeth on her horse, Winston.

Earlier during the year, after twelve years of a childless marriage, David Addison Butler was born on 17 February 1955. Ross and Ruby had long given up hope of having a child, for Ross was almost fifty and Ruby now forty-two. But Ruby was no stranger to mothering. When her own mother had died at an early age, Ruby had taken on the responsibility of bringing up her sister and three of her four brothers. Ross had never been around small children, except for his brother Carl,

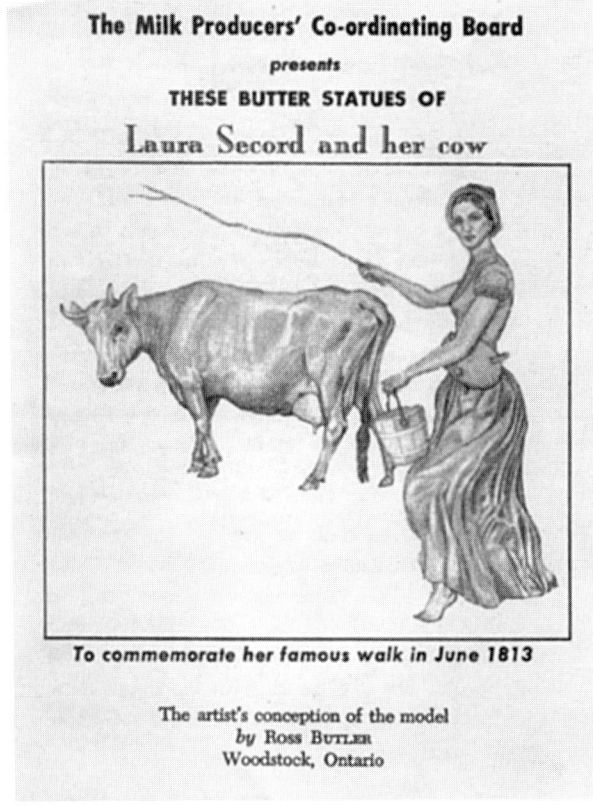

The Milk Producers' Co-ordinating Board
presents
THESE BUTTER STATUES OF
Laura Secord and her cow

To commemorate her famous walk in June 1813

The artist's conception of the model
by Ross Butler
Woodstock, Ontario

and he found the idea of fatherhood a bit daunting.

With the arrival of the new baby, the Butler's little home became very cramped. They contemplated moving into the big house with Ross's mother, whose health had been steadily deteriorating. Although Mary Butler was now in a wheelchair, neither she nor Ruby, both strong-willed women, wanted to share a house. For the next two years Ross's mother was in and out of a nursing home until she died in 1957.

Eight months after Mary died, Ross, Ruby, and their "love" child, as Ruby called David, moved into the big buff brick on Pavey Street. Everyone pitched in to help the family with the move. David faintly recalls his Uncle Earl pulling him across the snowy yard with the boy sitting atop a dresser. As David grew older, Ross often took the boy into town. Because he always immaculately dressed himself, Ross expected David to look like a perfect little gentleman. He also insisted that David be mannerly at all times, claiming that good manners were a sign of good breeding. Obviously, Ross sometimes forgot that David was just a little boy.

In 1960, Ross was asked by Meadow Brook Farm in Michigan to complete a statue of Firestone, one of the greatest draft horses of all time. In his lifetime, the Belgian gelding had won twenty-eight championships and was the wheel horse in the undefeated sixes class of that era. Eighteen years before, the gelding had been discovered working as a farm horse by Harold Clark, the new manager of Meadow Brook's breeding operation. Clark was so impressed by Firestone's massive, thick, deep body and his beautiful colouring that he literally stole the horse from the farm department and began grooming him for the show ring.

In all, Ross made four models of Firestone but only one was cast in steel-reinforced plaster and mounted, then dipped in bronze. Twenty-five years after Ross completed the sculpture of Firestone, he was contacted by the Belgian Draft Horse Corporation of America. They wanted a special gift for Matilda Wilson Dodge, the retiring owner of Meadow Brook Farm, and they asked Ross to try to find them a statue of Firestone. Fortunately, Ross had one in his gallery. On the day of the presentation, the statue was transferred from the trunk of Ross's car to the trunk of Harold Clark's car in a clandestine meeting on the Canadian side of the Blue Water Bridge at

Port Huron. Both men were afraid of delays and difficulties from customs officials, so they decided to sneak the statue across the border. The statue is now on display at Meadow Brook Hall, a part of Oakland University in Rochester, Michigan.

After completing the statue of Firestone, Ross's artistic career seemed to be on hold. His cattle buying-and-selling business was doing fairly well, but even this could not prevent a pile of debts. To secure greater financial stability, he invested in several ventures, including purchasing a Freightliner truck. Although he knew nothing about trucking, he contracted to haul freight to the West Coast for a London firm. This venture, like the others, was to bring huge profits. But when the contract was pulled a few years later, Ross was forced to sell the truck at a loss and he almost lost his home as well because he had mortgaged it to buy the truck in the first place.

During these years, Ross also acted as an agent for the Waterloo Cattle Breeding Association and was instrumental in importing cattle from the Jersey Islands at a cost of one hundred and fifteen pounds per head. Exporter William (Bill) G. Pritchard, Ross's contact in the Islands, wrote that if Ross could get enough orders, Pritchard would ship the cattle by plane. About this same time, Ross opened a weekly Jersey auction at Eastwood, a small community just east of Woodstock. His ad read: "Jerseys — all ages. We finance and deliver anywhere in Southwestern Ontario. Whole herds and springing cows a specialty."

Fortunately, the dairy industry was prospering. The Ontario Jersey Club had spent four million dollars on an advertising campaign to promote milk. This campaign was paying off and more dairy herds were needed to keep pace with the demand. Instead of financing the purchase of a few cows, Ross was now financing dozens. As the volume continued to increase, he turned the financing over to a finance company. He wrote up the agreement and the finance company purchased the contract. In the early 1960s, the economy began to cool and some of the breeders got behind in their payments. When the finance company couldn't get their money, they seized the cattle. After several seizures, the finance company told Ross that if he sold them any more bad contracts, they were going to sue him. The company contended that it

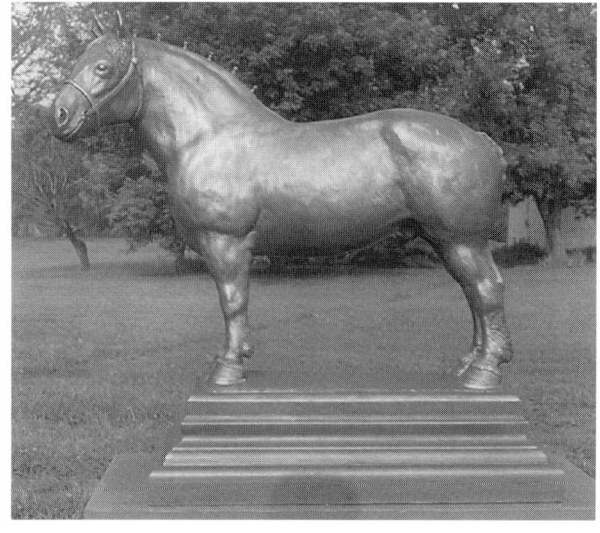

Quarter life-size model of the famous Belgian horse, Firestone.

had bought the contracts in good faith. When five more farmers reneged on their payments, Ross was forced to take the cattle back or be sued by the finance company. In desperation, he bought a farm at Huntingford, ten miles north of Woodstock, and hired one of the delinquent breeders to look after the stock. As payment delinquencies increased, Ross found himself in possession of more than one hundred cows. Because the purchase of the farm had come about quite suddenly, he had made no plans to grow feed. Everything had to be purchased and Ross found himself deeper and deeper in debt.

To make matters worse, his hired help left without warning. Now almost sixty years old, Ross was forced to take over the farm chores, everything from milking the cows to mucking out the stables. With the help of David, now ten years old, and a couple of David's cousins, Ross managed to cope. The milking machines were then seized for non-payment.

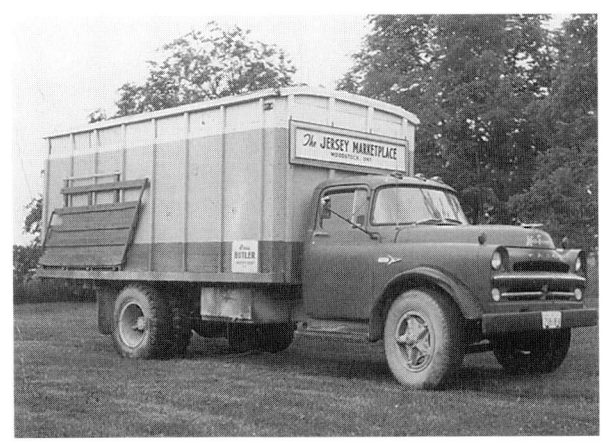

To buy and sell cattle, Ross Butler started The Jersey Marketplace.

The whole world seemed to be conspiring against me. I became so tired, so beat and frustrated that one day I walked out into the pasture field . . . and there among the cows, I cried my heart out.

Although his milking machines were gone, Ross still had his Sputnik, a stainless steel tank on rollers into which the milk was emptied. The Sputnik was normally used in conjunction with the milking machines, but since Ross and the boys had to milk by hand, they simply poured the milk into the top of the tank. The Sputnik held approximately 300 pounds of milk, and when it was full, Ross secured the twelve-inch lid with a clamp and wheeled it into the milk house. He inserted air pressure into the horn-type lid, and this pressure forced the milk out of a drain at the bottom of the machine into the bulk tank.

On one particular morning shortly after Ross pressurized the tank by inserting air into the lid, there was a hissing sound. The tank had developed a leak. Ross placed his finger over the leak and hissing stopped. Suddenly, with a rocket-like force, the lid blew off the tank, hitting Ross on the forehead and knocking him to the floor. The explosion was so powerful that the lid was blown through the milkhouse roof. Although the lid was only twelve inches in diameter and weighed only a few pounds, it had pressurized to a force of ten pounds per square inch.

The blow had shattered Ross's glasses and a piece of flying glass went into the eye of Don Leuszler, Ross's nephew. Don screamed and covered his face with his hands. Ross was both stunned and bleeding, but he somehow managed to stagger to his feet and get everyone out of the milkhouse before he collapsed on the ground. As David ran across the road for help, Ross managed to get to his feet, go into the stable, release the cows' stanchions, and drive all of them outside. When David returned with the neighbour, Ross was sitting on the ground holding his bleeding head. The neighbour immediately put everyone into Ross's car and drove them to the hospital. He then took David to get Ruby.

When the doctor told Ruby that Ross had a fractured skull and would be hospitalized for at least two months, she became so distraught that she had to be sedated. She did not even hear the doctor say that Don Leuszler had been sent to a hospital in London for surgery in the hopes of saving his sight.

By late afternoon, Ruby had pulled herself together. Although still terribly worried, she and David went back to the farm, where there were cows to milk and chores to do. When they arrived, Ruby was surprised to find her brother, Russell Leuszler, and his son already feeding the cattle. Shortly thereafter, several neighbourhood women from Pavey Street arrived to help with the milking.

Ruby knew she that couldn't depend on this volunteer help for long. When someone offered to buy a couple of the cows, she sold them for a quarter of their worth. Word quickly spread that there was a bargain to be had at the Butler farm and even more buyers came. When the finance company heard about the accident, they immediately stepped in and seized the cattle. They didn't realize that several of them had already been sold.

When Ross heard that Ruby had sold a few of his cows for a fraction of their worth, he was very upset. He firmly believed that a few good sales would have kept

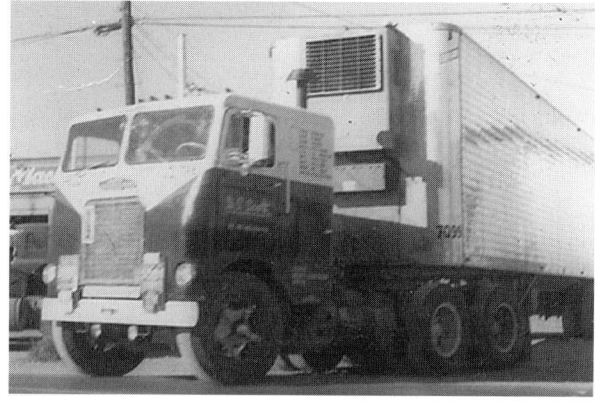

In another enterprise, Ross Butler purchased this Freightliner transport.

the finance company at bay. While Ross was convalescing, he had a lot of time to think. He realized that Ruby was right when she claimed they were deeply in debt. They had lost the farm and the cattle; their city property was heavily mortgaged and also in danger of being seized. The Butler's owed eighty-six thousand dollars, a staggering sum in 1966.

Ross did a lot of soul-searching, trying to figure out what had gone wrong.

Over and over again I asked myself where I had gone wrong. And it took months of soul-searching before I found the answer. I was an artist, and when I gave up my dream, I began to falter. Now, after twenty-five years, maybe it was time to renew that dream.

14 | Renewing the Dream

ONCE ROSS BUTLER HAD MADE HIS DECISION to return to his art, he couldn't wait to get back to his easel and canvas. He had been away from painting for almost twenty-five years and was not completely sure that he could begin again. With dogged determination and a feeling of rightness, he set to work on an oil painting of the Ella Cow, a record producing Jersey. Using his basic theory of proportions, one brush stroke flowed into another and it was not long before his work took shape and form.

He soon found that returning to his dream was the easy part. Establishing himself again as an artist was a little more difficult. Ross didn't realize that his paintings had lost something. Although they were perfectly proportioned, his new paintings lacked the special quality of reality or life-likeness that distinguished his work. They just didn't "walk off the canvas."

Ross's main worry, of course, was his unpaid bills. Rumour had it that there was a warrant out for his arrest for delinquent accounts and he knew that it would be only a matter of time before it was served. His debt hung like a dark cloud over his head and it certainly didn't help his strained relationship with Ruby. Every time someone knocked on the door, Ruby was afraid to answer it, lest it was the sheriff coming for Ross.

To add some extra money to the Butler coffers, Ruby became a Fuller Brush lady. Travelling throughout Oxford County, she qualified for many promotional sales incentives and earned enough money to buy her own car. "She enjoyed visiting neighbours and friends as much as she did selling," said Sharon Rounds, another Fuller Brush lady. "Maybe that is why she was so successful."

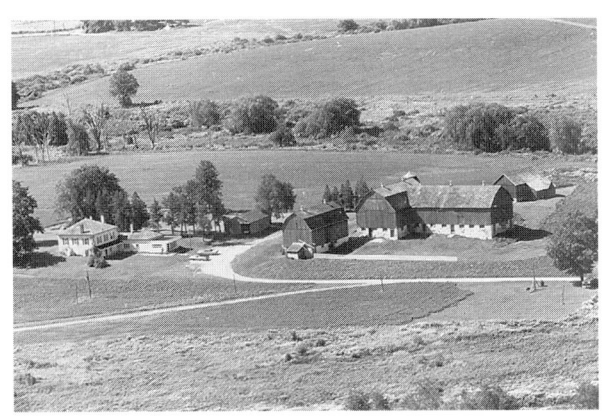

The Butler farm, a former Bible college, with the studio now located in the barn in the foreground.

Ruby's interests were quite varied. As a result of Ross's accident, she became a volunteer in the Farm Safety Association. She was also active in the local Home and School Association, rising in later years to be vice-president at the provincial level of the association. Through this organization she became involved in UNICEF (United Nations International Children Emergency Fund). David was one of the few neighbourhood children who collected for charity instead of trick or treating. "My mother was always involved helping people, whether it was through an organization or on a one-to-one basis," David recalls about those years.

Despite his financial troubles, Ross managed to stay one step ahead of his creditors. In 1968 he was invited to exhibit at the flower display at the Royal Winter Fair. The display was an outstanding success. Ross's eye for colour and texture helped him arrange an eye-catching display of flowers, sculptures, and greenery. David, now thirteen, went along to Toronto to help his father.

About that same time, Ross was approached by a real estate man who was looking for a large parcel of land within the city limits. The perimeter of Ross's property was too small, but if he could acquire some land from his neighbours or a written promise of some land, it would make the site more attractive to the potential buyer. The rumour around Woodstock was that the property was needed for a senior citizens apartment complex. It was too good of a chance to miss. Ross contacted all the neighbours whose properties adjoined his. While several were quite willing to sell fifty or sixty feet, some were not willing to part with an inch. They felt Ross was trying to make money off them. The truth was that Ross needed the sale to get out of debt.

With the pending sale, Ross decided to "spruce up" his own property. The first thing on that agenda was to dispose of his former studio, the small building that had been Ross's and Ruby's first home. Any buyer of the building would have to move it, of course, but perspective buyers found that the cost of the move was greater than its value. When the building didn't sell, Ross's only alternative was to have it torn down. He promised David and a couple of his friends $500 if they would knock down the old building and salvage the good lumber. At first the boys found it fun to knock out the walls, but when that fun turned into work, they quickly tired of the job. In the end, Ross hired a man to finish the work and haul away the scrap.

Negotiations progressed quietly and Ross finally sold the property to Harold Freure Construction (Ontario) Limited of Kitchener for sixty times more than what he had paid for it. They, in turn, built the senior citizen apartment complex. The sale did not include the bull barn and art gallery, which was later sold to Dr. Roy Mitchell, who immediately sold that property for a huge profit.

The sale of the main property could not have come at a better time, for Ross's creditors were still beating a path to his door. The "miracle," as Ross called the sale, enabled him to pay off all his debts and buy a hundred and eighty acre farm in East Oxford, approximately one and a half miles south of his Pavey Street property.

In April 1970, the Butlers moved into their new eighteen-room house, which had once been a dormitory for a Bible College. As well, the farm had two hired-man houses and three barns, one of which had a large stable, but only about half of the land was tillable, the rest being flood plain.

With the acquisition of the farm, Ross was able to rekindle an interest in poultry, an interest that had developed when he had helped on his father's farm in Norwich. Many early pictures of poultry were black and white etchings, but Ross wanted to paint them in their true colours.

While attending a poultry show in Beamsville, Ontario, he saw two almost perfect Buff Orpingtons — father and son. He immediately wanted to buy one, but the owner would not sell. So Ross decided to develop his own birds of perfection. He joined the Oxford Poultry Association and systematically began raising different breeds. Using the same method of breeding, feeding, and caring that he had used with his Jerseys, he developed his own poultry True Types. He studied their faults as well as their characteristics from egg to maturity. When he felt his birds were ready, he took them to exhibitions, beginning with the Beamsville show, one of the most prestigious. With twenty-five entries, Ross earned twenty-four firsts and one second.

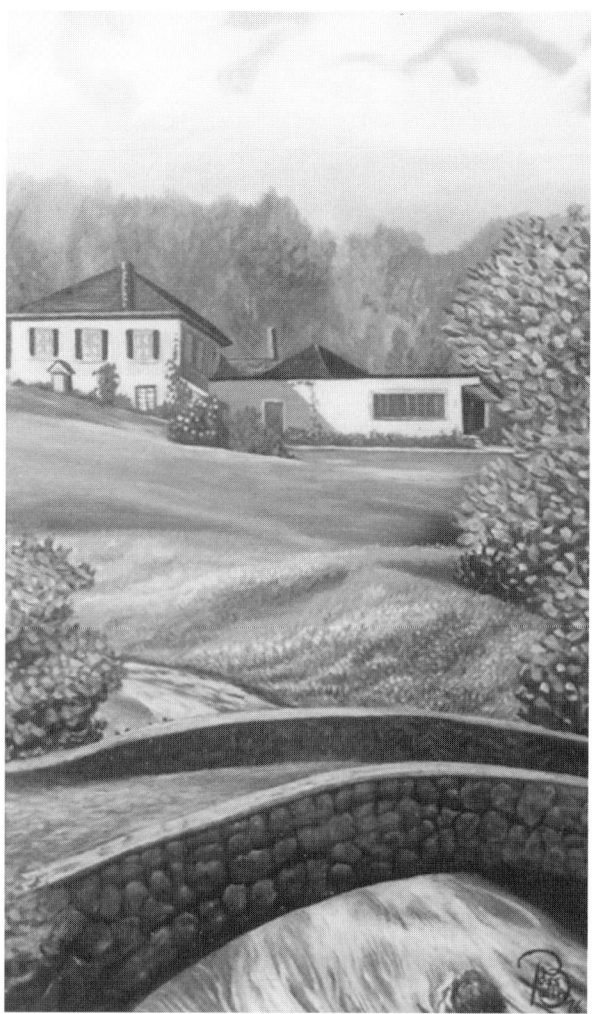

Where the Artist Dwells, (16.5 x 28", oil on board, 1976), Ross Butler's painting of his home which he later named "Southwood."

Before he came home, he traded his second place bird for the cock that had beat him.

Ross soon had eighty-six varieties of birds, three hundred pens, and five hundred chicks. His feed bill was over one hundred dollars a week, but it was not all loss for a hatchery in Blenheim had agreed to take all his eggs. Once a week, Ross would make a trip to Blenheim to deliver the eggs and return with a load of feed. There was nothing Ross liked better than to barter for trade, whether it was eggs for feed or labour for a free house.

Painting the True Types of the poultry breeds almost became an obsession for Ross, but he still had to prove that his breeds were the best. When the American Poultry Association celebrated their centennial in Columbus, Ohio, Ross decided to enter twenty five of his finest birds. His entries received sixteen first prizes as well as several lesser ribbons. More important, however, eleven of his breeds were judged as grand champions. On the heels of this success, the American Poultry Association asked Ross to paint all the poultry True Type breeds.

Ross selected an Australorp for his first True Type and set up a specially-built cage in his studio for the rooster. Ross later discovered that the American Poultry Association were only interested in the True Types if he painted, financed, and published the pictures on his own.

Right then I decided to give up on the whole idea of painting True Types of poultry. I was just too old to gamble any more.

He decided to get out of the poultry business. In the end, all Ross had to show for his poultry business efforts was one True Type painting and hundreds of ribbons and trophies. No profits had been made; in fact, the venture had cost him a good deal of money.

Yet with a new home free and clear of payments and a place where he could work without interruption, Ross's artistic future looked very bright. Several commissions to paint prize-winning cattle and horses materialized. When the Holstein

Friesian Association of Canada wanted their models of the breed updated, they contacted Ross. The breed had evolved over the years and was now stronger, bigger, longer, and better knit-together than the animals of the 1930s.

The Holstein Friesian Association formed a committee of seventeen to work with Ross. Chaired by Abner B. Martin of West Montrose, Ontario, this diversified committee was made up of judges, breeders, classifiers, and staff members. Three area breeders — Gordon Innes, Fred Griffin, and Wally Knapp — were on the committee. Their task was not an easy one, as opinions about what constituted a True Type Holstein were strong and varied. It took months and dozens of meetings at Ross's studio to bring the paintings and sculptures up to the desired standard. When the committee asked that a little more depth be added to a shoulder, or that a leg be shortened, or the muzzle broadened, they found that it threw the rest of the animal out of proportion. "Despite all the desired changes," Wally Knapp later said, "Ross always co-operated one hundred percent with the committee."

The first four models were put up for auction at the Royal Winter Fair's "Sale of Stars" by the Holstein Friesian Association. The arena was packed with breeders from across Canada, plus several from United States and Europe. Ross expected this first plastic model to sell for approximately one hundred dollars. He was flabbergasted when a bid came in at one thousand. Three simultaneous bids quickly followed it. The model was finally purchased by Bob and Lee Shore of Glanworth, Ontario, for six thousand three hundred dollars. The second model brought four thousand and the third and fourth both sold for three thousand five hundred dollars each. These three were purchased by Attilio Ladina of Pandina, Italy. Everyone seemed extremely pleased by Ross's creations. The only criticism he heard was that his True Type cow was a little on the young side, more like a four-year-old than a seasoned cow.

Now released from his debts, Ross's pleasure and relief overflowed onto his canvasses. In 1971, Ross completed his painting of the ABC *Family at Pickland* for Claude Picket. The original canvas was sixty-nine inches by seventy-nine inches and represented seven hundred hours of work. A seemingly endless task because Ross had to

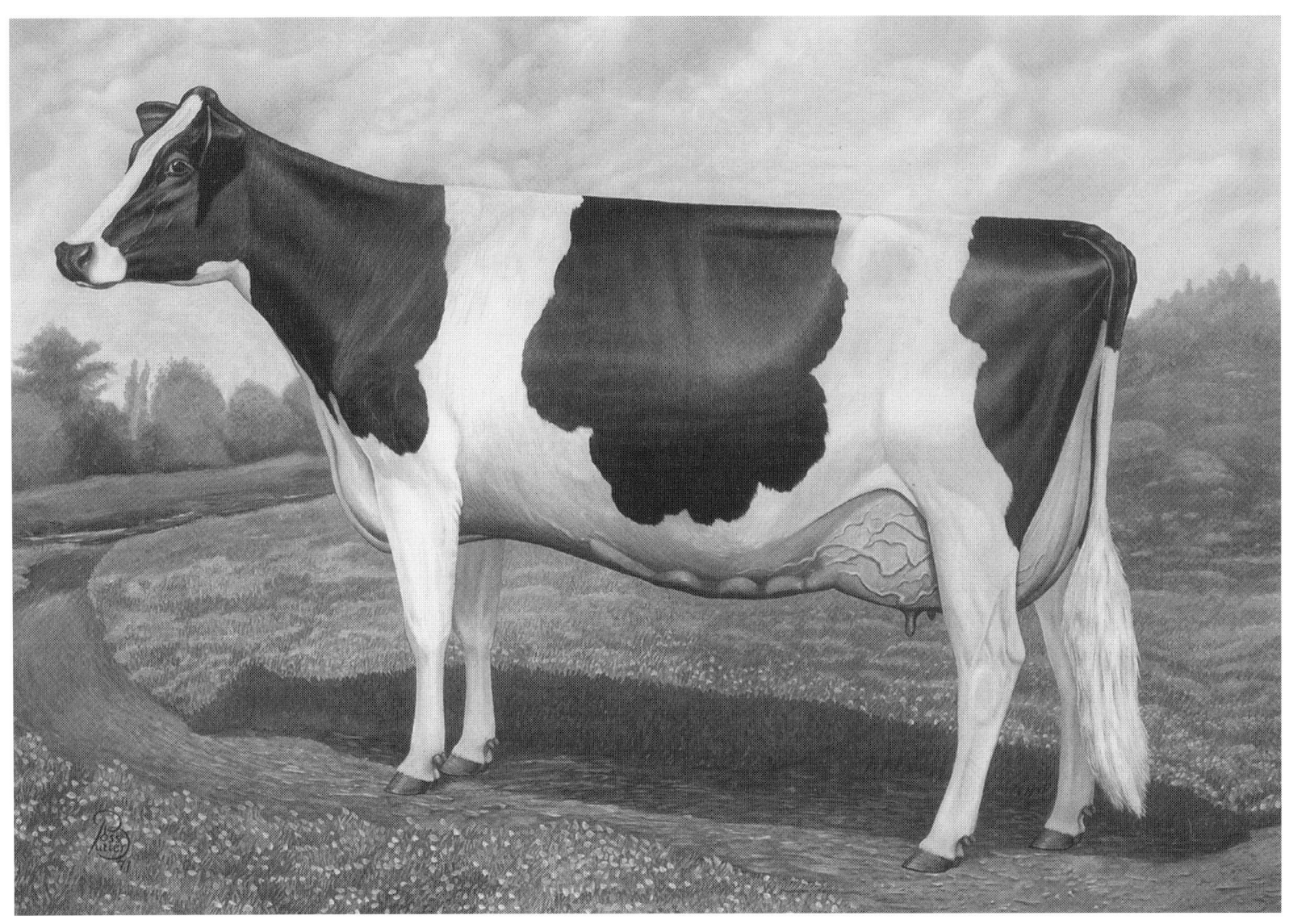

True types, painted for The Holstein Association of Canada, 1971.

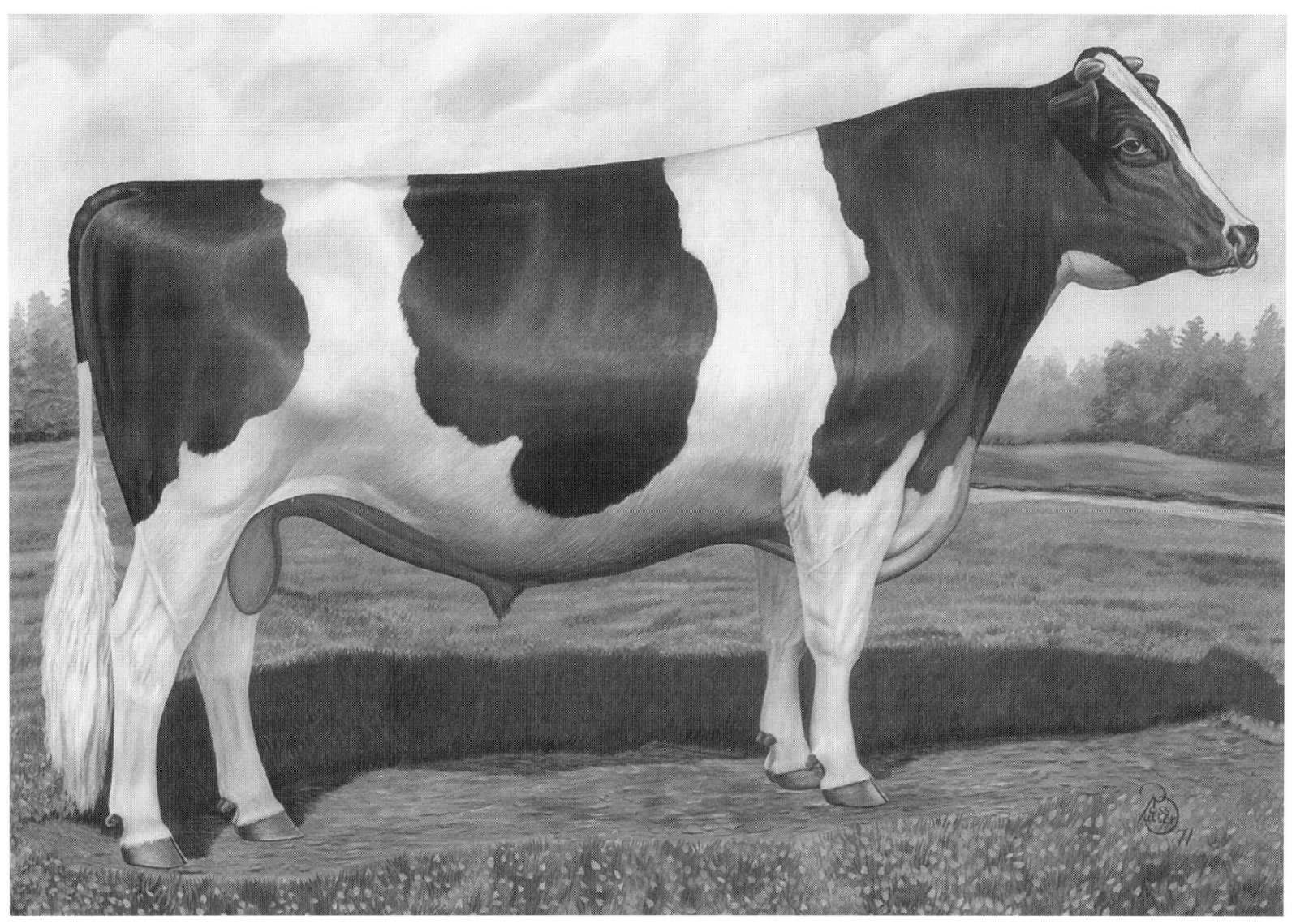

travel many times to the Pickland Farm to refresh his memory of the landscape, the painting earned him ten thousand dollars. Picket later donated this painting to the Holstein Friesian Association head office in Brantford.

Now comfortable with large paintings, Ross began *Royal Review*, a panoramic study of many of the better known breeds of poultry and livestock as they made their way from the breeder's barn to the show ring at the Royal Winter Fair. It took Ross one full year and an estimated three hundred thousand strokes to complete this large four-by-eight foot painting. Every stroke was done to the beat of classical or easy-listening music.

Royal Review was first displayed at the flower show exhibit at the Royal Winter Fair in 1974. Banked by thousands of blooms, the masterpiece captured the attention of more than 200,000 people. Ross was so caught up in the success of this painting that he had five thousand coloured reproductions made. The reproductions sold well, but they didn't sell in the quantities that Ross visualized. Although orders came in from around the world, Ross's expectations for sales fell quite short. As with some of his other paintings, hundreds of reproductions are still on shelves at the Ross Butler Gallery.

Following *Royal Review*, Ross completed *All Canadian Holsteins — The Cattle upon the Thousand Hills*, a painting of the Royal Winter Fair champions. He again printed five thousand reproductions, and, again, sales fell short of expectations. Ross had yet to develop a marketing mind to match his artistic talent.

The publicity generated from Ross's paintings brought hundreds of visitors to Woodstock. In one month alone, Ross had busloads of tourists from South America, Switzerland, and Great Britain come to his studio. In addition to these international visitors, there were school groups, judging contestants from the Royal Winter Fair, church groups, and Women's Institutes. Ross loved the attention and personally escorted all of the groups around the gallery. He would tell his visitors little stories about the paintings and, occasionally, would throw in an anecdote that was exaggerated a little. After all, Ross was not only still a great artist but also a good story teller.

15 | Southwood

ROSS BUTLER ALWAYS PAINTED early in the mornings before visitors or duties distracted him. While he painted to the sound of classical music, his mind often wandered. Usually his thoughts were centred around the farm, how best to utilize the flood plain area and how best to make the farm pay. He envisioned a historical village, much like the one he had planned for the fairgrounds just after World War II. He could see his property and adjoining acreage as part of a memorial and development park. This one thousand two hundred acre park would be home for a museum, zoo, children's playground, and, of course, a fitting home for his own art collection.

Ross became so obsessed with the idea that he took two months off from his painting to develop an outline for "Southwood," a tourist attraction that would be second to none in Ontario's agricultural heartland. He developed a prospectus and had three hundred copies printed which were mailed to the Prime Minister of Canada, the Premier of Ontario, other government officials, businessmen, and local officials.

The reaction was immediate and responsive. Letters of congratulations and encouragement came from almost everyone. I contacted Wintario. Three of the men came to see me. They liked what they saw and instructed me to get prominent local people involved, form a corporation and work out a cost.

Ross worked out a plan for the buildings, roads, and picnic areas. When Southwood was completed, it would have thirty buildings, among them a sports facility, a museum with a replica of every known farm implement, an art gallery, domestic zoo, and Hall of Fame with over one hundred portraits of famous citizens of Oxford.

However, when the project topped twenty-two million dollars, interest waned and Ross's dream of Southwood fell by the wayside.

Disappointed, Ross's interest turned to more mundane activities. Since childhood, he had loved Sundays because they were a day away from responsibilities. He and Ruby now visited flea markets in the area, where Ross bought picture frames and Ruby couldn't resist the little flower arrangements. They now seemed to find a closeness that had been missing in their relationship.

Ross still continued to paint, but commissions became the norm instead of the exception. Occasionally he painted portraits for a change, and Eugene Whelan, then Minister of Agriculture, became one of his subjects.

In the mid-1970s Ross met fellow artist and avid history buff Murray Killman. Killman was a descendent of Jacob Killman of Butler's Ranger fame and Ross was the great-great-grandson of Colonel John Butler, after whom the Rangers were named. John Butler, son of Old Walter Butler and his second wife Deborah Ely, was a staunch British loyalist living in the colony of New York at the time of the American Revolution. He believed that the Thirteen Colonies' dispute with Great Britain was not a question of infringement of civil rights or religious freedom but related to a single article of commerce — tea. When hostilities came, he organized a group of backwoodsmen and settlers into a formidable loyalist fighting unit known as Butler's Rangers who attempted to defend the property rights of fellow loyalists by raiding "rebel" strongholds and farms in the Mohawk River valley from British positions at Fort Ontario and Fort Niagara.

It was probably through his ancestral connection with Colonel John Butler that Ross developed his love of history. When Murray Killman was asked to go on a speaking tour of New York state for the American Bi-Centennial Year, he invited Ross to go along as well.

In Rome, New York, the two were treated as visiting celebrities. Murray had brought a portrait of Colonel John Butler with him on the trip and a comparison of the portrait to Ross showed a remarkable likeness. The Americans made much of this

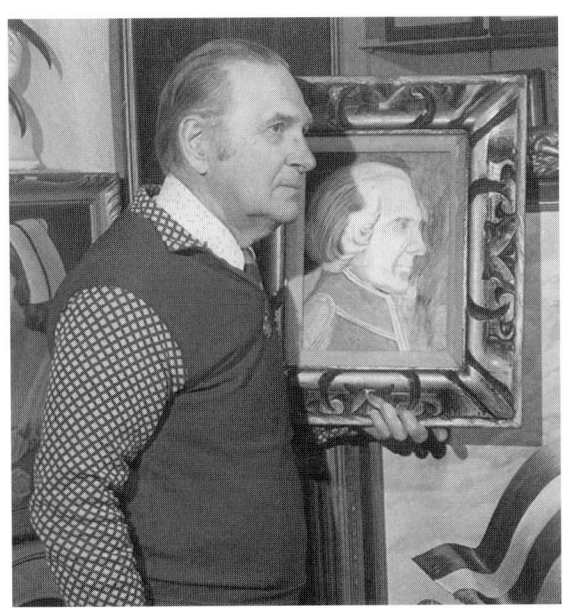

Ross Butler posing with a portrait of Colonel John Butler, his great-great-grandfather.

resemblance. Two American friends took Ross and Murray two hundred miles to see a powder horn that was used in the American Revolution. Written on the horn was the name of the owner, the date, a picture of some Indians, and the mounted figure of the Commander of Fort Stanwix. Pictured above the Indians and the Commander was a crude drawing of the Stars and Stripes. Based on the date on the horn, the flag in the picture was believed to be the first Stars and Stripes flown in battle.

Ross was so impressed with the powder horn that when he returned home he painted it with an unfurled flag in the background. The Americans loved the picture and asked Ross if he would present it to President Jimmy Carter on the 200th anniversary of the Battle of Oriskany in Rome, New York. Because Ross looked so much like his ancestor Colonel Butler, they also asked him to play the Colonel's part in a pageant reliving the battle. Both artists were asked to exhibit their paintings at the John F. Kennedy Arena which was adjacent to the pageant battlefield. Ross was so enthusiastic about this event that he invited two busloads of people from Woodstock and Oxford County to accompany him to Rome, where they were supposed to be included in the celebration. When this didn't happen, many were disappointed.

Believing his painting of the *First American Flag* would sell well, Ross had ten thousand reproductions made. Yet again, he had misread the market and only a few hundred sold. To make matters worse, the man who was acting as his agent in Rome, New York, took off with both the money and the unsold reproductions.

Ross was so impressed with the Butler family history that he became determined to see it in book form. He joined a writer's group, and Ruby, who rarely shared his activities, accompanied him. They both loved both the camaraderie of this writer's group.

I was inspired by the exchange of ideas sparked by our meetings. These ideas opened up a whole new world to me.

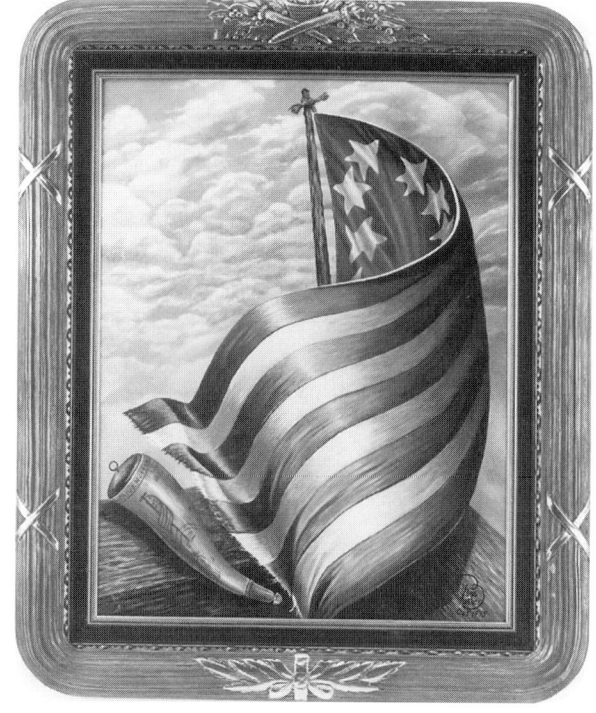

First American Flag (24 x 36", oil on masonite, 1975), what is believed to be the first Stars and Stripes to be flown in battle, with the Hutton Horn bearing inscriptions proving that this flag did indeed fly above Fort Schuyler on August 3, 1777 when the fort was under siege by British and Loyalist forces, including Butler's Rangers.

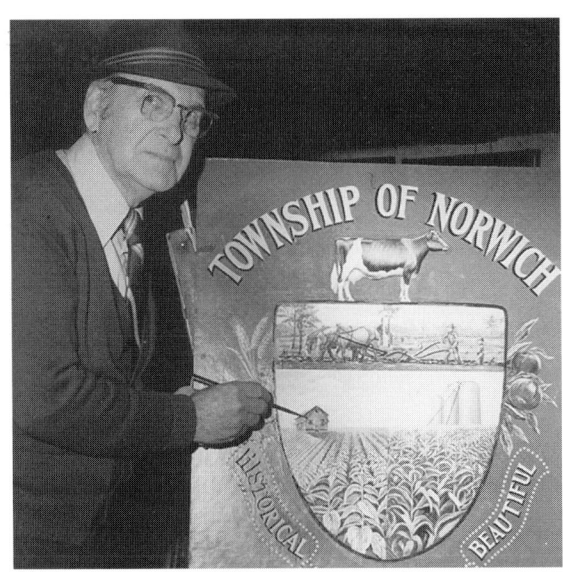

Ross Butler posing with the Township of Norwich Crest, 1977.

In 1975 Ross was asked by the Township of Norwich to design a crest for their amalgamated township. Two years earlier, the township had invited local county school children to participate in a "design a crest" contest. Tamma Losee won the contest and received a prize of twenty-five dollars. She also received a letter of congratulations from Dr. Bruce Halliday, then Member of Parliament for Oxford. Halliday wrote in his letter, "Your crest will appear on letters and other means of identification for Norwich Township for probably many years to come." However, Halliday didn't know at the time that although Tamma had won the contest, the crest committee had not found her crest suitable for their needs. Instead, the committee asked Heraldic House Limited of Toronto, an international coat of arms firm, to design a crest for the township. When the crest designed by Heraldic was also not suitable, the committee appointed Ross. Years later, the contest would cast a doubt in some people's mind as to who actually designed the Township of Norwich crest, Tamma or Ross. This came to the fore after Ross's death but research has proven that the design of the crest was Ross's exclusively.

His design combined the township's prosperity, its historical past, and its agricultural landscape. At the top of the design was a picture of Calamity Jane, a champion cow whose picture had been painted on the side of a barn at Curries. Beneath the cow was a picture of a settler ploughing his field with a team of horses. On the perimeter of the crest, Ross painted the township's agricultural products: corn, tobacco, clover, grain, and apples. He framed the crest with the words "HISTORIC, AGRICULTURAL AND BEAUTIFUL." During that same year the township council passed a resolution to offer Ross two thousand seven hundred and fifty dollars for the exclusive rights to the crest and the transparency to reproduce it, and although Ross had wanted to retain the original and the transparency rights, he settled for the original.

On 14 April 1978, just nine days short of his seventy-first birthday, the Western Ontario Breeders Association honoured Ross with a "recognition" dinner attended by over three hundred people. There were many accolades for Ross that night. Dr. R.J. McDonald, the general manager of the Western Ontario Breeders, drew the audience's attention to the unique contribution that Ross had made to the livestock industry in Canada. Dr. Bruce Halliday, M.P. for Oxford, added his praise. Dr. Claire Rennie of the Ontario Ministry of Agriculture agreed that it was an honour to pay tribute to Ross Butler, a man who had made such a contribution the agriculture industry and society in general. "Ross, through his paintings and sculptures, has demonstrated to thousands of people the importance of having goals of perfection." Rennie also said that the Ontario Agricultural Museum planned to develop a permanent display of Ross's work, an announcement confirmed in a letter from R.W. Carbert, general manager of the museum. W.P. Watson, general manager of the Royal Winter Fair, added that with originals and copies of Ross's paintings being distributed overseas, new markets for Canadian cattle had been opened. A letter came from the Federal Minister of Agriculture, Eugene Whelan, who congratulated Ross and said he was proud to call Ross a friend.

Ross was very moved by this outpouring of goodwill and affection, which was so different from that first testimonial held in 1952.

My greatest reward is to look at you people gathered here on my account. It's just unbelievable!

At the close of the testimonials, Ruby was given a bouquet of roses and Ross a set a luggage for a proposed trip abroad, which, because of a lack of money, never took place. And, unfortunately, the sale of his art to the Ontario Agricultural Museum in Milton never took place. At the time, Ross's collection was considered to be culturally significant, valued at $1,161,460. He asked for one million dollars for his painting *Royal Review* and promised to donate the rest of his collection to the museum in exchange for a receipt for income tax purposes.

At the time, both Ault Dairies and Labatt's were corporate sponsors of Ontario Agricultural Museum and the two companies wanted an independent appraisal of Ross's work before sanctioning any deal. They hired a woman who was skilled in art appraisals, but who had little knowledge of domestic animal paintings or sculptures. As soon as the museum's Robert Carbert and Ross saw her, they knew they were in trouble.

Another dream fell by the wayside.

16 | Agri-Cultural Connections

ANOTHER ACCOLADE CAME to Ross Butler on 7 March 1980 when he received word that he had been awarded an Honorary Membership from the Ontario Institute of Professional Agrologists. Although affiliated with the Agricultural Institute of Canada, the Institute is an overall body that provides continuity and encourages the attainment of higher standards in the many phases of agriculture. Ross's award was based on his creative ability to sculpt the True Type models.

The previous year Ross and Ruby Butler were overjoyed when their son David married Mary Conlon in a double wedding ceremony in Stoney Creek on 28 July 1979. They were joined in the ceremony by Mary's sister and her fiance. Ruby now had the daughter she had always wanted and Ross looked forward to the prospect of becoming a grandfather.

During these years Ross met Beth Deslippe, a former teacher whose agricultural background extended back to her childhood. Like most rural women, Beth believed that not enough education was given in schools about Canada's agricultural industry. She saw a way to bring art, education, agriculture, and heritage into the classroom with Ross's art.

Beth took her idea of using Ross's art to promote agriculture in the classroom to the North and South District Women's Institutes. These women had also long recognized the gap in rural-urban education. "Ross uses art as the medium to promote an aspect of our natural and rural cultural experience," Beth told the women. "He uses these artistic skills to record in many mediums the vitality, beauty, proportions and utility of the livestock history." The women liked Beth's idea of putting prints of

Ross's domestic animals in the schools of Oxford County, but they developed her idea several steps farther. The North and South District Women's Institutes became the catalyst that put together "Agri-Cultural Connections," a bilingual packet of information which linked together agriculture, science, history, art, heritage, and the environment. Ross Butler and his paintings became the link that tied the program together.

The women knew that this would be a long-term project costing a great deal of money. They obtained the backing and support of the Boards of Education, the Ministry of Agriculture and Food, the Ministry of Citizenship and Culture, the Ministry of Education, and municipal and county governments. They also found sponsors like Pioneer Seed, the United Co-Operatives of Ontario, and the Oxford Holstein Breeders Association.

The project was divided into two phases, the first dealing with the marketing process. This process took on many forms, including rural theme displays at several galleries and museums, personal appearances by Ross, a fund-raising dinner, and television, radio, and newspaper exposure with Ross always as the focal point. The show "Animals I Have Known" at the Lynwood Art Gallery in Simcoe was especially successful. Opened officially by Eugene Whelan, the show featured thirty paintings and twelve sculptures on display. Students were caught up in the process with activities that included field trips, pioneer crafts, and sports days. These activities were designed to bring rural and urban students a greater appreciation of their agricultural heritage.

While the "Agriculture in the Classroom" project was taking shape, Ross and Ruby celebrated their 40th wedding anniversary. At their celebration party Ross paid tribute to Ruby.

No one else could have weathered all the hardships entailed in being married to a temperamental artist. Without her, I would have failed time and time again.

Life during these twilight years was good for the Butlers. David, Mary, and their son

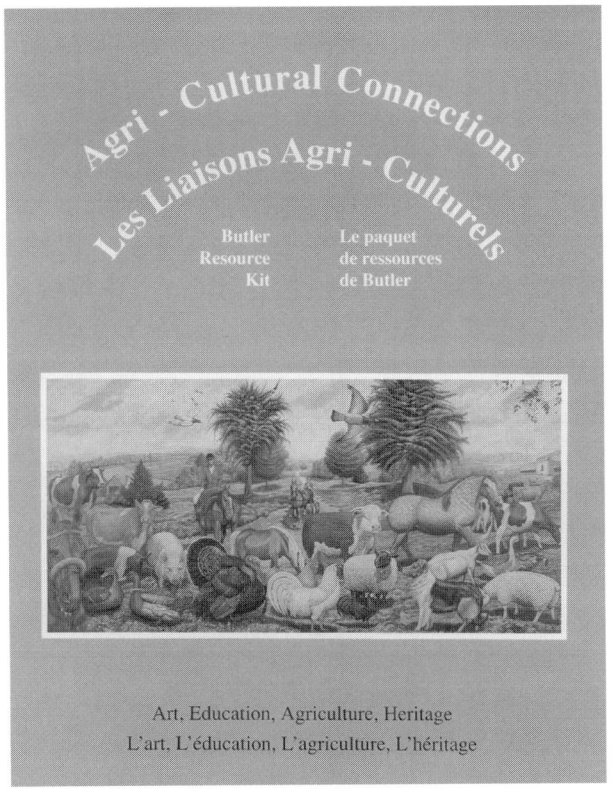

Art, Education, Agriculture, Heritage
L'art, L'éducation, L'agriculture, L'héritage

John had moved into one of the hired man's houses on the property. Ross now had the opportunity to get to know his grandson in a way he had never known his son. Grampy and Grammy, as Ross and Ruby were called, found a more relaxed lifestyle that was much to their liking, although Ruby persisted in keeping most of her charitable duties. She enjoyed a simple life-style, not desiring fancy clothes or a lot of money, but just needing to be needed.

Ross also needed to be needed, but in a different way. Like Ruby, he needed his family, but he also craved the accolades of being an artist of repute. He hosted Professor W.S. Young's day-long diploma study group from the University of Guelph. For the Canadian Jersey Cattle Club, he designed a new logo which gave his beloved Jerseys a new and distinct identity.

Ross received a pat on the back when Peter Lewington's book entitled *Canada's Holsteins* was published in 1983. In the chapter called "Pursuit of Perfection," Lewington said, "Ross was one of the most industrious and innovative characters to grace the dairy industry." Even abroad, breeders had great respect for Ross Butler and his True Type paintings. When British painter and sculptor John Harper was putting together his True Types of the breed for the British Holstein Society, he came to Canada to meet Ross. Harper was accompanied by a British television crew who filmed Ross at work in his studio, walking about the farm, and relaxing in the evening with the family which had recently grown. David and Mary had another son, Paul.

The British film crew was not the only one to visit the Butlers. Bill Bramah of Ontario's Global Television came with his cameraman, Terry Culbert. Bramah's warm and friendly interview showed Ross at work on one of his paintings, *The Three Sisters*, which had been commissioned by Cecil Deslippe of Meadowbridge Holsteins of Kintore and Great Lakes Harvestores. The commission was said to be worth ten thousand dollars.

Ross was still willing to try new things. In 1984 he painted a collector's plate of Brookview Charity, a grand champion owned by Hanover Hill Holsteins of Port Perry,

Ontario. This plate was the first in a series called "Top of the Fair" by City View Associates of Woodstock. While Ross received a hefty commission for painting Charity, City View Associates did not fare as well. During that same year, Ontario's bi-centennial year, Ross received the Bi-Centennial Certificate of Merit Award in recognition for his contributions to agriculture. He was also made an Honorary Life member of the Canadian Holstein Association and awarded a Certificate of Recognition.

Ross's awards were overshadowed in the mid-1980s when he was diagnosed with Parkinson's Disease, which causes the degeneration of nerve cells deep within the brain. Although the disease progressed slowly, Ross eventually found it difficult to hold a paint brush and extend his arm to the canvas. Instead, he began to write his memoirs. Ruby, too, was having health problems — she had been diagnosed with cancer. Despite their health problems, Ross and Ruby were overjoyed when Tommy, another grandson, was born. Both tried to put their illnesses aside and get on with a lifestyle that was filled with family, love, and support.

Ross's interest in agriculture and art was kept alive by the North and South District Women's Institutes who were putting the final touches to "The Butler Resource Kit." Spread over five years, this promotion had taken on many shapes and forms, everything from hands-on animal displays at museums to the final gala salute at the Royal Winter Fair. The main focus of the project, of course, was agriculture in the classroom program. Each "Agri-Cultural Connections" packet contained a uniform set of 8 1/2 by 11 inch coloured prints of twenty-four different breeds of livestock and poultry with bilingual information about the breed on the back of each print. Included in the packet was a bilingual resource booklet, showing both rural and urban students the importance of agriculture in Canada. Five thousand Agri-Cultural Connection packets were distributed to Boards of Education across Ontario, which, in turn, were to deliver them to the classroom.

In early 1986, a representative of the Royal Winter Fair approached Ross about honouring him at the fair. Ross assured the representative that he was feeling up to

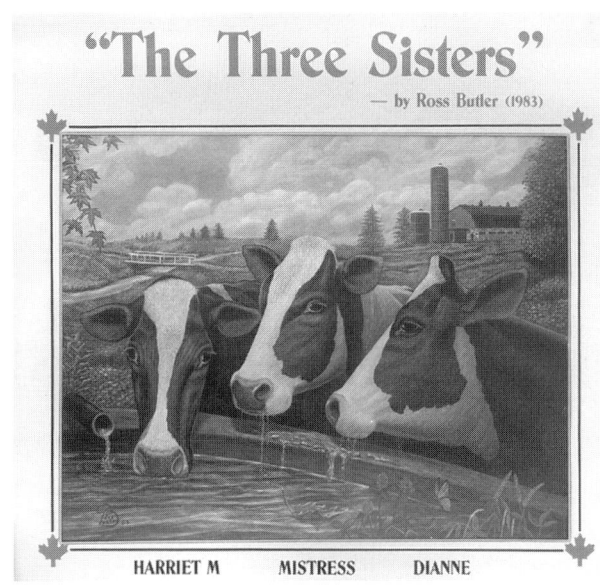

Painting commissioned by Meadowbridge Holsteins and Great Lakes Harvestores.

the task and was soon visited by the manager of the Fair. The publicity for "The Royal Salutes" would be in the hands of promoter Ivan Goring, who would co-ordinate the event. A display would be located in the upper portion complex near the East Annex VIP headquarters. As well, several of Ross's paintings and sculptures would be featured in the flower show display at the complex entrance. In Dairy Lane, there would be a life-size butter sculpture of Ross himself created by Windsor sculptor Chris Rees.

Everything came together in November 1986, just a few months before Ross's 80th birthday:

The Royal Salutes Ross Butler on his Eightieth Birthday

In the upstairs VIP lounge, which was not open to the public, Ross's portrait of Queen Elizabeth was strategically placed. It was hoped that this painting would inspire patrons of the lounge to donate to the Agri-Cultural Connections project. The Ross Butler Gallery was set up in the East Annex close to the VIP lounge. Knowing that Ross's health was deteriorating, dozens of volunteers gave their time and energy to make the "Salute" a success. These volunteers included Brenda Wenstob, the curator of the Woodstock Art Gallery, and her husband Jim Mathieson, who carefully packed all of Ross's paintings and sculptures into a moving van, delivered them to the coliseum in Toronto, and installed the various displays.

Ivan Goring and the women from the North and South Districts Women's Institutes took over from there. They got royal blue backdrops from the Ontario Ministry of Agriculture and Food and set them up in the gallery where the paintings *Royal Review* and *All Canadian Holsteins — The Cattle upon the Thousand Hills* as well as the statue of Firestone were displayed. The women also answered questions about Ross and his career when Ross could not be there to talk about his life's work. Ivan Goring helped them set up a fifteen minute video on their bilingual Agri-Cultural Connections packets. Mount Elgin's Linda Hammond, the president of the Oxford South District Women's Institute, told visitors that "Ross Butler's art has played a key role in conveying what life on the farm is like."

One of the biggest highlights of the Royal Winter Fair was the Governor General's VIP banquet, where Ross, with Ruby at his side, was acclaimed as the "world's most famous painter of domestic animals." Ross expressed his thanks to the Royal with these words:

In all the world, I could never have dreamed of a better setting to display my models and canvasses.

In 1987 Ross was nominated for the Ontario Citizenship Award by Winnie Roach Leuszler of British Columbia, the first Canadian to swim the English channel. Unfortunately, Leuszler's letter arrived in Oxford County only four days before the cut-off date for nominations, and Ross's family and friends had to scramble for letters of support to accompany the nomination. Twelve were inducted that year, but Ross was not one of them. However, he was not dismayed.

Whether I won the medal or not is immaterial. Having all those letters of support is what counts.

That support, especially from their family, was unwavering as the health of both Ruby and Ross suffered. Ruby's cancer progressed and Ross underwent surgery to remove his gall bladder, then was also later diagnosed with prostrate cancer. One of the few bright spots during this period came in 1991 when Ruby received the Communication Achievement Award from the Woodstock Toastmasters Club for her charitable efforts as Volunteer of the Year.

Ruby died in 1993 and Ross was devastated. He had never really believed that he would lose her. Realizing that his own death was on the horizon, he enlisted David to set his affairs in order. David asked Brenda Wenstob to complete an appraisal of the assets of his studio. In her summary of Ross's work, she said: "In his works Ross had accomplished an integrity and truth of attitude and form which has survived the test of time. He gave the agriculture community in Canada a vision of the future; a map of what the various breeds could and did achieve."

Ross passed away on 11 July 1995. He did not live to see his greatest honours. In June 1997 he was posthumously inducted into the Ontario Agriculture Hall of Fame at Milton, Ontario. Six months later, at his beloved Royal Winter Fair in Toronto, he was inducted in the Canadian Agriculture Hall of Fame.

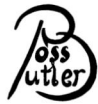

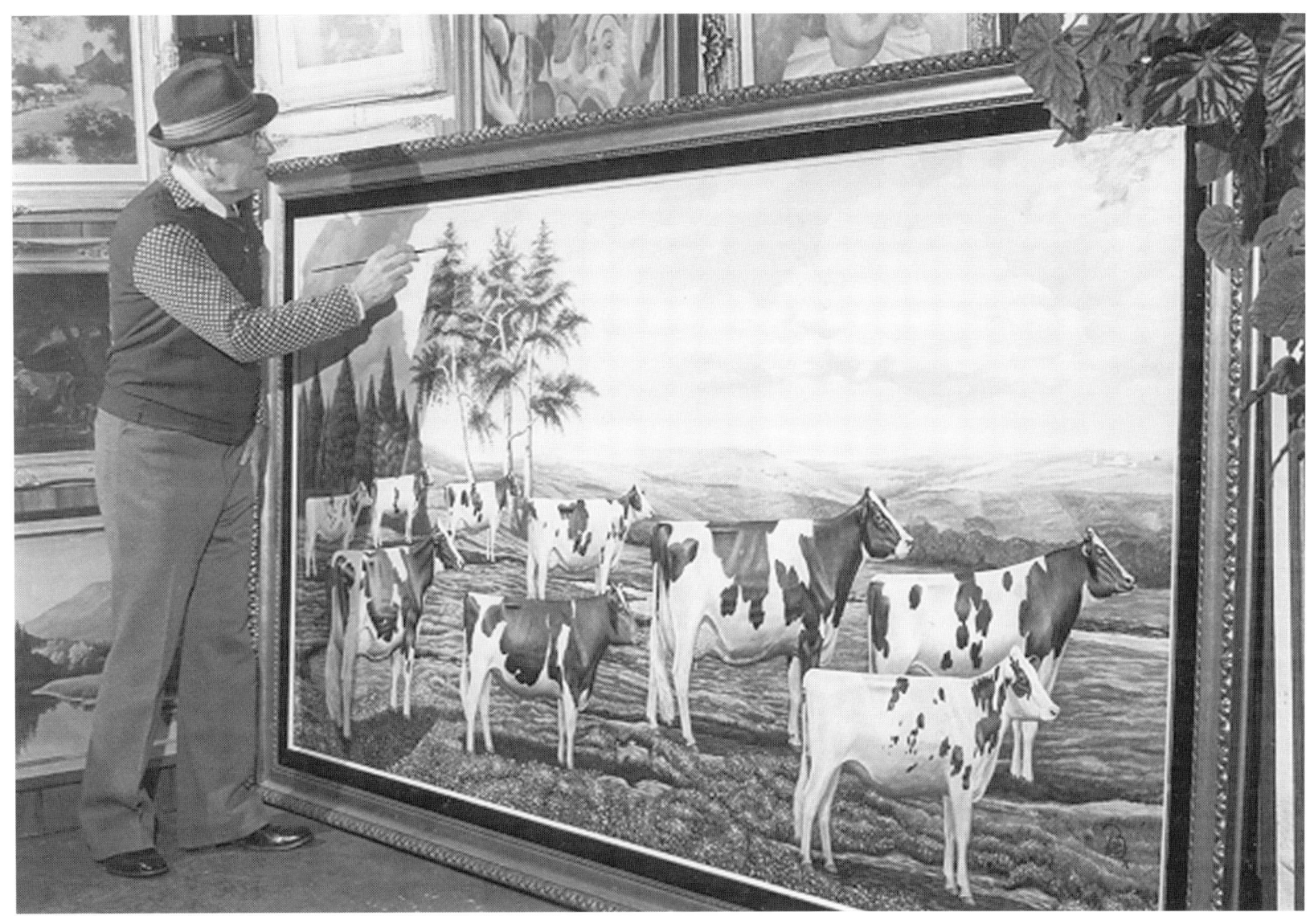

Ross Butler painting All Canadian Holsteins —
The Cattle upon the Thousand Hills.

Further Reading

Carter, Major General William Harding. Illustrated by Edward Herbert Miner. *Horses of the World*. Washington: National Geographic Society, 1923.

Gaunt, William. *Stubbs*. London: Phaidon Press, 1977.

Gilbey, Sir Walter. *Farm Stock 100 Years Ago*. 1910; rpt. Hillbrow, Liss, Hampshire, UK: Spur Publications Co., 1976.

Harper, J. Russell. *A People's Art: Primitive, Naive, Provincial and Folk Painting in Canada*. Toronto: University of Toronto Press, 1974.

Johnson, Paul S. *Farm Animals in the Making of America*. Des Moines: Wallace Homestead Book Co., 1975.

Lewington, Peter. *Canada's Holsteins*. Toronto: Fitzhenry & Whiteside, 1983.

Lord, Barry. *The History of Painting in Canada: Toward a People's Art*. Toronto: NC Press, 1974.

Morris, George Ford. *Portraiture of Horses: A Few People, Some Dogs and Other Animals*. Shrewsbury, NJ: Fordacre Studios, 1952.

Periam, Hon. Jonathan. *The Farmer's Stock Book, 1887*. Toronto and Chicago: International Publishing Co., 1887.

Quinn, Michael S. "Corpulent Cattle and Milk Machines: Nature, Art and the Ideal Type." www.http://envirolink.org/arrs/pseta/sa/sal.2/quinn.html

Webster, Michael. "Perfection on Canvas: Canadian Ross Butler's Images Set Husbandry's Highest Standards." *Harrowsmith*, Volume 59: 62-71.

Prescott, Maurice S. and Frank T. Price. *Holstein-Friesian History*. NP: Holstein-Friesian World, Inc., 1930.

Ross Butler Studio

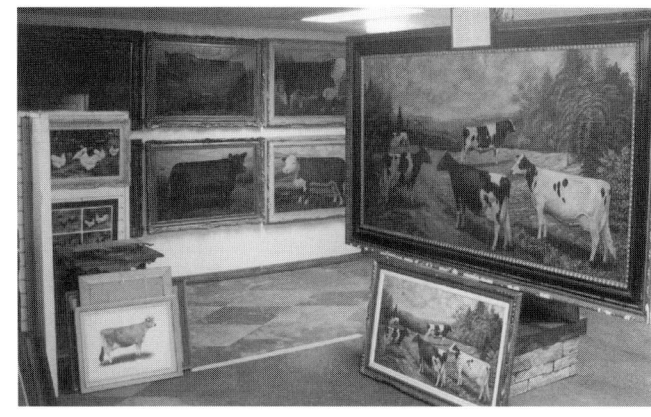

Located on an 180-acre country estate officially designated as an environmental protection area, the Ross Butler Studio and Agricultural Art Gallery offers visitors from around the world a glimpse of the vision of a unique figure in Canadian art and agriculture. Recognized by both the Canadian and Ontario Agricultural Hall of Fame, Ross Butler is considered one of the world's foremost livestock artists and an authority on animal proportions. The Canadian and Ontario governments commissioned this self-taught artist to develop "true type" portraits of farm animals for educational use. This resulted in the distribution of Butler prints across Canada and around the world. His studies of animal proportions and his true type pictures were used by judges, classifiers, and breeders in the development of domestic livestock breeds. Ross Butler was also the founder of the The Oxford Breeding or Central Unit, the first all-breed artificial insemination barn in Canada, and a founding member of the Oxford Museum and Historical Society. The Ross Butler Studio maintains his legacy: a collection of original art and archives of agricultural pictures, sculptures, and books.

Trails meander throughout the Butler Farm on Cedar Creek and Southwood Fen, enhancing a leisurely visit to the Studio and Gallery. For those who wish to extend their stay, a three-bedroom country cottage is available as a peaceful, rural retreat in the heart of one of the nation's richest farming regions in Oxford County, near Woodstock, Ontario, the Dairy Capital of Canada. The Ross Butler Studio and the Butler Farm are operated by his son, David Butler.

Limited edition reproductions of many of Ross Butler's works of art featured in *Journey To Perfection* are available directly from the Studio.

For more information, contact Ross Butler Studio, R.R. # 4, Woodstock, Ontario N4S 7V6, Tel. (519) 456-3025, Fax. (519) 456-5364, E-mail: dbutler@oxford.net.

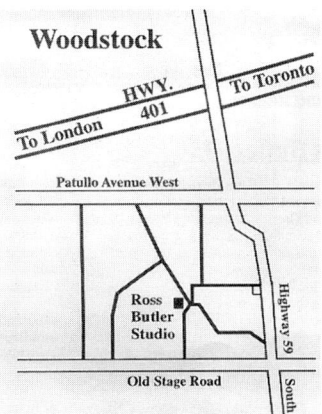

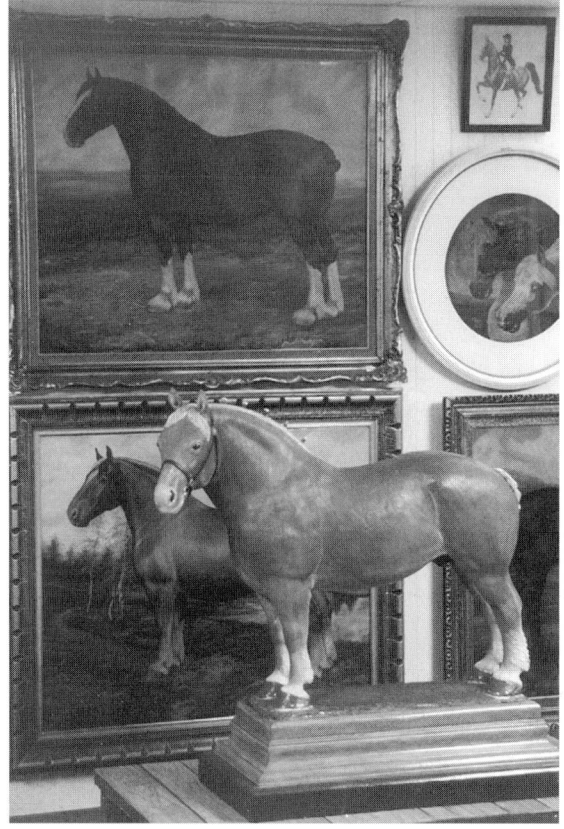

Quarry Press Art & Heritage Books

By the Labour of Their Hands: The Story of Ontario Cheddar Cheese
by HEATHER MENZIES $19.95

Rivers of Oil: The Founding of North America's Petroleum Industry
by HOPE MORRITT $19.95

Legend of the Lake: The 22-Gun Brig-Sloop Ontario, 1780
by A. BRITTON SMITH $34.95

The Three Faces of Molly Brant
by EARLE THOMAS $19.95

Seven Years with the Group of Seven: A Memoir in Words and Pictures
by JOYCE PUTNAM $24.95

J.E.H. MacDonald: New Views on Canadian Artists
by BRUCE WHITEMAN $19.95

Tom Thomson: New Views on Canadian Artists
by JOAN MURRAY $19.95

F.H. Varley: New Views on Canadian Artists
by MICHAEL TOOBY $19.95

A.Y. Jackson: New Views on Canadian Artists
by DOUGLAS FETHERLING $19.95

Arthur Lismer: New Views on Canadian Artists
by CAROL MARTIN $19.95

Franklin Carmichael: New Views on Canadian Artists
by CATHARINE MASTIN $19.95

Lawren Harris: New Views on Canadian Artists
by JUDITH STOFFMAN $19.95

Available at your local bookstore or directly from Quarry Press, P.O. Box 1061, Kingston, ON K7L 4Y5, Tel. (613) 548-8429, Fax. (613) 548-1556, E-mail: order@quarrypress.com.